The Heroine in Western Literature

For Gabriel,
and his brother

The Heroine in Western Literature

The Archetype and Her Reemergence in Modern Prose

by

Meredith A. Powers

McFarland & Company, Inc., Publishers
Jefferson, North Carolina, and London

Acknowledgments: I acknowledge the help of those who never seemed to doubt my ability to complete this task, and in so doing made me doubt it less myself: Dr. David Stineback was first among these. Susan Kaplan and Andrew Levkoff with their solicitous support mitigated the isolation of the last few months. Ron Pies and Austin O'Toole revived me with their consistent encouragement. I am especially grateful to Cat Viens and Gerry Cyr whose faith in me has survived births and deaths and other distracting phenomena, and was always there when I needed it, like a gentle following wind,

And John McNally Powers who puzzled and proofread and encouraged, all the while praying furiously to shorten my stay in Purgatory,

And Gabriel McNally Powers-Cyr who is the only person I have ever lived with who both respects and encourages my need to write,

And Dr. Alan Rappaport who was simply the best.

Library of Congress Cataloguing-in-Publication Data

Powers, Meredith A.
    The heroine in Western literature : the archetype and her reemergence in modern prose / by Meredith A. Powers.
        p.   cm.
    Includes bibliographical references and index.
    ISBN 0-7864-0830-8 (softcover : 50# alkaline paper) ∞
    1. Women in literature.   2. Heroines in literature.   3. Goddesses in literature.   4. Archetype (Psychology) in literature.   5. Myth in literature.   6. Feminism and literature.   7. Literature—History and criticism.   I. Title.
PN56.5.W64P69   1991
809'.93352042—dc20   91-52597
                                                     CIP

British Library Cataloguing-in-Publication data are available

Cover image © 2000 Artville

Manufactured in the United States of America

McFarland & Company, Inc., Publishers
  Box 611, Jefferson, North Carolina 28640
    www.mcfarlandpub.com

Table of Contents

Part One
The Prehistoric Goddess

Introduction:
In Search of the Heroine

Some years ago while reading Joseph Campbell's *Hero with a Thousand Faces,* I was distressed by the discovery that there is no archetypal pattern therein which traces the activities of the heroine in literature. Campbell goes so far in that work as to suggest that Daphne's transformation into a tree to escape rape by the pursuing Apollo is a refusal of the call to heroism.[1] It occurred to me at the time that that would certainly not have been Daphne's assessment of the experience and that subsequent, nonmythic rape victims might well express envy of Daphne's timely metamorphosis, might judge her escape heroic.

How does the conceptualization of heroism function within the individual's imagination? Within the larger cultural vision, mankind's collective imagination? One can so easily imagine the frightened woman envisioning her own escape—outrunning, metamorphosing, triumphing over her adversary, yet tradition has already decided. It is the god bent on rape, the rational Apollo, who is the hero of the myth, not the woman who escapes.

A child tethered in a car seat survives, unhurt, an automobile accident in which the driver, the child's mother, sustains a serious head wound and unconscious, bleeds into her child's lap for the ten minutes it takes help to arrive. All ends well and what follows is a curious process. The child who was the only conscious witness to the event begins to spin a mythic rendition that grows and alters like an organic substance over time. But one thing is consistent, from its first draft the myth features the child as hero. Transformative of necessity, the three-year-old describes venting rage like the Incredible Hulk, bursting forth from the helplessness of circumstance and avenging the mother's injury by soundly trouncing the driver of the other car. By the time help arrives the child has magically reappeared in the car seat and is ministering to the wounded mother. Each revision increases the child's heroic vision of the self, each helps incorporate the episode which has become in story not a profoundly disturbing confrontation with

2

existential helplessness but an opportunity for the child to express innate heroism.

Coming up against that which threatens to overwhelm the self, we avert it with mental constructs, with fantasies. We help ourselves to supernatural powers, we banish anxiety and lure courage, simultaneously evolving a vision of ourselves which pulls toward life and away from the dangerous surrender to inadequacy or helplessness or mute fear. So the unconscious erects defenses of its own. The ability to envision oneself as heroic, to evolve a mythology of the self which is empowering and sustaining, functions as a primary psychic defense.

The process is at work in the imaginations of both girls and boys, men and women. How many of us have fought the fear of flying with fleeting scenarios of plane crashes, resolved in our imaginations when we deftly save ourselves and perhaps two or three others on the way out? We are each, man or woman, heroic in the stories of our own becoming, in the imaginative visions we construct, embellish, and sometimes tell. Yet what of Daphne? The raping god is the focus of the story, the fleet woman who escapes leaves both Apollo and the listener baffled, but her metamorphosis has never been viewed as the stuff of heroism. Despite the fact that she comes from the oldest stratum of myth, the very stories to which Western culture has turned for evidence of human archetypes, of the archetypally heroic, Daphne's actions have been explicated as the stuff not of heroism but of magic, allegory, and gender.

Although in others of his works Campbell does acknowledge sympathetically that there is a paucity of scholarly analysis of the accepted feminine archetypes, in *Hero with a Thousand Faces,* his definitive study of heroism, the subliminal implication is that heroism, that innate conception of the human psyche is possible only for men. The absence of a discernibly autonomous heroine is disturbing, but a cursory review of Greek mythology suggests there were only limited possibilities for women. Heroism, that noble conception which is itself an outgrowth of the seminal conception of divinity, appears in myth to be an entirely masculine affair. In fact, the connection between the two ideas—divinity and heroism—provides the explanation for the absence of an autonomous cultural heroine.

> The two—the hero and his ultimate god, the seeker and the found—are thus understood as the outside and inside of a single, self-mirrored mystery, which is identical with the mystery of the manifest world. The great deed of the supreme hero is to come to the knowledge of this unity in multiplicity and then to make it known.[2]

But such a task is made almost hopelessly complicated if not theoretically impossible for the heroine because of Western culture's vitiation and eventual denial of the feminine divine.

The goddesses and mortal women who do appear in myth are mothers, wives, mentors, temptresses, ogresses, and victims. Occasionally, like Daphne, they are mysterious alien creatures without voice and whose motivation, power, and behavior thus remain enigmatic. These are promptly dismissed, placed outside the primary narration or they become part of that which the hero must overcome. The women who remain figures in the central narrative play supporting roles in the stories of heroes. Danae, for instance, was entombed with Perseus, but only Perseus emerged heroic. Neither Theseus nor Odysseus would have accomplished much without the intercession of Ariadne and Athena, but the stories are of the hero's triumph. There are stories which focus on women. The oft-analyzed myth of Psyche tells of a wife who learns to contain her curiosity and become deferential, and the tale of the hapless Atalanta tells first of her heroic behavior in the Calydonian boar hunt then discredits it as inappropriate for a woman. There seems to be no acceptable, self-determined heroine in the bunch. Women are props in the hero's drama or, as with Psyche and Atalanta, they are displaced souls in conflict with the restrictions of patriarchal culture who in myth learn lessons meant for all the world. Women are functionaries, backdrops in a mythology which insisted, sometimes with notable aggression, on the metaphoric centrality of the hero. Explication has perpetuated the bias. Daphne did not cleverly escape a villain, she "refused the call."

Yet what of Daphne's view of the experience? What she resists is the questionable privilege of being raped by the god. The rewards inherent in such a violent rite understandably escape the girl.[3] In modern times rape is recognized as an act of violence, of demeaning violation; the raped person is a victim, yet in myth it is accepted as a conduit to divinity or a variation on the marriage ceremony. But the women of myth do resist. Is that not archetypal behavior? Daphne fled, as did Arethusa and Britomartis; each clearly preferred metamorphosis and each was assisted in her escape by a shadowy goddess. But Daphne's version of the event is not told.

And what of Danae, the daughter betrayed by her father, the mother who gives birth alone and takes her infant to safety? Surely if told from her perspective, this would not have been the story of the birth of a hero, but of the heroism of a mother, one who perceived the mother-child relationship as the central bonded pair and whose ethics and actions evolved from that focus. But her story is not told; she is silent, passive, receptive, violated, victimized, finally rescued. Yet hers is the story of an ongoing conflict with the powers that be. Imprisoned by her father, she is subsequently impregnated by a god, eventually vindicated by her son. But what of her version of the story? Her mythology of herself? Might not Danae have been a tad more active, a tad less deferential, have had, in fact, a completely different view of the experience? Surely for both Daphne and Danae heroism was something which they too participated in. But women do not have a voice in the extant narrative of myth; their view of experience is to be inferred. The voice of the goddess is only a whisper in the hero's ear, commanding him to great feats while she herself remains in the background. Art itself is male; inspiration, the Muse, is female.[4]

Despite this slant, mythology has been viewed as the inviolate wellspring of information about ourselves. Subsequent to Carl Jung and his theory of archetypes, mythology became sacrosanct, a hallowed treasure trove thought to contain the ontogenetic and phylogenetic absolutes from which no human being could escape. In myth was to be found those "mental forms whose presence cannot be explained by anything in the individual's own life and which seem to be aboriginal, innate, and inherited shapes of the human mind."[5] In these ancient fictional constructions, long explicated solely by men,[6] we are directed to find revealed what is quintessentially inherent, and therefore appropriate, for individual men and women. As an intellectual conception archetypes have come to carry more cultural clout than the outworn prescriptions promulgated by religion. In fact, they have worked their way into discourse with an authority previously associated exclusively with divine revelation. Archetypes are seemingly infallible, inarguably, psychic *imperatives.* The thinking person dare not choose to question them. It would be intellectually unsound and as futile as denying biology.

Yet there has been a persistent aura of inscrutability and discomfort surrounding feminine archetypes. The absence of an autonomous heroine amplifies this. My examination of mythology for evidence of a heroine led to the discovery that the problem with feminine archetypes is a problem of gaps. It emanates in part from the baffling silence of so many mythological women, in part from the disingenuous voice of others.

While Athena may intercede at the trial of Orestes to announce that she is "in all things on the side of the father," and Psyche may sort her seeds and gain immortality by making her peace with a peculiar marriage, there is another, unarticulated view of feminine experience evident in myth. Injustice and victimization are inherent to the female experience in the evolution of a patriarchal culture, yet few admirable figures articulate that conflict. Prometheus, noble Titan chained to his rock, rages loftily against the tyranny that has victimized him, yet Danae is silent. When feminine voices are raised in the elation of rage or triumph, as are Medea's and Hecuba's, they are juxtaposed with deeds so heinous that there is scant inclination to label them heroic.

In her introduction to Jean Shinoda Bolen's book *Goddesses in Everywoman: A New Psychology of Women,* Gloria Steinem expressed an adroit skepticism concerning feminine archetypes, "because Jung and others who placed such archetypes in the collective unconscious ended with either/or, masculine/feminine polarities."[7] But the process of manipulating archetypes in the service of the goals of patriarchy is much older than Jung. It is, in fact, a historic characteristic of Western aesthetics which began in mythology with deprecation of the goddesses. Embellishment and revision of existing goddess myths employed narrative devices such as rape, marriage, and suicide to present metaphorically "the helplessness of women in the face of overwhelming male superiority."[8] Such retellings were prompted by powerful social anxieties and are prescriptions for the gender system rather than revelations of the archetypal feminine. These revisions have been accepted as cultural fiat, however, while the wail of the victim's rage has been mitigated or lost. In its final form mythology tells the hero's story and claims it to be the "universal" event; the heroine's task at best is a matter of learning deference. Contemporary enshrinement of all characterizations from myth explicated through a traditional male view of experience and then labeled "archetypal" continues the manipulation.

In truth, ethnohistory as well as mythology suggest that the single relentlessly recurring pattern of human behavior is ethnocentric conflict. This archetypal pattern is phylogenetic, aggressive, and goal oriented. Its success completely obscures any ontogenetic urges which may have opposed it. Conquering tribes seek to validate their ascendancy and make permanent their status by subjugating the values of the conquered. This is a dynamic linked to the physical superiority within the group. It immediately obfuscates the imperatives of the subjugated.[9] A mutation of this process in the prehistoric Aegean was between the sexes, with conquering tribes, who were patriarchal as a result of their Paleolithic hunting tradition, insisting on the righteousness of sexual dimorphism and social hierarchy. The conquerors sought to validate their own tradition by declaring what was appropriate or—more commonly—what was inappropriate for women; religion and aesthetics were both employed to this end; the empowered declared facilely that the *real* gods were on their side.

Conceptions, first of tribe, then of divinity, and eventually of heroism represent a continuum in the development of consciousness, itself a phylogenetic archetypal continuum that began in a period of prehistoric, preverbal sentience and preceded the later dynamic of ethnocentric conflict. The model begins within the tribal group and develops toward the individual. Sexual difference as metaphor may be employed at every step, but sexual polarity and gender injunction seem to have entered the continuum rather late. There is evidence that suggests that all tribes initially conceived of divinity as feminine: their first god was the tribal mother. Only later did the male divinity gain status in response to the ecological needs of specific tribes as the goddess's son and eventually when procreation was linked to copulation as her consort. Ecological factors in Paleolithic times contributed to much flux and movement, both geographic and conceptual.

The Northern hunting tribes who invaded the milder dominions of the Aegean agricultural tribes had already evolved a celestial hierarchy which mimicked their own internal social structure and preserved the special status of the male hunting elite. The native tribes who were conquered were agricultural tribes who still worshiped individual tribal goddesses but were themselves faced with compelling new needs, including a need for internal military elites to defend against invaders.[10]

As a conception of divinity the Aegean tribal goddesses threatened the status of the elite male subgroup. The interests of the conquerors were served by reconstructing the original goddess archetype, and the characterizations which appear in mythology after this revision begins are deliberate, prescriptive constructions concerned with crimping conceptions of divinity, of female power, and worth, not archetypes of the feminine. My attempt to locate an archetypal heroine called for a search into the religion that preceded the Olympian religion in order to locate the feminine divinity which had existed autonomously in that substratum before the needs of the dominant tribe were served by subjugating her to her consort and sons.

The question of whether matriarchy did exist in the prehistoric Near East continues to be debated. Evidence of archeology and ethnohistory suggests that it did to a degree. But the term itself is slippery. For my purposes in this study it refers to tribes in which conceptions of divinity and social organization centered around maternal affiliations. I do not intend to suggest visions of numerous Deborahs leading primitive hordes into battle nor to insist that men were of secondary status in these ancient tribes. The matriarchal tribes who were the original inhabitants of the Aegean conceived of divinity as feminine; a conception which undoubtedly evolved out of the attachment patterns I discuss in the first part of this study. That fact allows the speculation that their early aesthetics, their original myths, presented the goddess/heroine as the central figure, not necessarily in stories analogous to the later stories of heroic individuation, but certainly in stories which gave voice to the feminine divine.

Allowing this perspective, and considering the evidence culled from archeological excavation, it is possible to speculate on which mythological women were originally autonomous heroines, which stories are of tribal conquest, and, more significantly, which stories are of the usurpation of power from one sex by the other, as is the myth of Daphne and Apollo. That is the focus of the second part of this study, in which I suggest how the literary conventions, revisions, and the biases of specific iconists contributed to the process which resulted in the production of ersatz female archetypes whose primary function was to organize a view of experience which was devoid of feminine power and in which both free will and heroism for women were espaliered to social order rather than expressive of inherent ethics of their own.

Helen of Troy, for example, was once a powerful Spartan earth goddess, who evolved through patriarchal overlay into the passive and powerless victim of her own beauty, permanently etched in literature as the unfaithful wife. Ariadne, who plays a supporting role in the story of the heroism of Theseus, was actually a version of the great goddess of Crete, where she was worshiped as "the sacred one," unaccompanied even by a subordinate child god, yet she evolved through patriarchal revision into the abandoned and forsaken victim waiting passively on Naxos for another male to save and avenge her. Such specific analysis supports the conclusion that female archetypes as they exist are slanted at best. Stripping away the lawyers of patriarchal overlay imposed on narrative and juxtaposing those skeletal stories with the immutable images left in pictorial art begin to suggest an initial characterization of the prehistoric goddess.

The process of aggressively deprecating feminine principles by reducing the status and banalizing the powers of the goddesses began with revision of the earliest pre–Homeric myths, stories of the tribal goddesses, called *Kores*. It continued as a cultural imperative as tribes merged into the first cities where male elites dominated and culture evolved its first heroic figures, personifications of the Heroic Ideal. As a process, goddess reduction was a prodigious, unyielding march toward the obliteration of the conception of the feminine divine. Prompted by social concerns, it was facilitated first by changes in the nature of storytelling but also changes in the nature of language and the biases at the onset of formal literary criticism, that which Northrop Frye calls "the conscious organizing of cultural tradition."[11] Even though there is at least evidence of the machinations at work in the process in Aegean myth, it was much more summarily accomplished in the Levant.

As Greek culture evolved, every age seems to have produced and interpreted aesthetics which contributed to the process. In fiction the legendary and once autonomous tribal goddesses were overlayed with more and more heinous embellishments and then judged in a moral theatre. By the fifth century B.C. nonfictional women had reached the nadir of their social and political fortunes and were kept in Oriental seclusion while men conducted the "Golden Age." Analysis of mythological overlay from this period, as well as the evidence of pictoral art, suggest that while Classical Athens may have been unparalleled in contributions to the civilizing of the West, it was remarkable also for its manipulation of aesthetics in the service of a literal androcentrism which sanctioned sexual violence and pederasty to enforce social hierarchy and was wedded to notions of "necessity" and "natural" order which were imperatives for a cruel gender system. During this grim period in the history of women myth became permanent, immortalized in language recorded by an intellectual elite which took its place beside hunting and military elites in its enjoyment of the position of dominant subgroup. Notable craftsmen of Greek literature, particularly Euripedes, recognized and questioned the inexorable reduction of the matriarchal principle in cultural life. Beyond its immediate social significance, his dramaturgy brought into disquieting focus the polarities that such a course was fusing into the fabric of the evolving culture. But his insight proved to be anomalous. A generation later Aristotle would present Western culture with its definitive conception of divinity—a god in the image of the cerebral male.

This study begins with the assumption that extant mythology is patriarchal revision and then focuses on the literary and cultural conventions which facilitated such revision. By doing this we begin to see that concealed beneath the overlay are archetypally female characters, divinities, and heroines who were once powerful and autonomous versions of the great goddess of Near Eastern matriarchal religion. That figure is not merely an enigma, but an anathema to the goals of the dominant culture. Hers is a religion which was wholly aloof of formalism and characterized by spiritual principles which evolved out of attachment patterns and a mystical, pre-rational sense of continuity between the life of the tribe and the life of nature. Unlike subsequent theological orders, it was a religion which accepted humanity's place in the flux of phenomena and did not subscribe to ideas of guilt or necessity in order to countervail the sense of helplessness inherent in that. Instead, it acknowledged the process by which the unconscious erects its own defenses against such helplessness and is made stronger by the process. Elaine Pagels has suggested that guilt is more acceptable to the human psyche than is helplessness, that "guilt is the price to be paid for the illusion of control over nature."[12] Such control was apparently less significant to the ancient goddess worshipers.

Archetypal patterns of heroism for women come from this matriarchal period, and remain connected to it and to the idea which the scholar Jane Ellen Harrison called "Themis," that ancient imperative which compelled the earliest of our ancestresses toward a social order, deeply rooted in the oldest social unit, mother and child. This focus is at its heart in conflict with the patriarchal goal of the metaphoric centrality of the male. The great goddess of this ancient religion and the archetypal heroine who is her outgrowth are discernible in revised mythology and have continued to trucu-lently exercise their own ethics, amaranthine if misunderstood. Daphne herself was a tribal goddess and her confrontation with Apollo mimics the historic confrontation of the patriarchal and matriarchal systems. Apollo is perfunctorily occupied with the issue of subjugation; aggressive sexual violence is his right. Daphne resists victimization, preferring her autonomy to this rite of initiation into patriarchal womanhood; metamorphosis through retreat into the irrational is her right.

But since Daphne is mute in myth and Danae's version of events is not told, the task of understanding the behavior and fleshing out the motives and goals of the archetypal heroine has to be undertaken with evidence offered from other sources. The wealth of contemporary scholarship on women provides a key to the explication of the goddess's story. I am convinced that she is a genuine archetype who has been a persistent, if muffled, voice in fiction. It is because her goals are often contrary to the primary interests of patriarchy that she is such a puzzle. Her rebelliousness is inexplicable to the powers which believe in the righteousness of the patriarchal order; her apparent discontent is unfathomable to traditional exegesis; her ethics and motives are inscrutable even to the men who tell her story. This contrary, often fascinating figure has remained on the periphery of cultural life, appearing and reappearing in Western narrative as did Hester Prynne, consistently enigmatic, but clearly motivated by discrete daemons inexplicably her own.

Contemporary fiction, especially that written by women, provides a forum which is not interested in perpetuating the sexist constructions of aesthetics, one which is specifically interested in explicating the stories of heroines. Contemporary women writers allow their female characters the voice which was denied mythological women, and at the same time retell the stories of heroines who first appeared as unsatisfying profiles in ancient narrative. By mortising the shadowy goddesses of the ancient stories with the articulate voices of contemporary heroines, a new vision of the lost archetype begins to materialize. In Sue Miller's *The Good Mother*, Anna Dunlap gives Demeter a voice; in Anne Tyler's *Dinner at the Homesick Restaurant*, Pearl Tull tells of Danae's heroism; in Toni Morrison's *Beloved*, Sethe offers a compelling explication of Medea's ethics. The process of juxtaposing the articulation of contemporary heroines with remnants of the archetypal goddess revealed in myth generates a fuller characterization of the lost goddess. This protean, syncretistic figure is akin to the shadowy Mother Nature, but she is much more complex, intricate, and wholly more satisfying.

The word *chthonic*, which comes from the Greek word *chthon* meaning earth, has been used as an adjective to describe the enigmatic religion that preceded the religion of the Olympians in Greece. Like the goddess religion which produced her, the chthonic heroine has been misunderstood partially because of her transformative energy and her use of irrational modes. This heroine is not primarily rational or logical and so has been labeled anticultural. She is often dismissed as was Daphne or deprecated as was Atalanta or simply redesigned as was Athena. Her divinity has been attenuated or obliterated or silenced. But she persistently reappears, remaining somewhat outside the primary narrative of Western literature. She prevails by continuing to make disquieting, elliptical appearances until she finds her voice in contemporary fiction.

Campbell tells us that the great task of the hero is to come to the knowledge of the divinity within, to thus resolve the "mystery of the manifest world." The manifest world of Western culture, however, is complicated by the fact that it has utterly obliterated the feminine divinity, replacing her with attenuated derivatives who are deliberate revisions; in her final manifestation she is not divine at all, but the human mother of the god whose task is to suffer serenely and whose only power is to intercede with her divine son. The first task of the archetypal heroine is to overcome her culture's denial of the feminine divine and then refuse the silence; she begins having to transcend the "impact of the world." In the ancient matriarchal religion it was the task of the goddess to seasonally arise; the ritual "Anodos of the Kore" is the rising of the young goddess out of the earth, the first step in a divinity of cycles in which she merges with her mother and gives birth again to herself.

This feminine divinity includes a commitment to a harsh but lofty justice, to a Grundanschauungen which is daemonic and irrational and more primally compelling than the dictates of the superego or the restrictions of man-made law. Her commitment is to *thesmoi* (holy codes), rather than *nomoi* (man-made laws), to *eros* rather than *logos*. The strength and renewal of the goddess comes from her comfort with nature, the irrational, and her empathy with others. She is evident in the stories of Medea and Hecuba as well as of Antigone. She is upsetting to the dominant order because she is alien to its goals; she is labile and syncretistic; she has no interest in perpetuating the polarities which have become entrenched in Western thought and does not share man's excessive emphasis on individuation as the goal of development. She is not predictable according to accepted cultural paradigms; this goddess metamorphoses. Her ethics are foreign, yet they will not be subjugated. So she remains a threat to the rational order of the patriarchy and continues to be suspected, dispatched, or deprecated.

In contemporary fiction she tells her own story, revealing her own connate ethics, explicating her own motives in her own voice, a voice which Daphne and Danae and even Medea were denied. This new articulate heroine seduces the reader to question long accepted conceptions of divinity and righteousness and offers illumination on her enigmatic mythological predecessors. Her heroism returns to us a conception of the lost divinity, the ancient goddess of the Near East, that indiscriminately nurturing mother: "From forth [whose] robe a fragrance shed, that makes the heart to yearn."[13]

Chapter I

Motherhood in Prehistory: Attachment Patterns and the Origin of Religion

The problem of establishing patterns of heroism for women in Western literature goes back to the time before the Neolithic revolution when the artists of the Paleolithic hunters and food gatherers carved faceless figures in the darkest recesses of their cave dwellings. These were distorted and exaggerated figures of women, often featuring peculiarly oversized sexual organs. Undoubtedly harbingers of the mother goddess, these figures themselves were not so much representations of specific goddesses as the amorphous images ancient artists conceived to suggest their peoples' appreciation for fertility, that magical power of woman which counters man's most ancient fear. The carvings come from a time when culture was embryonic and tribal. That they were hidden in the darkest recesses suggests that they were secret and endemic to individual tribes who associated them with some magical power thought to make one tribe more prolific than its neighbors.[1]

Sometime during the Pleistocene period, Homo sapiens established itself as an outgrowth of his primate relatives. To understand the tribal organization of hominids and early Homo sapiens, scholars have turned to the social grouping of lesser primates. The most common primate social organization is based upon the mother-children community, with the natural biological foundation of the initial dyad often extending past the infant's nursing years, past the point where there is another and yet another nursing sibling. The result is a social organization which is matriarchal. Some scholars speculate that in hominids the attachment to the mother was prolonged beyond the period of actual dependency by an attachment to place.[2] Hominids needed to store food, and that storage place was also the place where mothers had their children and where older children returned to store food, and eventually, to share food. The biological imperative of motherhood developed into a psychological imperative to protect and nurture her dependent and semidependent offspring and may well have provided the incentive to design the first containers and tools to help prepare plant food for small children.[3] The association between mother and child and food and place was strengthened; as hominid became Homo sapiens, this social formation remained, rooted in the mother-child relationship and developing into the basis for both culture and the tribe.

But what of the onset of human consciousness, the beginning of culture? At what point did mankind perceive itself as mortal and move beyond instinctual operation to a cerebral plane which included consideration of the metaphysical?

Neanderthal tribes buried their dead with tenderness and accompanied by accoutrements which indicate a conception of death as a journey; beyond that they left no clear indication of a religious life or mythology.[4] The temple caves of the Paleolithic period, however, testify to the fact that Cro-Magnon tribes had realized their first religious stirrings beyond a primitive death cult and that these were closely associated with their mothers. The Aurignacian figurines uncovered just north of Anatolia beyond the Black Sea are predominantly figures of animals and procreative females; the females are sexually exaggerated, often obese figures without feet—characteristics which underlined the connection to fertility and the earth. Joseph Campbell writes: "And so we can say that in the paleolithic period, just as in the much later age of the early agricultural societies of the Near East, the female body was experienced in its own character as a focus of divine force, and a system of rites was dedicated to its mystery."[5]

The little that is known of the rites themselves come from the temple caves of the Paleolithic sites in southern France and northern Spain, offering asymmetrical drawings of scenes of bull copulation with attendant dancers. Such scenes indicate the practices of religious rituals—rituals involving the veneration of fertility, perhaps including recognition of the male role in conception, and certainly generating a mythology.

Campbell describes the Paleolithic period as having three embryonic cultures, each with a separate character determined by its food source. The hunting cultures were dominated by the male hunters who enjoyed enhanced social status because of their position as food providers; the tropical gardening cultures were matriarchal, with women increasing their already high social status as they orchestrated the transition from plant collecting to plant cultivation; a third variant was formed by the tribes which combined hunting and gathering and in which economic power and social status was probably shared by both men and women.[6] Campbell, like many other scholars, associates the presence of goddess artifacts with a planters' mythology, and suggests that by the late Paleolithic period the goddess was already associated with symbols like the bird, serpent, and labyrinth, which would be connected in the late Neolithic period with the cults of the great goddess Ishtar-Aphrodite.[7]

The goddess who appears in the hunting shrines of the Paleolithic period came into her own during the Neolithic period. The gatherers of the tribe were the women, and as such they were the ones most likely to have stumbled onto the art of deliberate cultivation. Campbell suggests an intersecting of hunting tribes and tropical garden cultures during the proto–Neolithic period, during which domestication was passed from one to another and the seeds of higher civilizations were planted. This transpired in the area called the Fertile Crescent.[8]

The economy of the Neolithic era was an agricultural economy, with a village life that included pottery and weaving; it has been recreated quite vividly by archeologist James Mellaart who excavated Catal Huyuk, the ancient Neolithic village of Anatolia. Catal Huyuk has revealed itself to have been a settled beehive community which existed during the transition from hunting to agriculture. Evidence suggests that as agriculture replaced hunting as the prime source of food for the community, the status of women, who were associated with agriculture, increased, and female religious images dominated.[9] In her oldest representation at Catal Huyuk (dated 6200 B.C.), the goddess appears in a bass relief on a constructed wall giving birth, but arrayed beneath her is a combination of plaster breasts and animal skulls, indicative of her early characterization as the goddess of death as well as life. As goddess of death she is pictured with vultures; the vulture mask was apparently used in her ritual.[10] As goddess of life she is pictured in pregnancy as well as birth, as a dancing maiden, amid leopards as protectoress of wild things, and amid floral designs as patroness of weaving. As a mother she appears with both son and daughter. She is the primary resident of shrines, and those who attend her are female. Scholars speculate that these shrines were sanctuaries for women in childbirth.[11]

The appearance of the goddess, accompanied by certain recurring symbols including the bull, occurs not just in the vegetarian agricultural phase of Catal Huyuk which prospered in the shadows of the Taurus Mountains, but also in the other ancient Anatolian settlement of Hacilar, as well as later in Crete and pre–Achaean Greece, always in similar constellations. Such factors suggest that Anatolia was an early wellspring of civilization, a civilization characterized by the worship of the goddess, which was eventually disseminated throughout the Near East and the Aegean.[12] Campbell supports the single base theory suggested by archeology and ethnology by pointing to the similarity of form in myth and ritual. At the same time he cites the variety of symbols as indicative of the amalgamation of numerous mythological systems, probably of tribal origin, merging in the Near East where governing elites of the high Neolithic period strove to categorize.[13] Campbell writes:

in the neolithic village stage . . . the focal figure of all mythology and worship was the bountiful goddess Earth as mother and nourisher of life and receiver of the dead for rebirth. In the earliest period of her cult (perhaps c. 7500–3500 B.C. in the Levant) such a mother-goddess may have been thought of only as a local patroness of fertility, as many anthropologists suppose. However, in the temples even of the higher civilizations . . . the Great Goddess of highest concern was certainly much more than that. She was already, as she is now in the Orient, a metaphysical symbol: the arch personification of the power of Space, Time, and Matter, within whose bound all beings arise and die: the substance of their bodies, configurator of their lives and thoughts, and receiver of their dead. And everything having form or name—including God personified as good or evil, merciful or wrathful—was her child within her womb.[14]

This great goddess and her cults came to Neolithic villages from tribal origins during the Paleolithic period or earlier. As a deity she was conceived by separate and discrete tribes, especially those with agriculture as a food source but also by hunting tribes. As archetype, she is maternal and nurturing but subordinate to neither her children nor their father.

As already noted, these Paleolithic tribes were organized around maternal connections with women and their young children banding together into tribes which did not necessarily include adult males, at least not initially.[15] As the arts of agriculture and stock breeding were developed they produced "an epochal mutation in both the character of human existence and its potentialities for development," according to Campbell,[16] although more recent scholars disagree.[17] Let us assume that between the late Paleolithic era and the onset of the high civilizations, women were allowed a certain status in tribes and tribal communities. They would have been honored as the foci of tribal connections, sources of tribal fertility, perhaps as inventors of agriculture, along with pottery and the loom.[18] Like the later Neolithic women in agricultural communities such as Catal Huyuk and Hacilar, Paleolithic women were likely to be unfamiliar with notions of gender. Although physically smaller, they were not yet the assignable chattel of men, but mothers of the tribe. Until conception was connected to coitus, women would have been afforded particular status because birth was thought to be parthenogenetic. Myths of a much later period suggest the covetousness of the ascendant sky god, as Zeus awkwardly aped maternal power in the stories of the parthenogenetic births of Athena and Dionysus. As propagators of the tribe the women of prehistory must have enjoyed sexual freedom; they were certainly not valued for virginity.[19] As individuals, however, they would have had no more freedom than their male counterparts, for the structure of these early vegetal civilizations centered around group needs and obligations, thus fostering rigid taboos and inflexible punishments which did not allow for extenuating circumstances.[20] Consciousness itself may have been limited, particularly in its ability or willingness to conceptualize the self as separate from the group.

The point at which human consciousness originated is an issue which has prompted much speculation by scholars in various fields. Theories connect this evolutionary watershed to brain size, adaptation to the needs of the hunt, and numerous other less significant factors. One characteristic of the origin of human consciousness is indisputable: consciousness originated in an era of group imperatives. As mankind took notice of his uniqueness in the cosmos, acted out primitive aesthetic inclinations, and used language to communicate as no other primate could, he functioned as a social being, a participant in a primate social grouping. This was essential to his survival in an antagonistic environment and had at its heart the central emotional connection to his mother and her tribe. Elizabeth Fisher has pointed out the poignant conflict inherent in this dawning of consciousness. This social primate, Homo sapiens, discovers with his individual consciousness the immutable reality of self against a harsh universe, and with that consciousness comes the discovery of the initial other, his mother.[21] For the twentieth-century infant the discovery is thought to be fraught with deep anxiety; it can have been no less so for the species as a whole.

The connection between the mother-child bond and the onset of culture has also been the subject of some discussion. The patriarchal focus of most scholarship resulted in speculation as to the evolution of the *male*, with a remarkable paucity of discussion given to the essential mother-child component in that process. One nineteenth-century scholar, Johann Jakob Bachofen, whose theories were initially scorned by his contemporaries, expounded the view that the mother-child bond is the common denominator in cultural evolution. Bachofen suggested that the biological imperative inherent in mothering is inseparable from a spiritual principle which propels the relationship to a loftier level than that of other primates, and thus forms the groundwork of human culture. To Bachofen this affection between mother and child infused the evolving Homo sapiens with Grundanschauungen, the spiritual principle which generated culture. Bachofen wrote:

> The ethical aspect strikes a resonance in natural sentiment which is alien to no age: we understand it almost spontaneously. At the lowest, darkest stages of human existence the love between mother and her offspring is the bright spot in life, the only light in moral darkness, the only joy amid profound misery ... The relationship which stands at the origin of all culture, of every virtue, of every nobler aspect of existence, is that between a mother and child; it operates in a world of violence as the divine principle of love, of union, of peace. Raising her young the woman learns earlier than the man to extend her loving care beyond the limits of the ego to another creature, and to direct whatever gift of invention she possesses to the preservation and improvement of this other's existence. Woman at this

stage is the repository of all culture, of all benevolence, of all devotion, of all concern for the living and grief for the dead.[22]

Bachofen's contemporaries, clinging to the theory that the patriarchal family was the first social institution, dismissed his work as the rambling of a man who had been inordinately influenced by a saintly mother. A needs-of-the-hunt theory was widely accepted in the nineteenth century as the explanation for the origin of culture, and, indeed, it held center stage well into modern times. Bachofen's writing did at least begin an intellectual dialogue which brought into discussion the previously unquestioned idea that the patriarchal family unit was a historic and universal characteristic of culture.[23]

In the last twenty-five years, however, evidence has confirmed the existence of the three separate types of embryonic cultures operating in the Paleolithic and Mesolithic periods, with hunting providing the primary food source for only a limited number of tribes. Because of this clarification by archaeologists, the theory that the origin of culture is linked to men and the hunt has been largely abandoned or modified. Consequently, Bachofen's ideas have received new attention; the mother-child dyad, after all, is an ubiquitous characteristic of all cultures, now as in the prehistory. Bachofen's own mother may well have been influential, but what is unusual is not the influence or benevolence of his mother but the scholar's own clear-headed willingness to acknowledge her particular influence as a microcosm, a universal theme common to all cultures and a possible catalyst of cultural evolution.

But Bachofen's theories are more than just fodder for feminist polemic. Although he did hold that matriarchy preceded the ascendance of patriarchal culture, he was no feminist. He viewed matriarchy as a necessary and inferior stepping-stone toward the ultimate fulfillment represented by the patriarchal status quo; he assumed, as so many cultural analysts have, that history has always been essentially progressive. Further, he divided the matriarchy of prehistory into two periods: the later period being the era of the great goddess; the former, an era of mother-dominated tribes which were sexually permissive, godless, without familial formations and quite base—according to his nineteenth-century sensibilities. Yet he saw these two epochs as necessary in the process of "psychological mutation" which brought mankind to its apogee in nineteenth-century patriarchal culture.[24] Despite his error and bias, Bachofen's writings provide a valuable source work which recognized the influence of spiritual principles in the evolution of culture and the connection of those spiritual principles to the symbol of the great goddess. The first deity, she is representative of the mystery of woman and nature which was inseparable from the moral and social order generated by mothers in the earliest kinship groupings.

In his early writings Sigmund Freud clearly undervalued the infant's close tie to his mother, couching it in his theory of instinctive sexual drives; he failed throughout his life to recognize the relationship as expressive of a primary social drive, irrefutably linked to the individual's ability to master language and form affiliative relationships, and therefore having social as well as individual significance. The psychoanalysts who followed Freud continued to identify the mother-child bond as a primary behavior system connected to the infant's physiological needs but secondarily connected to sociality.[25] It was not until the groundbreaking work of John Bowlby, in *Attachment and Loss,* that psychoanalytical scholarship coordinated its own ontogenetic interests with the findings of ethnologists who had studied the social interaction of other primates.[26] Bowlby recognized that the attachment between infant and mother was something resembling Bachofen's interpretation and eventually evolved his fascinating theory which must be included in any subsequent discussion of the origin of culture.

Bowlby's studies of infants who were deprived of maternal association, although supplied with sufficient sustenance, led him to recognize their failure to thrive as reflecting a social need which is as much a biological imperative as the need for food. Operating in the human infant concurrent with the drive for food, but independent of it and also of the sexual drive, is a primary social drive similar to that seen in other primates and having its antecedent in animal instinct. Bowlby dubbed it "attachment behavior." In order to activate this drive even the well-fed infant must be presented with the stimuli of nurturing: breast feeding (or equivalent bottle feeding), cuddling, eye contact, smiling, and vocalization to and from the mother or her substitute. The drive itself has as its goal not the satisfaction of hunger but the simple proximity of the mother and, although it begins during the early period of utter dependence, it extends long after the infant becomes able to satisfy many of his own needs elsewhere. Bowlby writes: "This early dialogue of 'need' and an 'answer to need' becomes a highly differentiated signal system in the early months of life; it is, properly speaking, the matrix of human language and of the human bond itself."[27]

Attachment behavior as a human characteristic is not limited to the relationship between mother and infant, but is clearly a characteristic of the species, persisting throughout the life of the individual despite changing foci. Bowlby counters the suggestions of other psychoanalysts that attachment behavior fades with age, insisting instead that it persists in the healthy individual into adult life, although it is redirected in maturational steps from its origin in infant-mother bonding.[28] After that first essential bond, attachment behavior is demonstrated toward others as well. Bowlby writes that "in the early months of attachment the greater the number of figures to whom a child was attached, the more intense was his attachment to mother as principal figure likely to be."[29]

It is not necessary to assume that the attachment behavior of the mothers and infants of prehistory excluded the presence of fathers, although they were not necessarily included and were certainly not the indisputable patriarchs of nuclear or extended family groups. The tribe necessarily included mothers and their infants and older children, grouped together because of this maternal association and propelled by attachment behavior and known blood ties, which for the ancients meant only ties to mother and siblings. Bowlby's theory is that this social drive existed to protect the tribe from predators, the nursing mothers, infants, and young children being most in need of group protection. He connects these primitive human bonds with the beginnings of conscience.[30]

Accepting this prehistoric setting of tribal associations centered around mothers and held together by attachment behavior and group needs, we move on to consider mankind's first creative urges—the beginnings of religion.

In his book *Five Stages of Religion,* Gilbert Murray suggests that anxiety was the raw material of religious strivings and that angst was infused with significance by its outwardness, its connection to the good of the tribe rather than the individual.[31] Jane Ellen Harrison, in *Prolegomena to the Study of Greek Religion,* has dismantled the religious rituals of the ancient world to uncover the rites of the most primitive stratum. What she discovered in this bottom stratum of religious development is a collection of rites of aversion, revealing deep primitive fears which demanded expiation through the magic gesticulations and kinesthesis that eventually developed into religious ritual[32] One cannot help but connect these tribal urges to the individual's behavior systems identified by Bowlby: the first being attachment behavior, which kept the tribe together, and the second being separation anxiety, which propelled the tribe to avert alarming situations.[33]

There is a gloomy, gothic tone to the seminal fragments identified by scholars who have examined the mysteries of ancient Greek religion. To the primitive tribes who evolved these rites, the world was fraught with malevolent, alien entities, spirit things called Keres, which the tribe needed to avert and placate. This was the nature of the early chthonic religion, which included worship of the tribe's dead ancestors, as well as exercises of purification against the spirits of the world. Over this chthonic base, which was initially without any god but whose first deity was the great goddess, later strata would be superimposed, with each layer developing a more complex set of rituals and more elaborate mythology, each absorbing and altering the mythology of the last in order to verify and validate the new status quo.

Jane Ellen Harrison uses the example of Zeus-Meilichios to illustrate this stratification. As Meilichios he was a pre–Homeric deity, but even earlier he had been Maimaktes-Meilichios, an ancient earth deity who was worshiped at first as a snake, the recurring chthonic symbol of earth and rebirth. The name itself, Meilichios, means "Placable One," indicative of the fact that in his original form he was a Ker, a spirit whom the tribe needed to placate.[34]

At the bottom-most level it was the Keres who motivated religious ritual. These entities eventually became ghosts or sprites, but to the ancients they were the amorphous catalysts of both evil and good in tribal life.[35] They would eventually be recrafted into the daemon Furies, but even after revision would continue to be associated with blood ties and primal obligations, especially between mother and child, that generative connection which spawned and then held together the tribe. The blood-for-blood reckoning represented by the Furies was necessary for survival in the tribal epoch; as a social compulsion it was intricate to what Jane Ellen Harrison identified as "Themis," that aspect of the collective unconscious which was a social imperative toward a sophisticated, uniquely human order and which raised man inexorably above the level of his primate relatives.[36]

The rites of these ancients were primitive, magical exercises organized to avert the profligate Keres which brought evil into man's life, but they also recognized the duality inherent in nature and so courted the presence of the benign Keres which brought benefits to the tribe.[37] It was believed that Keres brought disease, nightmare, blindness, madness, old age, death, and strife, but also harvest, good winds, healthy children, deliverance from evil, and prosperity to the tribe. By the time Hesiod's Pandora released the sprite-like creatures in her box, the evil Keres had come to outnumber the good in man's consciousness; but the fact that the last of them was the beneficent hope reflects back to the time when Hesiod's wiser, albeit more primitive, ancestors saw quite clearly the duplicity prevalent in all nature.[38] The sense of duality characteristic of the Keres would infuse the personality of the first deities as well.

Harrison's theory of the origin of religion, developed throughout her lifetime and recorded in three of her books, was not particularly popular in the late Victorian Age, which cherished its paternal monotheism. Harrison saw religion as a product of man's social drive, its function to conserve the common life of the tribe and its initial expression in tribal rituals. Out of these rituals arose a by-product, the divinity, which was significant but not essential, and did not always contribute to the primary goal.[39]

The primary goal of the religious rituals was the preservation of the group, the totem group, and the tribe, which was a consanguineous entity developed out of the mother-child dyad and connected by matrilinear bonds. This social factor contributed to the evolution of religious notions by first uniting the group in self-aggrandizement through its communal rites. At this stage of cultural development, divinity was a quality of the group, a sense of itself as sacred and larger than the individuals who composed it. Ancient religious rites, prototypes of the later mysteries which long preserved the traditions of purification and banishment, were sometimes directed against the individual when his action threatened the life of the group. As long as one avowed the group rituals by participating, by continuing in the tribe's ancestral customs, the individual participated in a social process which identified divinity as within itself.[40]

The emotive nature of these ancient rites has led them to be interpreted as secular, even profane, an impression that was heightened by the inclusion of sexual acts and the fact that participants were transported to an altered consciousness; yet it was the freedom of consecration, not desecration. In later times, by the period of Orphic religion in Greece, these ancient rituals were condemned as orgiastic and lawless; actually they were forms to confirm the unwritten law, the law which preserved the social order of the tribe, and they expressed duty toward that order which included divinity as a quality of the group.

This collective sensibility was strongly rooted in the emotionally powerful bond between mother and child. Existing as an entity long before it spurred a specific divinity, it encompassed conscience—as Bowlby suggests—and Grundanschauungen—as Bachofen suggests—and reflected mankind's sense of the supernatural, his knowledge of something larger and more mysterious than the self, as Harrison suggests. She writes: "The thing greater than man, the 'power not himself that makes for righteousness,' is, in the main, not the mystery of the universe to which as yet he is not awake, but the pressure of that unknown ever incumbent force, herd instinct, the social conscience."[41]

At first the rituals were apotropaic exercises to banish the Keres, but later they were employed to supplicate or bless. These were rituals of sympathetic magic, imitations of natural processes to stimulate nature through simulation. So the megara, the deep crevices of the earth, were stirred to stimulate and simulate spring, and the life-giving of the earth was only a step away from the personification of the earth as a life-giving mother, eventually the goddess.

The earliest rituals employed the curse as a conduit of aversion. "The curse is the essence of the law," wrote Harrison,[42] because long before any divinity had been conceived the tribesmen could compel one another to behave as the tribe wanted, in accordance with the needs of the group through curse and magic ritual. Harrison writes: "The curse on its religious side developed into the vow and the prayer, on its social side into the ordinance and ultimately into the regular laws; hence the language of early legal formulas still maintains as necessary and integral the sanction of the curse."[43] For the tribesman, the ultimate curse was a social punishment, with the offender ostracized from the tribe as was Cain or Orestes. Murray suggests the enormous anxiety felt by the sinning tribesman: "The savage who is breaking the laws of his tribe has all his world—totems, tabus, earth, sky and all—against him. He cannot be at peace with God."[44]

So the rituals to avert and lure the Keres were the seminal stages of religious rituals, and they included the use of the apotropaic masks, like the mask of the Gorgon's head, and imitations of natural processes, including birth and later copulation when its significance was understood. Harrison suggests that when the primitive tribes no longer knew why they practiced these rituals, "they made a goddess their prototype,"[45] and that the earliest goddesses were the Keres themselves, initially addressed because they were dreaded but later developing into the spiritual beings who presided over curses and resided with the honored dead as did their later chthonic counterparts—Kore and Hecate.[46]

The earliest deification to appear out of the miasma of inchoate religious impulses was a consanguineous figure, the clan mother, a distaff ancestress, eventually the tribal goddess. She was conceived by separate tribes, amid the tribe's rituals of anxiety, and closely linked to its sociality, and took power from her connections to the prodigious emotional force of the mother-child bond and the chthonic powers of nature. She appears on the walls of Catal Huyuk and amid the potsherds of Minoan Crete, as well as in Phrygia and the Levant. Her stories were told for generations before the patriarchal cultures of the north superimposed their male sky gods on her cults, and left us only remnants of the original myth; yet it is fair to conclude that she was a powerful heroine long before the appearance of Abraham or Zeus, with her myths linked to the promotion of the life of the tribe, to familial connections, to natural law. Hers would not have included stories of the promotion of the individual or of the righteous ascendancy of patriarchal constructs. There is evidence of her tenacious influence in popular religious cults which coexisted or competed with the patriarchal religions which those in power sought to establish. She was a powerful cultural figure and continues as part of our collective unconscious, despite the efforts of patriarchal overlay. In her initial manifestations is the authentic expression of the archetype of the heroine.

Chapter II
The Nature of the Goddess: Ominous, Transformative, Nurturing; Three Persons in One Goddess

To draw conclusions about the nature of the archetypal goddess, we must return first to the peculiar Keres. The spirit immanent in the thing, its Ker, whether benign or menacing, was initially thought to be separate from the thing itself. These prerational, prelogical essences were associated with birth, death, illness, recovery, accident, and old age, but also with good harvest, plentiful rain, blight, and drought. Ancient people sought to placate and avert those which threatened their survival and food supply while luring and courting those which benefited. Gradually they began to see themselves less at odds with their environment and began to see the spirit of the thing as a metaphor for aspects of themselves. Sir James Frazer wrote of this process in *The Golden Bough;* "As men emerge from savagery the tendency to humanize their divinities gains strength; and the more human they become the wider is the breach which severs them from the natural objects of which they were at first merely the animating spirits or souls."[1] These Keres, prototypes of the divinities, were spirits who encompassed the continuity of nature, birth as well as death, planting as well as harvest or drought. These seemingly contradictory associations remain evident in the enigmatic characterizations of revised goddesses, particularly the often inscrutable Artemis and the shadowy underworld figures of Hecate and Persephone. In story these "dread" goddesses execute and avenge; they preside over the dead, yet they are just as likely to be found assisting in childbirth or blessing spring planting. The Paleolithic figurines, already mentioned as harbingers of the great goddess, may have been representations of Keres, talismans thought to impel food and fertility rather than actual representations of the later tribal goddesses. The distortion of their figures to exaggerate the sexual tends to suggest that they were charms thought to promote precreation, not just within the tribe but in the wild as well.

23

It was logical for primitive omnivores to conceive of the earth itself as divine as well as maternal. Earth became the metaphoric mother, the generative entity associated with all life who simultaneously provided the womb which took back the tribe's worshiped dead. Aeschylus wrote: "Yea, summon Earth, who brings all things to life / And rears and takes again into her womb."[2] As a conception of divinity this idea evolved within each separate tribe; the particular characteristics of the anthropomorphism no doubt stemming from the individual needs of the distinct tribe, but connected always to the goals of food and fertility since promotion of these was essential to the continued life of every tribe and therefore deemed sacred. Harrison emphasizes these goals as making up the drive toward life, that which propelled ancient tribes to perform the rituals which became religion.[3]

Eventually the earth itself was the single mother-deity, in whose charge was procreation as well as the care of the dead; it is as such that she is pictured on the wall at Catal Huyuk, thousands of years before the first myths of extant literature tell anything of her story. Envisioned as an entity of such comprehension, in her earliest manifestations the goddess was not a model who was wholly good, not model at all by later moral standards, but rather a figure who transcended and encompassed the human, while reflecting in her presence the duality inherent in nature. Ever representative of the renewal of vegetative life, as an idea she necessarily included the death that attends renewal in nature. To the matriarchal consciousness the goddess reflects a "continuum in which different states are simply experienced as transformations of one energy."[4] She was ancestress of the tribe, guardian of the newly dead, as well as succorer of women in childbirth. As such she was an awesome figure with the potential to be as suddenly capricious, suddenly volatile as is nature itself. She combined both good and bad aspects, and was remarkable for this syncretism, merging in a single deity the contradictions which are inherent in life: the ferocious and immutable with the loving and benign, the ominously chthonic with the nurturingly maternal. These are her principal features: she is regenerative, yet she is infernal. From these two connections came her initial power, a power so threatening, so potent and mysterious, that a large part of the energy of Western man has gone into the process of reducing and disarming her. Although the prototype, the great goddess of prehistory stands in stark contrast to that benign and passive remnant, the Biblical Mary, whose sorrowful virginmotherhood is without sexual passion or chthonic overtones, and whose only power is as a suppliant interceding with her divine son for other suppliants.

The original mother goddesses were unnamed and nonspecific tribal conceptions. Imaginative outgrowths of man's awe of both nature and human fertility, they were originally more attribute than individual. As the

Neolithic era waxed and tribes merged in urban centers, tribal goddesses also merged, and were absorbed into one another, their syncretistic natures giving birth to merging myths and revised versions of themselves. Edwin Oliver James, in *The Ancient Gods,* suggested that the birthplace of the great goddess was Phrygia, and from that western Asiatic source her cults fanned out through the Near East into the Aegean, where she would appear as Cybele, Rhea, Asherah, Isis, Ishtar, Astarte, and Ge.[5]

Apuleius wrote of her, allowing her to define herself:

> I am she that is the natural mother of all things, mistress and governess of all elements, the initial progeny of worlds, chief of the powers divine, queen of all that are in hell, the principal of them that dwell in heaven, manifested alone and under one form of all the gods and goddesses. At my will the planets of the sky, the wholesome winds of the seas, and the lamentable silences of hell are disposed, my name, my divinity is adored throughout the world, in divers manners, in variable customs, and in many names.[6]

The Mountain Mother of Asiatic origins may well have evolved from Anatolia to Cyprus and the Cyclades to appear again in statuettes of the Middle Neolithic period in Crete, but there is evidence to suggest that her worship and an associated matriarchy characterized the mainland population during this time as well.[7]

By the Middle Minoan period she was a fully developed, multifaceted goddess in Crete. Initially worshiped alone,[8] she was the first significant deity in the cultural heritage of Western civilization. But the mythology of this goddess is obscure and elusive. There are no written records of her story, although the evidence of artifacts, of signet rings, sarcophagi, frescoes, gems, and seals suggests a developed mythology stemming from cult rituals that included the serpent, the tree, the bird, the bee, the bear, the butterfly which would become the double axe,[9] mythological animals, the labyrinth, and, eventually, the sacrificial bull, and the young god, a male child of the goddess who would become the dying god of later vegetation ritual.

The developed culture of Minoan Crete has been revealed through the archaeological enterprises which began with Arthur Evans. There is much more known about the everyday life of the sophisticated, urbane Minoan culture than that of Anatolian Catal Huyuk, or Central Balkan Vinca, yet the three are clearly connected. Various factors contributed to the conclusion by ethnologists and archaeologists that Western culture originated in the Near East, with both races and tribes merging in Neolithic centers like Catal Huyuk. Whether there evolved a parent culture, which then diffused from Anatolia through Crete and the islands to mainland Greece or whether the Old Europe culture of Balkan origin filtered down into main-land Greece before influencing Crete and the islands, is unclear. Burial customs of the Minoans on Crete resemble the burial customs of Catal Huyuk. There is also evidence of links through language and race, as well as religion.[10] Marija Gimbutas argues that the evidence of costume and theatrical mask connect Crete to the Old European culture at Vinca through liturgical ritual.[11] However it evolved, Crete represents a far more elaborate bequest than do Catal Huyuk or Vinca; at the zenith of its culture, Crete was magnificent, with an urbane sophistication and a developed aes-thetic sense. Although it has left no extant literature, Crete was clearly a culture which had a literature. As such, Crete offers to this study the earliest intimations of the goddess as heroine.

Will Durant emphasizes the Cretan artists' connection to nature in his discussion of that culture in *The Life of Greece*. This closeness is obvious in the art, but it is also reflected in the religion of Crete, which, in its near-ness to the time when religion consisted of rituals to avert or allure the Keres, bequeathed to later culture a panoply of dryads, sileni, sylphs, and nymphs, all of whom had evolved during the tribal days of Crete when tribesmen saw in every stream and glade a distinct spirit, powerful but placable. These were eventually anthropomorphized into female divinities and magical figures, who persisted as children or subalterns of the encom-passing earth goddess and even then were often indiscriminate in their nur-turing.[12]

Before and long after the growth of the urban center at Knossos, one manifestation of the goddess was a rustic figure connected to fertility in the natural world. As Mountain Mother or Mistress of the Wild Things her en-compassing aegis extended to animals in the wild, but she was a huntress too. Artifacts present her bedecked in a short skirt, and accompanied by spear and hunting dog. In this manifestation she foreshadows her own progeny, the huntress Artemis. But she was honored long before the Olym-pian goddesses. Throughout the hills and grottoes in ancient unrecorded times she was associated with the tree, an ancient symbol which connected the earth and sky and nether lands and which can be connected back to the Paleolithic statuettes of the feetless, rooted mothers and forward to the fer-tility rituals which followed the realization of man's role in conception and therefore called for a phallic element to fructify the earth.[13]

As urban center evolved in Crete, the goddess became a sophisticated and awesome extension of the Bird and Snake Goddess and tribal ances-tress. In Knossos she is pictured in the company of snakes, ancient do-mestic talismans, but instead of the grass snakes which served as household protectors,[14] the snakes which entwine her are vipers, and she proffers them to her worshipers. The vipers emphasize her chthonic connection, as snakes represented the souls of the dead,[15] and in presenting them, she reminds her worshipers that the connection between life and the renewal of life is through death, the annual death of nature, the ongoing deaths of the tribe. Otherwise, her figure is quite fashionable. Naked to the waist but for her jewels, she offers her breasts in the tradition of the Paleolithic statuettes, but, unlike them, she is realistic and lovely. Her skirt is elaborate and decorative, with tiered ruffles and the suggestion of crinolines. In urban Crete her rule is evidenced everywhere; her shrines appear in every palace and house, her influence was intricate to the Minoan hegemony.

The syncretism of the original tribal goddess complicated the confusion about the goddess's name and her nature as the world of the tribal village became the larger urban center. It undoubtedly contributed to the process of specification which would eventually help to disempower her. But initially at least, her syncretism was a natural aspect of her complexity. The goddess was the first deity to incorporate multiple persons in one god.

On Crete, as at Catal Huyuk, she was first a dual goddess, having two versions of herself, mother and maid. The agrarian order demanded a new symbolism which reflected its interests and the duality of the goddess supplied this. The earth mother gave way to the corn mother who produced the harvest but was again a nubile maiden in the spring.[16] The original cults had grown up around the generative processes, and human fertility continued as a hallowed priority in Minoan Crete, so it was but a short step to conceptualizing the maiden as daughter to the corn mother. Storage of grain was underground in containers called *pithos;*[17] harvest was referred to as the bringing down of the corn maiden,[18] so the idea of the "Anodos of Kore," the rising of the maiden, developed easily into the cycle of myths that include the story of Britomartis and Minos, as well as the story which has come down to us with the names of Demeter and Persephone. Always in these stories the period of anxiety, of famine or winter, is associated with the separation of mother and child, the severing of the most sacrosanct tribal bond.

But even as the corn mother and her maiden daughter evolved, the goddess herself remained inherently plural, in conception preserving some of the collective nature of the group emotion which had produced her.[19] She was ever generative, giving birth to versions of herself, yet remaining still able to generate others. The corn mother, traditionally called Demeter, may have been called Dikytanna on Crete. To an extent, at least in the cycle of myths which portray her as the sorrowing mother, she is separate from her own chthonic aspect, although we shall see that Demeter's ruthlessness has chthonic roots.[20] When a personality emerged from the goddess which was devoid of chthonic characteristics, however, as is often necessary for myth to compensate with a chthonic counterpart, and so Persephone became both Kore and Queen of the Dead. Britomartis, sweet maiden daughter of Diktyanna, has no chthonic aspect, but Diktyanna is also associated with and later called Artemis, whose chthonic counterpart was Hecate,[21] another deity who originated in Cretan myth.

These chthonic deities are ominous, expressing the misunderstood, dark side of the goddess, but that may not always have been the case. In the traditional myth of the separation of Demeter and Persephone, the mournful silence of the daughter comes from the fact that her sojourn in the underworld is not by choice; it is expressive of the deadening grief which is her response to separation from her mother. The Neolithic mind did not separate the living and the dead with the same stark delineations that were later common, but they recognized the debility of grief. Harrison suggests that Persephone as Queen of the Underworld is an extension of her role as Lady of the Wild Things.[22] Death, so common in the wild, is not accompanied there by human grief and so can be viewed as a more benign aspect of the cycle of nature. In fact, it is from Crete that the idea of Elysium, island of the blessed, originated.[23] According to that vision, the afterlife is yet another life, transformation to a subsequent life of peace and pleasant fraternizing among the great. It was a compelling idea which Socrates, an unbeliever, alluded to years later when, at the moment of his condemnation, he sought to comfort his supporters and defy those who intended to punish him: "Wherefore, O Judges, be of good cheer about death, and know of a certainty, that no evil can happen to a good man, either in this life or after death."[24] It has become the promise of subsequent religions as well.

From the same etymology came the words Eleutho and Eleusis.[25] The first is the epithet of the goddess as she succored women in childbirth. During the later period, after specification had attenuated the powers of the great goddess, she emerged in one variation as Ilithyia or Eileithyia, goddess of childbirth, who was one of the daughters of Hera. More accurately, however, the goddess as Eleutho is part of her role as Lady of the Wild Things, where she both aided in the struggle of birth and cared for the dead. It was as an extension of this aspect of the goddess that Artemis rose just moments after her own birth to assist her mother, Leto, in the birth of Apollo.

In her earlier manifestation in Neolithic Crete, the goddess who is midwife is also mother. The Anatolian Lady of the Wild Things holds leopard and lion pups. The Neolithic vegetation goddess is pregnant. On Crete the image is *Kourotrophos,* mother, an extension of the attribute of maternity, of nurturing, which led easily to the later abstraction involving her motherhood in the story of Demeter, where she is ever nurturing as the grief-stricken mother of Persephone, wet nurse of Demophoon, mentor of Triptolemus, grandmother of Zageus or Dionysus. Neolithic man connected agriculture and child rearing and motherhood; his creation of the personality of the corn mother Demeter fuses these aspects in a single personality.[26]

Tribal imperatives propelled this culture to its greatest achievements, achievements which apparently included the open participation of women in city life. Archaeologists suggest that the island's success was predicated upon an efficient interaction of subsystems which included the manufacture of tools for metallurgy and centers which organized agricultural enterprises, including stock breeding and exportation of crafts. The efficiency of these interdependent systems testifies to group cohesion of a tribal nature; scholars suggest it was closely linked to the aesthetic sensibility promoted by the Minoan religion,[27] a religion dominated by the mother image and supported by a society which was matrilineal if not matriarchal.

Campbell writes:

> The culture, as many have noted, was apparently of a matriarchal type. The grace and elegance of the ladies in their beautifully flounced skirts, generous decollete, pretty coiffures, and gay bandeaus, mixing freely with the men, in the courts, in the bullring—lovely, vivid, and vivacious, gesticulating, chattering, even donning masculine athletic belts to go somersaulting dangerously over the horns and backs of bulls—represent a civilized refinement that has not been often equaled since: which I would like . . . to fix firmly in place, by way of a challenge to the high claims of those proudly phallic moral orders, whether circumcised or uncircumcised, that were to follow.[28]

The fact that Crete was a civilization of united tribes, with a common ancestry as well as common social goals, was an important factor in its success. Although Crete made its influence felt upon the ancient world through control of the sea and exports, no invading cultures affected Crete until after some natural disaster weakened the island around 1450 B.C. Previous to that, the Minoan culture had been of unified stock for 1,500 years,[29] during which the female principle dominated in religion and had influence in society, and during which there was apparently neither war nor weaponry.

The fact that the women of ancient Crete were vibrant participants in public life, does not necessarily relate to their dominance as cult figures, as many feminist scholars have argued.[30] The female divinities of other cultures, such as Hindu and Oriental, have not enhanced the social status of living women, at least not beyond the Neolithic period. The fact that a female deity was paramount in Minoan religion while Minoan women enjoyed great personal freedom does, however, contribute to this study. Such social practice suggests a way of organizing experience which did not concentrate completely on the metaphoric centrality of the male in cultural life. Myths were composed partially as an outgrowth of ritual and religion, partially as a means by which ancient peoples explained matters of natural phenomena, but also as a means by which they validated the status quo.

One scholar tells us that there is "reason to suppose that the stone seat in the Throne Room at Knossos was the throne not of Minos but of Ariadne, used in ritual by the queen as representative of the goddess."[31] The status quo in Minoan culture clearly included social and political power for women, and this fact, as well as their worship of the chthonic mother goddess, would have necessarily been reflected in the lost stories of that age, in myths which might have revealed what was authentically archetypal for the goddess-heroine.

The Minoan goddess was Ariadne; her name reflects her days as a Ker. It is an epithet, "the sacred one." In her rural manifestations near Cretan mountains, she is called Britomartis or Diktyanna and she is associated with sylvan nymphs and worshiped in orgiastic dances.[32] The goddess, who is also called Rhea or Cybele when she resembles the great Asian nature goddess, was everywhere worshiped by groups, indicative of the continuum by which tribal ritual became liturgical process and eventually developed into both religion and art.

The dance is the key factor to making this transition. The rituals which developed into worship of the great goddess were tribal exercises. It is likely that they were led by the mothers of the tribe, who were the social center of the tribe as well as the identifiable ancestresses. The emotion of the dance was the lofty, cohesive goal and became closely associated with the chief dancer.[33] The emotion of the group, its immanent divinity, was enhanced by the loss of the individual's ego in the rhythm of the music. The group's ecstasy reenforced itself and created the deity, the anthropopathic conversion of that emotion into a deity. Campbell writes in *Primitive Mythology* of the power of all these primitive religious exercises:

> Through such half-mad games and plays ordered human societies were constellated in which the mutually contradictory interests of the elementary and social urges were resolved. And the higher principle according to which they were thus resolved was not in any sense a function or derivative either of any one of them or of their combination, but an actually superior, subordinated principle *gui generis,* . . . that principle of disinterested delight and self-loss in a rhythm of beauty, which now is termed aesthetic and which used to be called, more loosely, spiritual, mystical, or religious.[34]

The masks of the aversion rituals became incorporated into the liturgical rituals. The vulture masks of Catal Huyuk may have developed into a vulture goddess, with the chief dancer of the original ritual becoming the representative of the divinity. Harrison has pointed out that the Gorgon Medusa was originally a ritual mask, not a goddess or the profligate villainess of later myth.[35] The use of the ritual masks suggests the element of liturgy which Marija Gimbutas cited as the most obvious link between the cultures of Old Europe, Minoan Crete, and Hellenic Greece. "A liturgical use of masked participants, the *thiasotes* or *tragoi,* led ultimately to their appearance on stage and the birth of tragedy."[36]

Both the ancient tree cult and the advent of agriculture were associated with orgiastic dance worship. The Lady of the Wild Things, who had first been associated with fertility of wild animals and fertility of the tribe, extended her aegis to cover the fertility of the earth as the tribe came to depend on agriculture as its food source. The religious mysteries of Greece originated in Crete, where they were not mysterious but rather the open supplication of agricultural tribes, who looked to the sky and prayed for rain and to the earth and prayed for crops.[37] In Crete the original spring song of the *Kouretes,* a sacred ritual, was for healthy children as well as for good crops.[38]

Various scholars have connected orgiastic dance worship with the goddess.[39] Eventually she was most closely preserved in Artemis, but that was only after the trend toward specification had split the goddess into many narrow versions of her original syncretistic self. On Crete she had not yet been circumscribed when her attendants danced in worship with sacred boughs in mountain rituals. As Ariadne, "the sacred one," once the multifaceted goddess, she was worshiped in urban Knossos; Homer tells us in the *Iliad* of a dancing floor "like that which once in the wide spaces of Knossos Daidalos built for Ariadne of the lovely tresses."[40] There she had, no doubt, danced accompanied by the Cretan *Kouretes,* protectors of the child, in mother worship of the first order.

This old order was the traditional tribal order, consisting of mother, child, and initiated youths,[41] the core elements of the tribe itself. This group of worshipers developed rituals to increase agricultural production and tribal fertility, and because of the close connection between these liturgical rituals and agriculture, they conceived within these rituals the idea of the possibility of immortal life, a marvelously consoling idea first ritualized in the Cretan mysteries, which remained the essence of their heartening message as they evolved and migrated to the mainland, where they became the Eleusinian Mysteries of Demeter.

Up until a certain age, the individual child is unable to fathom the permanency of death. He conceives of death as a seasonal disappearance and expects the lost loved one to return as do the flowers in spring.[42] This psychological process is not unlike the conceptualization of primitive agrarian people who worshiped the goddess. In Crete the idea was incorporated into religious rituals which honored the goddess as corn mother and was bequeathed to later religions through the conduit of Demeter's Eleusinian Mysteries,[43] where it was clearly akin to the notion of later religions that man can transcend his mortality by his faith and be rewarded with a blissful afterlife.

> Happy is he among men upon earth who has seen these mysteries; but he
> who is uninitiate and who has no part of them, never has lot of like good
> things once he is dead, down in the darkness and gloom.[44]

The liturgical ritual of the early Cretan religion was sophisticated and aesthetic in nature. Fifteen hundred years before the Greeks attended the
Theatre of Dionysus, citizens of Knossos attended dramas which were, no
doubt, an urbanized extension of the original mountain dance, reflecting
the primary interests of the now-agrarian people. The story of loss of the
goddess's child, who is eventually reunited with her because of the goddess's own power and ingenuity, was almost certainly one of the dramas
presented in Cretan theatre. This is obvious from visual adumbrations in
Cretan art, from the fact that it is the essence of the story told in the ritual
drama of the later Mysteries of Eleusis, but also because it is a story which
has been told and retold in various Near Eastern cultures and had been in-
scribed on Akkadian tables dating from the first millennium B.C.[45]

In Sumerian mythology, Inanna is the generative nature goddess;
Ereshkigal her chthonic counterpart, the queen of the underworld. The lost
child of the goddess is the shepherd god Dumuzi who is rescued when his
goddess mother submits to death.[46] But she has cleverly left behind an
elaborate plan for her own rescue. James notes new evidence that suggests
there was another subplot to Inanna's story which had perhaps been repressed by the patriarchal cultures who inherited her story. In this the
rescued child is not sufficiently humbled by the heroism of his rescuer, the
goddess-mother. Instead, he is rather perfunctory about the event. His
divine mother summarily disciplines him by handing him over to the
daemons of the underworld, Ereshkigal's creatures, "presumably to carry
him back whence he came."[47] Variations of this story characterize much
Near Eastern mythology. The crux of the goddess's heroism can be seen
in Inanna's story; she has power over life and death, and that power is com-
plemented by her natural acumen. She orchestrates her own rescue by leaving a detailed plan with her underlings. In this aspect she is a forerunner
of Ariadne, who has the secret knowledge to rescue Theseus from the
labyrinth; but by the time Theseus mimics Dumuzi in his arrogant ingrati-
tude, the goddess has been disempowered, and she is merely a supporting
actress in the story of a misogynist's heroism.

In her response to the kidnapping of Persephone, Demeter shows a
chthonic power similar to Inanna's. Although Demeter's story undoubtedly originated in Crete, it was altered by later mainland storytellers, and
there is ample evidence of their overlay. The Cretan origin of the myth is
suggested by the fact that in the Homeric Hymn Demeter herself testifies
to the daughters of Metaneira and Celeus that she has been kidnapped
from Crete, but had managed to escape her kidnappers through her own

ingenuity. The name Demeter is not Cretan,[48] but Da Mater was the term the Minyans used in Attica to refer to their corn mother and the Minyans were thought to have been emigrants from Crete.[49] There is further evidence that the culture which existed in Attica at the time of the Cretan immigration was also matriarchal, no doubt having migrated south from the Balkan Peninsula. So in Attica there appears to have been a meeting of matriarchal cultures, one Cretan, the other the Old European culture studied by Gimbutas. Harrison writes, "In a word, mythology is *pre*-history and when it is confirmed by archaeology . . . we may venture to trust it."[50] The myth of Demeter as well as the Mysteries of Eleusis survived because of this merging and despite the later patriarchal influences which would alter the original plot with complications reflecting the ascendancy of male gods. Despite the overlay, the plot remains essentially a remnant of the earlier matriarchal cultures, with the insertion of the sky gods an almost perfunctory exercise that does not effectively diminish our ability to focus on the heroism of the goddess.

Although the effort to attenuate the influence of the original multifaceted goddess had certainly begun by the time of the composition of the poems which were incorporated into the Homeric *Hymn to Demeter,* the generative archetype who had preceded the corn goddess had not yet been completely separated and there is evidence of her in each of the female characters who appear in the poem. Earth as a separate goddess is present in the poem; she is the one responsible for the growth of flowers which lures Persephone into Hades' trap, but she is not autonomous and produces her harvest not for the good of the tribe, but at the bidding of the male sky gods who have usurped her power. Furthermore, she is apparently a willing accomplice in the abduction of Kore, who is lured by

> violets, irises also and hyacinths and the narcissus,
> which Earth made to grow at the will of Zeus and to
> please the Host of Many, to be a snare for the
> bloom-like girl—a marvelous radiant flower.[51]

This goddess had long ago surrendered her power at Delphi, first to Themis, her daughter, and a Kore version of herself, but later irrevocably to Apollo. She is hardly a fully realized character in this poem; she is but a paltry shadow of the powerful Goddess Creatrix, the primary goddess of Minoan, Minyan, and Old European mythology. Instead, she is a remnant of the Indo-European tribal mother, not a powerful generative goddess, but a limited, one-dimensional figure who needed the male sky gods to be generative.[52] In the Indo-European pantheon, this figure had never been fully anthropomorphicized; she remained an abstraction.[53] Yet as skeletal as she is in this poem she is also key. It is Earth who has the cunning to lure the young Kore and so guarantee the snare which Hades and Zeus have set. In this she has either retained or been assigned one of the recurring attributes of the Minoan-goddess tradition, a sagacity inaccessible to the Indo-European hero. As with Ariadne and Theseus, Hera and Jason, Athena and Perseus, even Athena and Odysseus, the complicity of a wise goddess was an oft-repeated and essential subplot in revised myth which developed into a fictional tradition, a motif which unfortunately helped to obscure the archetypal heroine as it facilitated a view of heroism as essentially a male experience.

The shadowy goddess Earth (Ge or Gaia) in this poem is typical of the Indo-European tradition. That she is distinct from the Minoan great goddess is obvious later in the poem with the entrance of Rhea, mother of Demeter, Hades, and Zeus. Rhea is clearly more of the Minoan tradition, although she too does the bidding of Zeus. Rhea's name was associated most often with Cybele in Phrygia but also appeared in Crete. In the poem she enters in the final stages of the conflict to intercede with her daughter for Zeus, who has been unable to compel Demeter to cease her revenge on gods and men. In this role Rhea is the Minoan mother; she is symbolic of the connections of the tribe and her intercession with her daughter is what finally does move Demeter to rejoin the Olympians. In addition, the intercession of Rhea prompts Demeter to teach Triptolemus and Celeus the secrets of her mysteries. Rhea is a forerunner of the Biblical Mary in this myths: although without her own power, the maternal figure has great influence on the divine child. The sacredness of the bond between them, and the fact that it mirrors her own with Kore, moves the goddess to acts of compassionate altruism, which result in unsolicited boons for mankind.

Rhea can be seen as an attenuation of the original goddess of matriarchal tradition, while Earth, as she appears in the *Hymn to Demeter* is the amorphous abstraction. The goddess of vegetation, this Demeter is an outgrowth, a more specified second generation offspring of Rhea. Demeter's closeness to her generative great goddess mother is clear from a comparison of her hymn to the shorter, less plotted Homeric *Hymn to Earth the Mother of All.*

The *Hymn to Demeter* ends with Rhea and Demeter exiting together toward Olympus. The poet seems unable to clearly distinguish mother and daughter.

> But when the bright goddess had taught them all,
> they went to Olympus to the gathering of the other
> gods. And there they dwell beside Zeus who
> delights in thunder, awful and reverend goddesses.
> Right blessed is he among men on earth whom they
> freely love: soon they do send Plutus as guest to
> his great house, Plutus who gives wealth to mortal men.[54]

The Homeric *Hymn to Earth the Mother of All* echoes this ending:

> I will sing of wellfounded Earth, mother of all,
> eldest of all beings. She feeds all creatures that are
> in the world, all that go upon the goodly land, and
> all that are in the paths of the seas, and all that fly:
> all these are fed of her store. Through you, O
> queen, men are blessed in their children and blessed
> in their harvests, and to you it belongs to give means
> of life to mortal men and to take it away. Happy is
> the man whom you delight to honor![55]

Demeter remains distinctly in the matriarchal tradition throughout most of the Homeric hymn to her. Although no longer chthonic, she still possesses powers which exceed those of Zeus or Hades, neither of whom can move her to behave as either of them dictates. Furthermore, she is displayed in her trinity in the poem as well, with Kore becoming Persephone as she merges with Hecate, the chthonic version of the goddess. In this poem, Demeter is inexorable and ruthless, unmoved by the will of male gods she is motivated by her own ethics to a righteous rage. As goddess of the harvest, Demeter still retains power over life and death for mankind, and consequently the power to cut off the sacrifices and homage so important to the vain Olympians, which she does without hesitation.

By the time of the composition of the poem, however, the sky gods of the Indo-European invaders were in ascendancy, having raped the tribal goddesses or metaphorically subdued them through marriage. For Indo-Europeans the institution of marriage somewhat resembled pair bonding, but in fictional representation called for fidelity and subservience on the part of the wife alone. Yet there is ample evidence that a complex power is still associated with the goddess, a power related to the mother-child dyad. When Kore is abducted she calls first to her father, but the shallow monarch god does not hear her or is able to ignore her as he accepts "sweet offerings from mortal men." Like the later hero Agamemnon, he is unmoved by the most compelling of cries, the cry of a dying child to its parent; or perhaps like Agamemnon, he chooses the accolades of men over the life of his child, and so is able to ignore the anguished shrieks of Kore, whose abduction he has helped arrange.

Because Kore "still hoped to see her dear mother and the tribes of the eternal gods," she continues to cry out, although no longer to seek the assistance of her father. Instead she calls on mother nature and her own mother: "so long hope calmed her great heart for all her trouble, . . . and the heights of the mountains and the depths of the sea rang with her immortal voice: and her queenly mother heard her."

Hecate, a chthonic version of Demeter herself, hears the cries and she alone goes to Demeter to tell her of the kidnapping, although Hecate too has been circumscribed and cannot tell her who has taken Kore. The night goddess, though prototype of witch and crone, is also associated with childbirth and fertility rites. Here she is called "tender-hearted Hecate, bright-coiffed," and throughout is the supportive companion of both mother and her daughter. Demeter herself has "rent the covering upon her divine hair" and reminiscent of her days as a Bird Goddess, has "sped, like a wildbird, over the firm land and yielding sea, seeking her child."

When she learns of Kore's fate from Helios, "grief yet more terrible and savage came into the heart of Demeter, and thereafter she was so angered with the dark-clouded Son of Cronos that she avoided the gathering of the gods." This is the reverse order of the traditional tribal punishment. She sequesters herself rather than banishing the offender from the tribe; the offender now controls the tribe.

With a poignant humanity, the goddess seeks comfort among human women, and there she finds it at the well at Eleusis where the naive daughters of Celeus offer her both compassion and employment, drawing her into their group without any inkling of her status. Metaneira alone suspects that the appearance of this crone disguises a higher rank; this prompts her to offer Demophoon, her own infant son, to be Demeter's charge and comfort. It is certainly why she offers Demeter her seat in the palace.

But Demeter still clings to appropriate and necessary grief, knowing the connection between suffering and wisdom and unconcerned with enhancing her own reputation or receiving homage. Demeter is *Kourotrophos,* child rearer,[56] so she accepts briefly the comfort offered by nurturing the infant Demophoon. She assures his mother that she is qualified to be nurse to her cherished late-life infant and promises to ward off the Keres that bring teething pain to infants. She is the ideal of the surrogate mother who would have rendered the child immortal in exchange for the brief reprieve his sweet infant needs brought from her debilitating grief.

Metaneira's understandable uneasiness leads to her nocturnal discovery of the goddess immersing the infant in fire. Demeter is enraged; Metaneira's intrusion has ended Demeter's interlude of comfort and dared to challenge her benevolent maternity. The Indo-European woman was probably unfamiliar with the primitive ritual of "saining" children against Keres,[57] a practice which was part of the Cretan ritual of initiation. But Demeter is furious, she casts the child away from her and turns her anger on Metaneira. It is the distaff tribe who hears Demophoon's wails and comes to comfort mother and baby as the goddess returns to her bereavement. But the surrogate mother has not repudiated her connection to the infant: "As for the child, he grew like an immortal being."

Demeter has "caused a most dreadful and cruel year for mankind" and "would have destroyed the whole race of man with cruel famine and have robbed them who dwell on Olympus of their glorious right of gifts and sacrifices, had not Zeus perceived." But Zeus can do little about it. He sends Iris, his messenger, first, and when she cannot sway the corn goddess he follows with numerous Olympian messengers, none of whom can prevail upon the grieving goddess to relent. In the end Zeus sends Hermes to convince Hades "with soft words" to set the young goddess free. What prevents Zeus's complete capitulation to Demeter's demands is the ruse of Hades, who slips Persephone a pomegranate seed at the moment when elation has made her forget caution.

Demeter knows of this trickery without having to be told of it. She knows too of the compromise which will separate mother and daughter for half of every year and make grief a rotating season in her life. Again there is the connection between suffering and wisdom, and now the goddess accepts the suffering as a natural part of the life cycle. But "their hearts had relief from their griefs while each took and gave back joyousness"; this cycle of grief and joyousness reflects the essential nature of this divinity and the balance within life itself. The goddess's seasonal grief is mitigated by Hecate, who offers to die with Persephone, and so the "bright-coiffed Hecate" becomes Persephone's "minister and companion," a surrogate mother in the underworld.

The poem ends with Demeter's own mother coming to comfort her daughter. The presence of the mother prompts Demeter to provide mankind with an unsolicited boon. In this last phase she is yet another version of mother; this time she is teacher, and Triptolemus, Diocles, Eumolpus, and Celeus learn the secrets of her mysteries, and through the death of the "Savior Girl," Persephone, mankind is given its first promise of immortal life.

The Hades to which Persephone goes is the Hades of the later Indo-European tribes; Crete's Elysian Fields were not the dark and gloomy kingdom of Hades. The two myths have merged but the Cretan mysticism has remained flexible: Paradise is when Persephone is with her mother.

The event described in this story, the separation of the mother and her child, and the heroism of the story, in which the divine mother actively sets about the task of saving her child from danger and death are expressive of concerns necessarily connected to the tribal drive for life. The dangers to the individual child and the efforts of the individual mother in protecting that child were matters at the heart of survival, not just of the tribe but of the species. The antagonist this mother faces is not just the god, but the inflexibility of male governance whose concerns are other than her own. This conflict and the relationships alluded to in the story, that of mother and child, foster mother and child, and between adult women, are all common aspects of female experience, yet as motifs they do not appear often in this constellation in mythology. The evidence in the story of the goddess's significant power and her righteous rage make it an unusual myth, as does the absence of feminine vanity. What is most unusual however, is that what motivates the heroine in this poem is explicit and ethical, as is the compassionate intervention of Hecate and the interaction between Rhea and her daughter. In this story the goddess's actions are neither banalized nor rendered inscrutable. Nor is there any suggestion of the bitter social competition that would later be so common to female characters as literature came to revolve around a central male experience.

Recent scholarship has attempted to burrow beneath the social constructions and cultural paradigms to examine the female experience as an entity unrelated to the goal of male centrality. Nancy Chodorow focused on the mother-child dyad as the pivotal period when values begin to diverge along lines of sex and she contends that this early relationship, at last recognized as the vital link to both phylogenetic and ontogenetic socialization, is experienced differently for boys and girls. Girls, "in identifying themselves as female, experience themselves as like their mothers, thus fusing the experience of attachment with the process of identity formation."[58] The result is an emphasis on empathy with others, which contrasts with masculine emphasis on individuation and separation. Carol Gilligan argues that beyond the emphasis on relationship learned from this social pattern, women possess an inherent tendency toward investment in others which generates a different ethical system, one based on facilitation of connection and care, not on individuation or autonomous achievement,[59] and validated by the emotional rewards of community. Such considerations suggest the archetypal goddess is one whose inherent priorities are like Demeter's—the mother-child dyad and the life of the tribe—and not the promotion of the male hero, the role she has been assigned in revised mythology.

If one accepts the possibility that the ancient goddess was less concerned than later generations with matters of heroic individuation, it is hardly difficult to conclude that the accepted pattern outlined in Campbell's *Hero with a Thousand Faces*, which includes a period away from the tribe—a period of isolated struggle outside the parameters of society— which culminates in a both personal enlargement and a boon for the society to which the autonomous hero returns, is not a pattern which would necessarily be followed by a heroine. The act of separation alone defines the pattern as a masculine endeavor. Campbell writes: "The hero can go forth of his own volition to accomplish the adventure, as did Theseus when he arrived in his father's city, Athens, and heard the horrible history of the Minotaur; or he may be carried or sent abroad by some benign or malignant agent, as was Odysseus, driven about the Mediterranean by the winds of the angered god, Poseidon."[60]

Gilligan reviews the works of Erik Erikson and Bruno Bettelheim to underscore the problems posed by traditional views of what is heroic for women, who are scorned for setting out on the equivalent of the masculine adventure (as was Atalanta), and instead are assigned a period of passivity before finding fulfillment with a husband:

> Since adolescent heroines awake from their sleep not to conquer the world, but to marry the prince, their identity is inwardly and inter-personally defined. For women, in Bettelheim's as in Erikson's account, identity and intimacy are intricately conjoined. The sex differences depicted in the world of fairy tales . . . indicate repeatedly that active adventure is a male activity, and that if a woman is to embark on such endeavors, she must at least dress like a man.[61]

Yet what of the heroism of Demeter? The boon she gave mankind was agriculture; in order to give it, however, she never left society. Instead, she remained within it, her lonely struggle an internal one—to work through grief—a task she completed by removing herself from the dominant social grouping—the Olympians—investing herself in another—Demophon. This story, which at least one scholar sees "as exemplifying the feminine attitude toward power," is a story of interdependence, of feminine networking, of a building up of strength through connection toward the ultimate achievement of a goal.[62] Most significantly, the goddess's actions do not result from the pursuit of personal aggrandizement nor are they a reaction to "some benign or malignant agent." She has not inappropriately challenged the power of Zeus, as Odysseus had the power of Poseidon, but instead reacted to the injustice of that power. It is a unique story in that it has "parental affection as its primary motivational theme."[63] Moreover, it is a story of parents in conflict. In its first rendition, the Homeric *Hymn to Demeter,* Persephone cries out to her father; he ignores her pleas, establishing the factitious right of his brother to seize the child at his whim over the ancient and more sacred right of a mother to raise her own child.[64] It is maternal emotion which propels the rest of the tale to its eventual end, which includes not just a boon for mankind but a reaffirmation of matriarchal ethics in the interacting commitments of Persephone and Hecate, Demeter and her own mother. There is no personal promotion, there is instead an emphasis on the tribe and its most elemental link, the mother-child dyad as well as the uniquely unqualified expression of appropriately feminine rage.

Gilligan uses this myth to demystify what baffled Freud and his followers. She writes:

> The elusive mystery of women's development lies in its recognition of the continuing importance of attachment in the human life cycle. Woman's

place in man's life cycle is to protect this recognition while the developmental litany intones the celebration of separation, autonomy, individuation, and natural rights. The myth of Persephone speaks directly to the distortion in this view by reminding us that narcissism leads to death, that the fertility of the earth is in some mysterious way tied to the continuation of the mother-daughter relationship, and that the life cycle itself arises from an alternation between the world of women and that of men.[65]

Yet there is little elsewhere in mythology which reflects this cycle. The tendency of Western culture, going back to its first extant stories, has been toward the suppression of feminine values and, therefore, feminine modes of thought and heroism, especially that which appeared ominous or irrational in that they conflicted with the Indo-European notion of gender, a system which was geared toward an exclusively male dominance.

Scholars have recently explored the ancient Greek predilection for defining in terms of what they were and were not: a prelogical, archaic pattern expressed in analogy and polarity which infused Western culture with its earliest self-definition by stressing exclusion and separation from others, from animals, from women, and from non–Greeks.[66] Such a tendency has a psychological motivation rooted in the earliest religious impulse of individual tribes, in their rites of aversion and supplication, in their vision of divinity as an outgrowth of their own sacral group. On a cultural level it coalesced as a hierarchy of human differences and a polarized vision which divided the universe of dialectics into opposites which exclude rather than complement each other and was almost indelibly impressed upon Western consciousness through the prescriptions of revised mythology. Campbell writes:

> Psychologically and sociologically, the problem is of enormous interest; for, as all schools of psychology agree, the importance of the mother and the female affects the psyche differently from that of the father and male. Sentiments of identity are associated most immediately with the mother; those of dissociation, with the father. Hence, where the mother image preponderates, even the dualism of life and death dissolves in the rapture of her solace; the worlds of nature and the spirit are not separated; . . . and there prevails an implicit confidence in the spontaneity of nature, both in its negative, killing, sacrificial aspect (lion and double ax) and its productive and reproductive (bull and tree).[67]

In this context the myth of Demeter is particularly rare, as it does not insist on the absolute separation of these worlds but retains the spirit of its Cretan origin, of the cyclic nature of all human experience. While the story conveys "the rapture of her solace," this maternal divinity is also powerful and ominous, empathetic and ethical. Though the story leans toward an insistence on the father as the inevitable if not the rightful shaper of events, it is an awkward learning which does not successfully diminish the heroine.

Part Two
Revision of the Archetype

Chapter III

Fiction as Process and the Deprecation of the Goddess: Atalanta, Cassandra, and Ariadne

If an elegant humanism flourished in Crete, one which did not insist on a gender system fostering polarity and the metaphoric centrality of the male, things were different elsewhere. But in a unique way Crete would influence cultures far beyond its own time and place. There was a hedonic character to Cretan culture which is underlined by the lack of military artifacts. The aesthetic principles of the culture, its curious religion, its commercial achievement, all contribute to a profile of Cretan character which suggests that the natural human aggression of the Minoan period was directed into hedonic rather than combative gestures.[1]

Cretan hegemony in the Mediterranean world and its documented influence on neighboring islands as well as on cultures as far away as Britain[2] suggest a preponderance which was the consequence of craft and grandeur rather than combative imperialism. This cultural phenomenon undoubtedly contributed to the lingering evidence of matriarchal principles in the Aegean and its revised mythology in contrast to their more sweeping obliteration in the Levant.

The Greek mainland, however, remained in a Paleolithic hunting mode long after Crete was an advanced civilization; while Crete and other high civilizations influenced its southern coastal populations, waves of hunting tribes were entering the peninsula from the north. Archaeological evidence suggests that the populating of Greece was not the gradual and rather pacific merger of homogeneous tribes as in Crete. The ruins of Mycenae and Tiryns testify that the earliest urban centers were feudal fortresses built with defense in mind; they also indicate a distinctly different attitude toward women than was prevalent in the Minoan culture. The early Mycenaean fortresses were designed with a "lasting principle of Greek architecture—the separation of the women's quarters, or gynaeceum, from the chambers of the men."[3] In addition to this segregation, these fortresses also suggest that among some mainland tribes a class distinction had evolved and had organized the social order along lines very different from those of the older matriarchal bonds.

In tribes which had pursued wild game as their primary food source, a second kind of bonding had evolved to ensure the continued life of the tribe. In his study, *Men in Groups,* Lionel Tiger outlines how male bonding evolved into the behavioral patterns of early man as they became hunters in the Middle Pleistocene period.[4] Tiger concludes that "male bonding is a function of aggression."[5] From the Middle Pleistocene until well into the Proto-Neolithic period, such hunting tribes were firmly dependent on such behavior, and therefore male bonding was an essential aspect of the drive for life, probably to the detriment of the religious impulse manifest by gathering tribes, and certainly to the detriment of the status of women within those tribes. "The cooperative groups involved with hunting would have been all male, and there would have been a strong selective pressure in favour of all maleness," Tiger writes.[6] For such tribes, according to Tiger's theory, the sexual dimorphism which guaranteed fertility was adapted effectively to include the special needs of the hunt. The elevation of the gladiatorial male in these tribes can be seen as a necessary aspect of survival and therefore was interwoven into their conception of divinity, and it is evident in subsequent mythology as is the related social anxiety of gods and kings who fear a violent dethronement at the hands of their progeny. It is conceivable that, once raised up by ecological circumstances, this tribal elite would strive to promote notions of social order which would preserve its privilege as much as possible.

From his study of mythology Northrop Frye distinguishes between three levels in the development of human consciousness which are reflected in language. The first stage, the metaphoric stage, yielded the earliest stories, including the ancient myths of the goddess. According to Frye's analysis, this first stage is linked to the plurality of gods and ancient people's somewhat undelineative relationship with aspects of nature. The most sophisticated cognitive operation it expresses is emotional and its connection to the early tribal rituals of aversion and supplication seems clear. The metaphoric stage, however, gives way, and a second phase, the metonymic phase brought to storytelling a new dimension, which Frye describes as intellectual, indicative of mankind's ability to grapple with metaphysics and "a sense that there are valid and invalid ways of thinking."[7] This second stage of language ushered in literary analysis which began as a function of storytelling itself. Revision restructured the original myths to interweave conceptual abstractions of perfection, including Indo-European notions of heroism and gender. Frye has pointed out the natural tendency of the novice critic to explain unfamiliar poetry in allegorical terms.[8] An essential aspect of the revision of the goddess myth is this human predilection to explicate in terms of what the critic knows and considers of value. By the time metonymic language came to the fore, Indo-European conceptions were prominent, and authority was in the hands of the hunters' male progeny, including the authority to interpret the story of the Aegean goddesses.

Mythology from this point has two components, its literary structure, that which is the heroic event, and its social function, that which is taught by the story. Frye explains this second function as concerned with "what it is important for a society to know."[9] With Aristotle, the analytical tendencies of revision developed into formal literary criticism, which has subsequently been the primary conduit in obfuscating the goddess's story by restricting hermeneutics to a model which regards only masculine experience as culturally significant.

The ancient story of Atalanta and her peculiar, unwelcome presence among the hunters of the Calydonian boar illustrates the clash between the hunting tribe's insistence on a gender system alien to the matriarchal Cretan tradition. In revision, this heroine is stripped first of divinity and subsequently of all logical or ethical motivation and is then evaluated in terms of her unwillingness to comply with certain social constructions. The story offers some insight into how revision as a process contributed to the obscuring of the goddess and the marginalization of her daughters in relationship to the heroic event.

Although a very ancient story, it has come down to us in the version told by Apollodorus in the first or second century A.D., long after the onset of metonymic language. The flexible nature of myth in this second stage of language allows embellishments which are allegorical, motivated by evolving social concerns. Originally myths were transmitted orally from generation to generation, with the individual storyteller freely altering the plot or speculating on character motivation so as to make the story acceptable within his own schema. It is an ongoing aspect of such storytelling, and we regularly engage in it when we present fairy tales and mythology to our own children. But the informal nature of the tradition also facilitates reconstruction, during which the additions and reinterpretations which adhere may obscure the original spirit or intent of the story. This phenomenon can be seen with Nathaniel Hawthorne in the nineteenth century who was the first to give Midas a daughter in his adaptation of that Greek myth in *A Wonder Book for Boys and Girls.* For some two millennia prior to that Midas had been repudiating his rashness, not on account of its moral consequence but because it had rendered him unable to satisfy his most rudimentary needs, hunger and thirst.

This same phenomena is evident in the story of Atalanta and the Calydonian boar hunt which was embellished as the two prehistoric social systems came into confrontation. The figure of Atalanta on the one hand, the primacy of the event and the characters' relationship to it on the other, suggests the story originated in the most ancient tradition. The hunt itself had come about because of the rage of Artemis, that Hellenic goddess whose persona most closely corresponds to the ancient Mistress of the Wild Things.[10] Oeneus, the male leader of an Indo-European clan, had made a sacrifice to his own pantheon but forgotten an offering for the local goddess, who responds in her inimitable way by sending a curse upon his cattle and crops. Oeneus answers in the heroic tradition of the Indo-Europeans; he calls together the noblest men of Greece to hunt the boar and promises to the individual hero who can land the prey the prize of its tusks and pelt, and perhaps the more subtle achievement of having thwarted the local goddess. Among the male hunters this single female huntress is a curiosity, more accurately she is an atavar. Scorned by the men, the huntress is the counterpart of Artemis herself, a remnant of the ancient Mistress of the Wild Things, another manifestation of "the pure maiden, shooter of stags who delight in archery."[11]

Atalanta, who had appeared earlier in the very ancient *Catalogues of Women and Eoiae,* was the free-spirited daughter of Iasus and had almost managed to retain her prepatriarchal autonomy by escaping the confining fate of marriage under the patriarchal schema.[12] By the time Apollodorus tells her story, he asserts, in an overlay characteristic of the classical period, that she had been an unwanted female baby exposed upon a hillside by her father. But consistent with the motif of the mysterious birth of the hero, Atalanta survived that attempted infanticide. Under the aegis of Artemis, she had been suckled by wild animals and raised by hunters. Moreover, Atalanta is no Indo-European daughter compensating for her father's disappointment at having had a girl. She is a heroine of the ancient order. The nature goddess of Asia Minor and Crete had traditionally protected and fostered young animals and humans indiscriminately. Even later when the independence of the Mistress of the Wild Things had been revised to an irascible virginity (as with Artemis and Athena) exegetical revision could never thoroughly suppress the ancient attribute of motherhood. The goddess even as Kore, was foster mother to living things, ever *Kourotrophos.* The Cretan notion of the dual goddess is evident also, for Atalanta is a Kore, another maiden version of her foster mother Artemis and granted certain powers by her, including both prowess with bow and arrow and the miraculous ability to bring forth a spring (life) from a rock (earth).

Atalanta was the first to wound the boar, after having single-handedly protected herself from rape by two of her fellow hunters. But she was awarded no accolades. Ancaeus, "who had disdained to go a-hunting with a woman,"[13] belittles her achievement. In Apollodorus's version he is killed by Meleager for his criticism of Atalanta, but in other, undoubtedly older versions of the same story, it was the boar of Artemis who castrated and disemboweled him for his unconscionable misogyny.[14]

Meleager, who finally killed the boar after a group effort, presented the pelt to Atalanta as her prize for having been the first to shed its blood. Meleager's uncles, "the sons of Thestius, thinking scorn that a woman should get the prize in the face of men, took the skin from her, alleging that it belonged to them by right of birth."[15] The conflict of the two social systems is obvious at this point with the sons of Thestius adhering to values espoused by bonded male hunters who are unable to acknowledge even heroic achievement when it is accomplished by a heroine. They turn on Meleager for his judicious recognition of the female (Apollodorus continues the exegetical deprecation attributing Meleager's fair-mindedness to lust: "he desired to have a child also by Atalanta, though he had a wife, Cleopatra"[16]) and intratribal bloodshed ensues, with the men of the tribe turning upon one another and Meleager himself dying in battle, although another version of the myth holds that his mother's curse was the true cause of his death. This last idea also suggests the merging of two traditions, for Meleager's disloyalty to his own kinsmen would have been among the gravest of sins in the matriarchal schema.

When the hunting tribe was threatened by an enemy or pursued an animal prey, the object of its aggression was clear and the interests of the group clearly served by a savage team opposition to that object. The pursuit of the Calydonian boar, which ended in such a botched and bloody melee, had been jaded by the ambition of each of the individual hunters who wished to gain the prize for himself. Although this conflict aborted the original hunt somewhat, the male group bonded immediately when it looked as though Meleager would give the prize to a woman. Tiger wrote that "males bond in terms of either a pre-existent object of aggression or a concocted one."[17] In the hunt, as in war, the enemy was clear and the group felt its cohesiveness, its inherent divinity through pursuit of that enemy. Such exercises would have been antithetical to the matriarchal tribe that felt its inherent divinity in the rituals of aversion and supplication connected to agrarian goals which led to the worship of the goddess and to heroines such as Atalanta. When the enemy was no longer clear, tribes which had been programmed with such agonic value systems necessarily "concocted" new enemies, enemies like Atalanta who were not originally evil, but who would eventually become, in Morgan's words, the "quintessence of evil."[18]

Atalanta belonged to the substratum of mainland inhabitants who had roots in the Neolithic horticulture tradition. Those people, whether originally from Vinca or Anatolia, undoubtedly worshiped tribal mother goddesses in their most developed religious phase and entertained values similar to those of matriarchal Crete. These were the Pelasgians, "sea people"[19] whose name suggests something other than a Vinca origin, but does not necessarily prohibit it. These were perhaps the oldest inhabitants of the peninsula, a fact which their ancient worship of Keres substantiates. Herodotus tells us that Homer and Hesiod named the gods and that before that definition, "the Pelasgians, on all occasions called upon gods—but they gave them no title nor yet any name to any of them."[20] Harrison suggests that this meant that the Pelasgians still referred to their deities by epithet as did the Cretans: Kore was "Maiden," Ariadne was "Sacred One." According to this theory it was the arrival of the Achaeans which began the naming process.[21] Such linguistic imperialism serves the reordering of experience and implies the subordination of the named to the namer who has established a subtle mastery through language. Frye writes, "This knowing the name of a god or elemental spirit may give the knower some control over it."[22]

Atalanta, who no doubt received her name from the later Indo-Europeans was once the unnamed Kore of a Pelasgian tribe at Calydon. The story indicates that she retained a tenacious influence even after the hunting tribes had begun to gain dominance there. Consequently, though incorporating the story of this significant figure into their own mythology, it was necessary to embellish it with their own assumptions about her behavior. The process was continued by Apollodorus who was prompted to speculate on Meleager's motivation while leaving Atalanta's enigmatic. In part this is an example of the manipulative possibilities of continuous prose, an innovation in the retelling of myth made possible as mankind moved into the metonymic phase of language.[23] With it myths became malleable, available for revision as part of the evolving culture's self-affirming mythology of itself. The more ancient myths, stories first of the goddess mother and the hero god, became instruments for inculcating the biases of the authoritative elite. In revision Atalanta has been allowed no voice at all. Since she has no access to language either through narrative or explication, she cannot offer any version of her mythology of herself. One wonders at her motives. How would she explain herself? What prompted her behavior which appears so unwelcome, contrary, and unrewarding? There are no intimations even; she is inscrutable. Despite her central achievement in relation to the event, in characterization she is anomalous, marginal, her heroism suspect and certainly not presented for emulation. In the end she is enigmatic and peculiar and deliberately left so. It was not until the twentieth century that a retelling of the story includes the perspective of Atalanta.[24]

Stories such as Atalanta's confirm the fact that the two cultures had evolved incompatible modes of organizing and evaluating experience. The social system of the Indo-Europeans was already an aristocratic order, including a gender system, in which leadership and social prominence were determined by the ability to increase the tribe's prominence through war and conquest,[25] goals infused into the fabric of their culture under the ecological constrictions of their Paleolithic past. That they were still in a hunting phase is evidenced by the artifacts found in the oldest of the mainland remnants.[26] Their leaders were men, and those who followed did so out of loyalty to the chieftain who provided effective aggressive leadership rather than out of the tribal affiliations characteristic of Aegean peoples. Women had no doubt been honored for their procreativity, but in tribes which lived on the meat provided by hunters—a commodity which was much prized even by tribes which were alternately dependent on stores from gathering, or where the ecology of their Paleolithic and pre–Paleolithic environments had offered little to gather—women became lesser with their social status decreasing as the status of the hunter-warrior group increased. Such limitations led to the need for expansion and fostered the formation of factions within the tribe, with military elites, administrative elites, and eventually intellectual elites gaining disproportionate power.[27]

The reduced status of women in these tribes did not necessarily mean that the tribes were less group oriented than were agricultural tribes in the Proto-Neolithic period, but for the hunting tribes, ascendancy depended upon the prowess of its military leadership, and was measured in the conquest and subjugation of other tribes, their substitute prey. Mastery through violence had long been a gainful pattern of behavior for this culture and military conquests quickly led to the practice of enslaving conquered women. Lerner has theorized, however, that subjugation of the women of their own tribes was the model from which men generated initial patterns of social hierarchy, that they learned "to institute dominance and hierarchy over other people by their earlier practice of dominance over women of their own group."[28] This first inclination to social stratification developed because it guaranteed Paleolithic hunters a privileged tribal position perhaps loosely akin to that enjoyed by procreative women in tropical gardening cultures, but more likely surpassing it. The rather understandable desire of that elite group to perpetuate its enhanced status continued to affect the social development of the Indo-European tribes and became a motivating element in their conceptions of certain values, including freedom. Herbert Muller wrote of them: "As barbarians and warriors, the Indo-Europeans may be said to have had a natural inclination to freedom—for themselves. As rulers, they showed no inclination to extend its blessings. Typically they established an aristocracy of warrior lords above a mass of peasant serfs—a pattern that left a lasting imprint on European history to this century."[29] It is a pattern which may clearly explain the unwillingness of the hunters in the Calydonian boar story to allow the deviant if judicious Meleager to recognize excellence in Atalanta, who was both a woman and a symbol of a conquered culture, as was Artemis and their mutual prototype, the ancient Mistress of the Wild Things.

That the Indo-Europeans had long been male dominated peoples is evident from archaeology. Both their pantheon of gods and their stratified social distinctions confirm this. They worshiped sky gods, predominantly male, who mirrored their own needs and promoted tribal interests by sanctioning the hunter-warrior code of courage and agonistic aggression and by emphasizing the feats of the individual. The result was a practical, anthropocentric religion, almost casual in nature, which glorified the dominant males and conflicted with the mystical, egalitarian worship of the powerful goddess.[30]

Nilsson writes of the fusion of the "emotional religion of the pre–Greek population, which seems to have been impressed with a mystic tendency, and the temperate religion of the Indo-Germanic invaders, who entrusted the protection of the unwritten laws of their patriarchal order to their gods."[31]

But Campbell's conclusion about this "fusion" was that it was

> a sordid, sorry chronicle of collision, vituperation, coercion and spilled blood. For in the Levantine sphere, as well as in the Greek, a deeply rooted contrast prevails between the pre–Semitic, pre–Aryan mystic-emotional religion of the agrarian neolithic and Bronze Age populations, and on the other hand, "the temperate religion" (let us call it so, for the time being) of the various invading warrior folk, "who entrusted their patriarchal order to their gods." Indeed, we do not merely "sense," we experience acutely in our souls, and have documented for every period of our culture, the force that holds apart in us these contrary trends.[32]

Thus we see that the ecological factors of the distant past which had determined the tribe's food source and what Tiger referred to as "prehistoric dietary changes" were coded into its earliest consciousness and first affected its conception of divinity and later contributed to a value system, a way of organizing and evaluating experience which was stubborn rather than malleable. For the Indo-Europeans infiltrating mainland Greece during the two thousand years before the beginning of history, this included an early generation of aggressive sky gods, offspring of their original tribal mother, who had usurped her power and influence and left her a shadowy and silent figure who functioned in mythology to emphasize the righteousness of their ascendancy. In contrast to the indigenous peoples, the invaders had a less passionate, less mystical sense of the continuity of life, death, and nature, an idea of divinity which had little to do with egalitarian group cohesion and more to do with preserving the elite status of the dominant male core, the hallowed tribe within the tribe. They were certainly a less hedonic, less aesthetically developed culture, nor did they strive toward aesthetics; James wrote of them: "Their métier is that of conquerors, and they behave as fighting chiefs."[33] What they did bring was a passionate appreciation of the magnificence of the individual in his opposition to an alien environment, which indicates why, despite their reluctance, despite her sex and tribe, despite later notions of gender, Atalanta's performance in the hunt was legendary and continued to afford her a grudging interest, a commitment to intratribal elitism; and a consequent social need to concoct prey when hunting prey was no longer the essential food source.

The two cultures differed most dramatically in their attitudes toward women and power, divinity and death.[34] Yet in Greece and Crete, in the period between 2000 B.C. and the classical period, these two very different groups met and engaged in prolonged cultural combat through open warfare and subsequently a more subtle struggle between conflicting value systems. Played out through numerous undocumented skirmishes and conquests, the conflict as process is most evident in the legends and myths which testify to the triumph of the more aggressive Indo-European values; dominant not because of their inherent moral superiority, but because of the fact that they were promoted by a people who were agonistically rather than hedonically aggressive, who were able to attain prominence through conquest and usurpation and then to declare their ascendancy evolutionary progress. One insidious component in evaluating historical experience in Western culture has been the tacit assumption that what has survived is best.[35] This specious undercurrent in exegesis propelled the biases evident in mythology into the belief systems of a later age, including belief in the nonexistence rather than the extinction of the feminine divine.

Let us consider how fictional devices contributed to this process with Atalanta. Her physical appearance and association with Artemis aside, she is nowhere called divine. In fact, her autonomy discomforts revisionists. Part of the story includes some debate over her virginity, certainly a peripheral consideration to the plot of the Calydonian boar hunt. Yet the insertion of this related detail is significant to subsequent perception of the woman. Included is the accusation that, despite a vow of virginity, she eventually married Melanion (after his goddess-inspired ingenuity in distracting her from her natural athletic achievement by an appeal to her aesthetic sense) and was subsequently unfaithful to him. Her son was called Parthenopaeus (a word with the same root as parthenogenic), and there is no certainty about who his father was. Some say it was Meleager, others Ares, the war god. All this confusion and speculation function to discredit Atalanta, who as a Calydonian Kore with roots in the matriarchal culture had different ideas about sexuality and marriage. The autonomy of the self-sufficient Kores was unfathomable to the invading culture who had already conceived a gender system which called for male control of female sexual practices. The autonomy of the Kores became virginity in later patriarchal interpretation, with mythological revision describing once-autonomous Kores such as Artemis and Athena as they request and are granted Zeus's permission to remain virgins. Promoters of the phallic moral order, which was fused with the notion of sexual dimorphism, eventually subjugated women's reproductive ability to the control of the elite male subgroup and in so doing called for the faithfulness of women in marriage as well as the complicity of women in a cultural obligation to arranged marriages. As tribes merged and developed agricultural systems evolved, marriage became a vital social system which was controlled by men, which may have assured sufficient labor and intergenerational cooperation through the exchange of women, but also contributed significantly to the dehumanization of women.[36] Atalanta, the Kore of the Cretan dual goddess who became mother and gave birth to herself in a cycle that increased the tribe but did not concern itself with paternity or the evolving imperatives of patriarchy, could not sustain good repute within these foreign restrictions.

Fidelity was a requirement for women because only through such restriction could descent be traced through the father, an alteration in social custom which the patriarchal tribes had implemented before their arrival in Greece, but which was unknown in matriarchal cultures like Atalanta's. The latter continued to trace descent through the tribal mothers even after the relation of coitus and conception was understood. The ability to establish lineage was earnestly defended by the Indo-Europeans who were no doubt threatened by the tradition of matrilinear descent they found among the autochthonic tribes of the mainland. In consequence, they insisted on a moral paradigm which included both female fidelity in marriage and virginity as fact not metaphor and infused into cultural analysis the subtle sense that matriarchal societies were primitive steps in a righteous progress toward patriarchal and patrilinear constructions. This was advanced through stories of heroines and local goddesses like Atalanta. Harrison wrote: "The intrusion of the patriarchal system, the practice of tracing descent from the father, instead of mother, tended to check if it was powerless to wholly stop, the worship of eponymous heroines. Conservatism compelled the worship of old established heroines, but no fresh canonizations took place."[37]

Yet the matriarchal cultures had long honored group fertility rites and connected copulation with religious expression. Matrilinear descent was itself an outgrowth of tribal affiliation and religious principle in cultures such as Crete. To these, the mystery of the natural spontaneity of life was focused in women, and even after coitus was understood, the male role was considered perfunctory. Sacred marriage as part of religious ritual on Crete included the periodic immolation of kings, an aspect of matriarchal religions which the male-dominated Indo-European invaders surely balked at. To believers in the goddess religion, virginity was not something to be kept, but was a seasonal characteristic—the goddess mother giving birth seasonally to herself again as maiden. Harrison wrote: "Virginity was to these ancients in their wisdom, a grace not lost but perennially renewed, hence the immortal maidenhood of Aphrodite."[38]

But the consequence of these cultural contrasts for Atalanta was a sullied reputation, despite the fact that her feats in the Calydonian boar hunt and among the Argonauts should have gained her a place of unquestioned repute according to the patriarchal standards of the dawning Heroic Age. But Atalanta was a woman, and one of the first and most emphatic innovations of intruding patriarchal cultures was to circumscribe women's ability to participate in the cultural conception called heroism. Despite her behavior and achievement *in the hunt,* Atalanta has been permanently alienated from the heroic event.

The stories of mythological women, even women as clearly heroic as Atalanta, are conveyed with the taint of disapproval, of distaste; clearly the connotation of heroism was altered in myth, altered toward a societal goal which was the besmirching of autonomous feminine behavior. The hunter is heroic, the huntress so peculiar she barely elicits empathy. Yet the story of this huntress remains prominent in mythology because of its powerful allegorical function. Increasingly the crafters of culture sought to categorize women in terms of the gender system, especially their complicity with the social practice by which men exercised control over the sexuality of women. Notions of what was respectable and appropriate for women were organized around this societal goal which was obviously alien to women's own inherent ethics or interests. The tale of Atalanta, what may once have been a myth of the Calydonian Kore, an authentic adventure of the goddess as Mistress of the Wild Things, has been attenuated so as to offer no insight into the archetype and instead offers itself as an example of the allegorical revision of the goddess myth.

But the stories of mythology evolved; they did not appear as did Athena fully grown from the head of Zeus, nor did they necessarily remain true to their original spirit. Composition itself is a process which for mythology allowed through revision the inculcation of ascending values and the reification of women was on the ascent. Despite such foibles, including the fact that revisions were finalized at a specific historic point, these stories have had compelling imaginative influence and still operate to confuse the search for an authentic, self-affirming mythology of Western woman.

We must remember that the first step toward mythology was the practice of tribal rituals; the stories which explained them came later.[39] Each generation that followed could reconstruct the plots and reinterpret the stories to suit its own biases. They could add irrelevant but defaming detail; they could eliminate that which might prompt empathy. One might argue the revisions themselves were expressions of group solidarity, and this is true, but the group which had attained dominance in the Aegean was a powerful male subgroup, already deeply entrenched in the sexual exploitation of women. They would rewrite and reinterpret myths in promoting, affirming, and enlarging this aspect of the status quo and garnish them with ideas of moral superiority. As the Indo-European tribes sought to impose their hierarchic order on autochthonic tribes, an aesthetic bias developed which focused on heroism as a function of the individual male hunter-figure and was suspicious and disapproving of equivalent behavior in women. Deprecation became an aspect of revision, with figures like Atalanta first silenced in story and then interpreted as outside the confines of what was appropriate, eventually outside the confines of what was civilized.

The use of fictional characterizations to marginalize those who did not foster the concerns of the dominant elite was not a practice limited to autonomous heroines. It extended to any group which seemed at odds with the goals of patriarchy. One such group, the centaurs, may have been mythological representations of Atalanta's own people.

Although the creation of half-man animals is traditionally thought to have been a fragment of man's early animalism, Harrison suggests that the centaurs and satyrs of Greek myth were late creations, the inserts of the Indo-Europeans who were characterizing in these strange creatures the autochthonic tribes they conquered, and then viewed with both disgust and awe.[40] During the Calydonian boar hunt, Atalanta spilled the first blood when she killed two fellow hunters, the centaurs Hylaeus and Rhaecus who were taking a brief break from the hunt in order to rape her. The centaurs, who can be connected back to the Minoan culture by the fact that they are half-horse, are remarkably salacious in mythology, where they are forever raping and carrying off the women. Yet in contrast, the most remarkable of them is Chiron, valued tutor to Achaean heroes and noble wizard, a pitiable yet magical, awesome creature whose death is an act of both vision and self-sacrifice.[41]

Exclusive of Chiron, who no doubt reflects Indo-European ambivalence toward the mysticism of the autochthonic tribes, the centaurs have been fused into mythology as representatives of that which is antithetical to the rising ideals of Indo-European culture. DuBois has pointed out that beyond their sexual promiscuity, these creatures were in seminal opposition to the crucial elements of Indo-European dominance, namely the guest-host tradition and patriarchal marriage.[42]

One of the first populations encountered by Atalanta and Jason and the Argonauts were the unfortunate women of Lemnos, probably a purely fictional rather than historical tribe, but one located emphatically outside the margins of civilization. Apollodorus explains that there were no men on Lemnos because the women had rebelled against the practice of exchange, when their husbands "took captive women from the neighboring country of Thrace and bedded with them."[43] Later interpretations of the myth include the observation that the Hellenes could not accept a matriarchal government as they had been unable to accept a valiant huntress and so were propelled to insert qualifications which fit their own schema. In this story the women are repellent because of their inexplicably offensive odor, a twist of plot which both excuses their husbands' disinterest and implies cosmic retribution for their behavior. They are certainly not presented for empathy, but elicit discomfort or disgust for their malodorousness which is juxtaposed with their rebellion against patriarchal constructions. These are not to be considered upright women, and the evaluation is affirmed by their trickery in seducing Jason and his companions. As with Atalanta's, their story operates to promote notions of righteousness which lure women's complicity in the gender system while simultaneously obscuring and alienating the archetypal goddess's multiplicity and autonomy.

We begin to see that the historic confrontation between Indo-European and Aegean tribal groups in mainland Greece and surrounding islands during the two millennia before the Age of Pericles permanently altered the mythology that has come down to us as the heritage of Western civilization, as the incontrovertible expression of our "collective unconscious." Yet it was clearly not collective at all but most adversarial. The Indo-Europeans did not understand the Minoan religion and were surely threatened by the ubiquity of powerful goddesses and heroines, yet they could not obliterate the goddesses. Some were silenced, others deprecated and dismissed. A combination of ignorance and fear led also to the characterization of women as ogresses: Gorgons, Harpies, Sirens, Graiae, Eryinyes.[44] These were the misunderstood, misinterpreted remnants of the goddess trinity. The conquerors saw only debasement and horror in the religion of the conquered[45] and the chthonic side of the great goddess allowed such emphasis to take hold. So the goddess became the female monsters to be killed by Indo-European heroes. "The highest divinities of the religion of fear and riddance," Harrison wrote, "became the harmful bogeys of the cult of 'service'."[46] The aggressive Indo-European culture would eventually squelch almost all obvious aspects of the more pacific matriarchal one and then interpret its remnants to suit its own bias, particularly the notion of its righteous ascent to dominion.

That the mainlanders were tenaciously influenced by the Minoan tradition is certain. Yet discernible factors, like the gynaeceum of mainland fortresses indicate that the intruding Indo-Europeans asserted their social patterns, despite the dominance of local goddess religions among the indigenous mainland tribes and despite their appreciation of the cultural superiority of Crete. Muller implies that the sophisticated concept of political freedom "reputedly natural to the Indo-Germanic genius," was actually the result of the Aryan tribes' encounter with the established Minoan culture. He concludes: "The Germanic, Celtic, and Slavic peoples of Europe neglected to become civilized until late in their history. For more than two thousand years the only Indo-European peoples to make significant history were those who entered the civilized world of the ancient East, and exchanged their language for a superior culture."[47]

The first Aryan intruders into the "superior culture" were apparently peaceful, but the trek from northern to southern Greece became a chronic pattern of migration for these northern tribes, these "brown haired Xanthoi conquerors."[48] First came the Arcadians, then the Achaeans by way of Thessaly, the latter having entered the Peloponnese by the middle of the thirteenth century B.C. The northern invaders seem to have been respectfully skeptical of the Minoan-derivative culture with its goddess religion and heroines like the Calydonian Atalanta. The newcomers then absorbed these tribes in an inexorable amassing of power which would eventually be focused in the throne of Mycenae.[49] These tribes were conquerors, elitists who believed that their own military superiority entitled them to the conquests they gleaned, and they strove continually to gain more.

> For the Achaeans were not content with the rich heritage upon which they had here entered and they pushed further afield. They seized Crete and ruled the island. In 1223 a band of them appears to have raided Egypt; and just thirty years later, we learn on Homer's testimony that they undertook a still more famous expedition of which Agamemnon was the legendary captain and the destination Troy.[50]

As these Aryan marauders absorbed the matriarchal cultures in their paths they had first to deal with the religion of the goddess. Although the mainland variation may not have been identical to the Minoan religion, much of the optimistic mysticism of the Minoan religion had touched the less advanced mainland cultures before the arrival of the Indo-Europeans, and the invaders found the worship of the multifarious, powerful goddess everywhere as they marched south through the peninsula. Her cults were firmly entrenched at Delphi, Delos, and Eleusis.[51] The shift of power that came about as a result of imposition of the gender system can be seen at Delphi, that sea of prophetic divinity which first belonged to Gaia, the mainland mother-goddess, then Themis, the goddess of justice and Gaia's less shadowy daughter, whom Harrison called, "the utterance, the projection and personification, of *the* religious principle itself";[52] Harrison points to the *Phiobas,* the priestess of the goddess at Delphi who prophesied for the goddess and identifies the priestess with Cassandra, the tragic Trojan princess whose first conflict was with Apollo. "She prophesied at the . . . shrine Apollo took over as he took Delphi. Her frenzy against Apollo is more than the bitterness of a maiden betrayed; it is the wrath of the prophetess of the old order discredited, despoiled by the new."[53] One version of the myth claims that Cassandra had the gift of prophesy from the sacred snakes of the temple when she and her twin brother were accidently left there as children. But another, later story, inserts a typically Indo-European overlay with Apollo lusting after Cassandra, tempting her with the gift of prophesy and then punishing her by spitting in her mouth when she withdraws her consent. The result was that no one believed her; Cassandra, powerful priestess of the goddess, whose gift was snake-given and chthonic, becomes disempowered and pitiful. A product of relentless deprecation in mythic revision, she is a madwoman by the time she is murdered in Agamemnon's hall.

Myth has it that the upstart Archaean hero god wrested the powerful temple at Delphi from his grandmother, and incorporates the Themis period by having her raise and nurture him. Apollo's motive for the seizure of power at Delphi is always connected in some way to his own mother, another pitiable disempowered local goddess, Leto. She had been raped by Zeus, and then persecuted by the outraged Hera, who sent the chthonic Python to harry her. Since the Python was the child of the protean earth mother Gaia, he sought refuge from Apollo's anger in her temple at Delphi. Apollo summarily seized the temple to avenge his mother, and so justified his usurpation of his grandmother and his foster mother at Delphi. Again the story is of the suppression of the autochthonic religion, told with a dusting of ugly theological animus. The results of these confrontations are always the same. A powerful goddess is rendered impuissant except through the violent heroism of her own son.

Within a generation or two of the conquest of Crete, the palace at Mycenae was greatly enlarged and the cities of Crete itself were revived as Mycenaean colonies. The Linear B tablets, which are dated during this period, give evidence of the presence on Crete by then of the Achaean pantheon as well as the retention by the Cretan people of elements of their ancient goddess worship.[54] Exactly what went on is unclear. There is some historic evidence that the original Cretan immigrants, after their amalgamation on the mainland with the intrusive pastoral-warrior tribes, returned to conquer Crete. Yet there is also the suggestion that Crete, perhaps after its Mycenaean transformation, demanded such high tolls from its subalterns on the mainland that the mainlanders, led by Theseus, rebelled.[55] His story also tells yet another version of the recurring conflict, the confrontation of the Indo-European individual hero with the Minoan great goddess. Theseus's heroism is only possible because of the guile of Ariadne, who knows where to find the answer and helps him maneuver through the labyrinth. But Ariadne, the "sacred one," the once-great Cretan goddess, has become through patriarchal overlay nothing more than a supporting actress. Her essentialness is downplayed, her foreignness emphasized, and like many other versions of the retelling of the goddess's story, she is used and then abandoned. There are various versions of her end. In the *Odyssey* there is evidence of the great-goddess duality:

> I saw ... Ariadne, the beautiful
> daughter of malignant Minos. Thesus at one time
> was bringing her from Crete to the high ground of sacred Athens
> but got not joy of her, since before that Artemis killed her
> in sea-washed Dia, when Dionysus bore witness against her.
>
> [11.321–25]

Other versions say she died in childbirth, others that she committed suicide. The most optimistic myths have her passively waiting on Naxos for another Indo-European hero god to rescue her so that she can live happily ever after, bearing him numerous famous children.

By the time of the Linear B Tablets, the pure Minoan culture has been transformed by the influence of the northerners and the result is Mycenaean culture on Crete. There is still the dual goddess of early Minoan religion, but she (or they) are now accompanied by a young male, the child of the goddess, no doubt, who correlates at least loosely with the Dumuzi-Tammuz figure of Sumerian-Assyrian mythology. Campbell refers to an ivory plaque which was found in the ruins of Mycenae and which represents the Mycenaean version of the divine family; consisting of two goddesses and the young god.[56] The dual goddess is Demeter and Persephone, with Triptolemus taking on a larger significance, or perhaps the babe is Iacchus (later called Dionysus, Brimus, or Plutus, even Zeus). While there is a connection to the Sumerian triad of Inanna, Ereshkigal and Dumuzi and their Assyrian counterparts, this is the first sign of the rise of the male in Cretan religion, and it suggests the beginning of the triumph of the phallic order of the Aryan pantheon which would rewrite mythology, permanently skew archetypes, and introduce rape and restrictive marriage as the major fictional elements in the subjugation of the original goddess-heroine.

One tribal goddess after another had to be subjugated by the Achaean pantheon, so the male Olympians (and their representative, Minos on Crete) became premier rapists and seducers and the tribal Kores became the legendary nymphs who struggled to resist their chicanery and violence. Britomartis was probably the first such victim; as Britomartis-Dicktyanna, she was the Cretan Mistress of the Wild Things who was pursued by Minos, a representative of the rising male in Cretan religion. She was the first to attempt to avoid rape by suicide; Artemis, another version of herself, deified her. The conflict is repeated in the tale of Daphne. Daphne was a Kore or priestess to the goddess, and she escapes the rape of Apollo with the assistance of the goddess, who transforms her into a tree just as Apollo is about to overtake her, and then allows her to be reborn again on Crete as Pasiphae. This is a story which retains a matriarchal flavor with its sense of continuity in life and death and nature. It is a rare instance of absurdly patriarchal illogic when Campbell uses Daphne's story as an example of one who refuses the call to heroism.[57] This is not a story of refused heroism revealing archetypes of lasting psychic value, no spontaneous revelation of truth. Daphne's story is of the confrontation between ideas of divinity, with the agonistic Olympian employing the hunter's time-honored means to dominance, while the hedonic goddess, now the hunter's prey, escapes violation by using her chthonic defenses of metamorphosis and rebirth. In Daphne's story the goddess escapes into the mysteries of her own schema, becomes a mystical enigma while asserting herself as a prevailing transcendence, despite her fall from power. Her rebirth speaks to the fact that there was something inadequate in a purely Olympian conception of divinity especially as it aspired, through violence, to suppress the immanent feminine. Using a power which transcended violence, the goddess in her generative spontaneity outsmarts the god.

Campbell himself has elsewhere polarized the spontaneity of the goddess stratum with the violence of the Olympians,[58] and disparaged Zeus's "long career of theological assault through marriage."[59] But it is the insistent insertion of rape as a motif in mythology which is most revealing as a chronicle of the imperative to establish a hierarchical conception of gender as an aspect of evolving culture. Zeus does not just marry the tribal goddesses. Again and again he rapes them, with a violence that becomes more perfunctory with each revision. The story of Daphne comes from Apollodorus; by the time of Ovid, rape had become a standard mode for subjugation of the remnant goddesses. This late revisionist made rape universal, inserting it where it was not previously present as in the stories of Persephone's abduction and of the sisters, Philomela and Procne. The rape of the goddess aptly expressed the domination of the brutish Indo-European sky gods. As gender polarity became more and more accepted during the centuries up until Ovid, rape became a more and more facile metaphor for the subjugation of the archetypally feminine to the central focus of the male in evolving culture. In Ovid, "rape is instantaneous in order to demonstrate the helplessness of woman in the face of overwhelming male superiority," writes Curran.[60] The rape of the goddess became the clumsy metaphor of the conquerors' theology to engulf and disarm what tenaciously refused to be obliterated.

What happened to the composition of mythology during the confrontation between these drastically antithetical cultures was a directed revision, with those who were triumphant imposing upon the stories fictional elements which would promulgate their values, then serve to impress the status quo. From mainland Minoan colonies the conquerors absorbed the local mother goddesses, but she was pushed into the background by the process of giving birth, the act which had previously affirmed her divinity among matriarchal tribes. In the new order she gave birth to the Aryan hero figure whose exploits would diminish hers, and one of whose tasks was to disempower or destroy her chthonic side. Her earlier sexual freedom, so essential to her inherent mystery, was precipitously restricted as she became an unwilling wife or violated rape victim of Zeus or one of his Olympian brothers. Campbell refers to the story of the overthrow of the Titans, who were the first, parthenogenetically produced children of Gaia, by the less stolid Olympians, whose superior acuity and cunning was only effective because of the guileful complicity of Gaia herself. It is a process of revision or "priestly device" called "*mythological defamation,* which has been in constant use ever since."[61]

Something must be said at this point about Hamilton and Graves, whose compilations of Greco-Roman stories provide the most common conduit of mythology, especially as supplements to the epics and certain of the tragedies which have continued to be popular in their original forms, although in differing translations. It is curious that Hamilton, whose little black *Mythology* has been the most widely used source for précis of the myths, knows nothing of the goddess while Graves, who does, has been somewhat criticized for his insistent attention to the matriarchal influence in ancient storytelling. Hamilton's method in compiling the stories was linear. She paid no attention to the chthonic substraum beneath the Apollonian religion or to the political interests at work in revision but, instead, approached the accumulation of facts as though the details overlaid by the later revisionists, including the Romans, were of equal significance. In fact, she accepts that these later interpretations clarify the original stories, as the revisionists of every generation certainly intended to do. It is an approach which adheres zealously to the Aristotelian bias of literary criticism, that what is universal and the proper focus of aesthetics is male experience. It included also the implicit assumption that a patriarchal social hierarchy was the righteous goal of all cultural history and inclusion of any detail which obscured that progress was superfluous, perhaps not quite scholarly, at least somewhat suspect, as was Grave's stubborn attention to the influence of matriarchal principles.

Because of this approach and the subsequent influence of *Mythology* as a sourcebook, Hamilton has contributed mightily to the process by which Western women were robbed of a self-affirming and authentic mythology of themselves. She describes, for instance, the conflicting reports as to who Atalanta's father was, assuming the imperative that the Kore be subjugated to paternal authority and writes: "Atalanta's father, whatever his name was, when a daughter and not a son was born to him, was, of course, bitterly disappointed."[62] In her introduction to Daphne's story, she claims that only Ovid tells it, although others have found it in Apollodorus and Plutarch. Embellishing Ovid, Hamilton has contributed to the banalization of the goddess, presenting Daphne as yet another tomboy, "another of those independent, love-and-marriage hating young huntresses" who begs her father's permission to remain unmarried and so retain a child's irresponsible freedom. Although she expresses sympathy for the unfortunate women who are loved by the gods, she does not use the word rape, nor fathom the girl's flights as a desire to escape violence. It is Apollo this author presents for our empathy. Pursuing the terrified runner, the rational god soothes and counsels capitulation: "Do not fear. Stop and find out who I am, no rude rustic or shepherd. I am the Lord of Delphi, and I love you."[63] It is her father Daphne calls to for help in both Ovid and Hamilton, not Mother Earth as Graves claims.[64] In Hamilton her metamorphosis is a horrible death: "a dragging numbness came upon her.... Bark was enclosing her; leaves were sprouting forth." In Graves's version it is an escape; Daphne triumphs in the manner of the goddess to be reborn again on Crete as Pasiphae.

While the first revisionists sought to validate a new pantheon and a new social order, they also engendered a powerful new psychology,[67] one which sanctioned the authority of one sex over the other and imparted notions of gender, which had enormous cultural influence and contributed to women's surrender to the system. As we can see from Hamilton's revision of both Daphne and Atalanta, this was an aspect of myth which continued long after the pantheon had been rendered comical. The most insidious component, which we will examine in the next chapter, was the fictional innovation of self-deprecation as a characteristic of those heroines who are given voice in revised mythology. As it is completely counter to the drive for life, self-loathing is obviously neither innate nor mythic to any human being, yet the insights from modern psychology suggest that on an ontogenetic level such diminished self-worth can be learned, especially when instruction comes from influential if dysfunctional authority figures.

Chapter IV

Self-deprecation and Ostracism in Homer

Despite the aristocratic social distinction Homer afforded many of his women, a cultural disposition toward imposition of the gender system is already obvious in his epics. The need to polarize the civilized and the chthonic is evident as is the tendency to juxtapose self-deprecation and righteousness in the articulate women who emerge. In Homer the heroic values of the Indo-European conquerors have gained the fore; the epics present a world of heroes, of individual men bent on self-promotion, engaged in admirable acts of agonistic aggression, pursuing wealth and immortality through reputation.[1] The women in his stories have been nearly shorn of their divine origins, the goddesses circumscribed, even the best among them has only a secondary status; many have become merely the props of men; all are tokens in a system of exchange which men control.[2] This exists despite the fact that there is recurring evidence in the epics of matriarchal and matrilineal remnants. There is evidence too of the chthonic heritage of the great goddess, who by the time of the epics has been fully diffused into the Olympian goddesses and lesser nymphs, each of whom has a specific and limited sphere, but no one of whom wields the power of the male Olympians.

Most remarkable of all is the absence of Demeter. She is barely mentioned in the *Iliad* and then only in analogy (5.500). She is not a full-fledged Olympian but a shadowy figure, as well she might be in a tale which emphasizes heroic values and allows the feminine principle expression only within the confines of patriarchal marriage. In the *Odyssey* her autonomy and power are clearly diminished; she has become the property of Zeus. Echoing, perhaps unconsciously, the traditional associations of goddess and fertility rites,[3] Calypso tells of how Demeter left the wedding feast of Cadmus and Harmonia to copulate in a thrice-ploughed field with Iasion. But this remnant of a much more ancient story with its religious ritual of human copulation to stimulate fertility in nature has become, through patriarchal overlay, an expression of inappropriate sexual freedom, offensive

61

to the tyranny of the patriarchal order (and incidentally attributed to the nectar consumed at the wedding). Iasion, once the honored consort of the goddess, is disciplined (as was Anchises for his affair with Aphrodite) by an enraged Zeus. The offense is multifarious. The hierarchy has been offered by the copulation of a female divinity with a human male, although this is obviously a moral restriction imposed only on the goddess as Zeus's endless violations of human women testify. Women and their children, whether human or divine, have already become a commodity of exchange used by men to facilitate a culture which kept men at its zenith. The once-ominous Demeter scurries away from the displeasure of an opponent whom she triumphed over in the earlier legend of the Homeric Hymn. If the Homeric *Hymn to Demeter* chronicles the rise of patriarchal values through violence and the imposition on natural rights of a factitious order based on male superiority, the fact that the once-powerful Demeter is nearly absent in the epics testifies further to the deliberate devaluation of authentic feminine morality and heroism, to the heavy-handed suppression of the immanent *she* by a cultural imperative which is its polar opposite.

Traditionally Homer has been considered the least misogynist of the Greeks,[4] if only because his women do not consistently threaten men with their uncontrollable passions. But the rules and values of heroic behavior celebrated in the epics are by their nature misogynistic and can be traced to the conflicts of tribal values which were the heritage of the Bronze Age confrontations. The society described in the *Iliad* and the *Odyssey* is not a clear or specific representation of an age. Instead, it is an amalgamation of images from societies going back to the period from the transitional pre–Mycenean until at least that of the late eighth century and probably to the sixth-century rule of Peisistratus. The legend of the Trojan War was itself an ancient one, but its relationship to historical fact may never be certainly established. What is known is that, between the event described and official recording of the epics of Homer, there occurred both the Dorian invasion and the Ionian colonization, historic events which testify irrefutably to cultural upheaval and an ongoing reorganization and reemphasis of mores and values by dominant tribes. There occurred also the "reforms" of Solon with their devastating legal effects for women.[5] Homer himself was working from a known legend, but how much he embellished that legend through invention and his own ideas of what was heroic can only be speculated.[6] How much detail was added, changed, or eliminated by revisionists is also a question. Consideration of techniques both of composition and preservation of the epics suggests the probability of ongoing revision and alteration of the text, perhaps not of the specifics of the legend, but certainly of embellishments which emphasized ascending values.

Just when Homer composed is somewhat unclear. Greek culture, at least until its adoption of the Phoenician script in the eighth century, was essentially a preliterate society (the Myceanean script of the Linear B tablets was apparently not used to record stories, and we have yet to decipher the Linear A tablets).[7] The *Iliad* and *Odyssey* were preserved through rhapsodes, or bards, although it has been widely accepted that they were also written down soon after their composition, either by Homer or by a contemporary or immediate successor.[8] The oral nature of the epics as well as the later additions of the Epic Cycle, however, make it clear that revision was a continuing possibility until finalized, edited, allegedly definitive forms were endorsed during the reign of the tyrant Peisistratus, whose rule followed Solon's and also included increasing social and political repression of women.

The epics served as a cultural imprimatur for the agonistic patriarchal tribalism which was later to become the elitist civic pride of Athens. Such a sociopolitical pattern makes it all the more likely that values of the later, more repressive periods were woven into the fabric of the original legend. Richmond Lattimore points to some of the omissions and revisions which characterize the story. Penthesilea, the Amazon, is said to possess *aristeia*, heroic excellence (as did Atalanta), yet her victories can only be inferred because it is only her defeat at the hands of Achilles which is described. The same reduction confuses the characterization of Hector, whose reputation "continually surpasses his achievements," according to Lattimore, and therefore suggests revision by composers of later epochs who were concerned with emphasizing a hierarchy which devalued foreigners. In Homer's own time those who were not Greek were not consequently inferior; Homer's treatment of the Trojans makes this clear. But an alteration in cultural bias took place between the original writing of the epics and their finalized form. This change allowed interim bards to diminish the exploits of the barbarian Hector, whose *aristeia* was obviously more appreciated by an earlier, less biased age.[9] A secondary objective of an interim storyteller was to emphasize the status quo, and by the time of Peisistratus that included the delineated hierarchy which placed both women and barbarians beneath the Greek male hero. Lattimore observes this reordering as he considers the author's final characterization of Hector. "Homer's success is somewhat left-handed. He has so industriously diminished his Goliath for the sake of others that we sense deception, and feel that Hector 'really was' greater than Patroklos or any other Achaian except Achilles."[10] But whether it was Homer or later revisionists who deemphasized Hector is unclear. The same point can certainly be made of Penthesilea.

The gradual polarization of masculine and feminine into adversarial rather than sympathetic positions is already evident in the epics. They are replete with parables which instruct women on how best to attain approval within hierarchical patriarchy. Those women whose behavior is approved are women, like Andromache and Penelope, who defer to the leadership of their husbands and do not attempt to challenge male centrality. Those whose behavior clearly challenge the hierarchy, notably Clytemnestra, are doomed to a miserable fate.[11] Even Helen, once a powerful earth goddess of Sparta,[12] and within the Indo-European frame still called the daughter of Zeus, is no longer divine in the epics but is instead tethered by patriarchal overlay. Although the kingship of Sparta was determined through marriage to her, she has evolved into the passive and powerless victim of her own tragic beauty who shows the self-deprecation appropriate to the Indo-European woman when she laments to Hector in the *Iliad*,

> Brother
> by marriage to me, who am a nasty bitch evil-intriguing
> how I wish that on that day when my mother first bore me
> the foul whirlwind of the storm had caught me away and swept me
> to the mountain, or into the wash of the sea deep-thundering
> where the waves would have swept me away before all these
> things had happened.
>
> [6.343–48]

Such is the expected remorse of the unfaithful Indo-European wife, but originally Helen was autochthonic, a once-powerful Spartan earth goddess, condemned for the sexual freedom which had once been her prerogative, an aspect of her fertility. The Trojan elders unconsciously allude to this connection when she approaches them on the battlements to help identify their Greek enemies.

> Surely there is no blame on Trojans
> and strong-greaved Achaians
> if for long time they suffer hardship for
> a woman like this one.
> Terrible is the likeness of her face
> to immortal goddesses
> Still though she be such, let her go away
> in the ships, lest
> she be left behind a grief to us and our children.
>
> [3.156–60]

Helen's name is pre–Greek and there were stories which insisted she was blameless, had been abducted against her will, had never even arrived in Troy. These stories were still told at the time of Euripides, who borrows from them for his *Helen*. One sixth-century B.C. poet, Stesichorus, was allegedly blinded for accusing Helen and wrote a poem of recompense which exonerated the woman, if not the goddess, by placing her in Egypt at the time of the war—an idea which Euripides picked up on nine hundred years later. Michael Grant points out that this aspect of the legend, the culpability of Helen, has been linked to the epics of Ugarit, which were themselves linked to the Old Testament—another document which proposed the inherent guilt of woman at seminal episodes of mankind's story.[13] The essential fact is that there were contradictory legends which were gradually abandoned or downplayed before the prodigiousness of the *Iliad* and *Odyssey*, but which reflect an attempt by some within the evolving culture to reject the misogynist bent which the epics were helping to make permanent.

Helen's marriage offers an enlightening vignette of the demise of the matrilocal, matrilinear tradition of the earlier cultures. Menelaus must fetch her back to Sparta to retain the kingship there, a root motive which has been buried in the legend, but which certainly helps explain why he took no vengeance upon her, despite her defection for the younger, more handsome Asian. The fact that Menelaus rallied the other Indo-European feudal lords to follow him and his brother Agamemnon, who ruled elsewhere, may have had more to do with his desire to remain the ruler of a rich, previously Pelasgian kingdom after Helen's defection than with the traditional mythological explanation. It is significant, however, that the oath of the suitors to Tyndareus is not mentioned in the *Iliad,* and the single, shadowy reference to the Judgment of Paris (24.25–30) smacks of interpolation.[14] But the legend recorded in the epics turns with the cultural tide toward patrilinear succession, and so we have the story of Menelaus attempting to beget a son through a concubine rather than pass on his wife's kingdom to their daughter Hermione. Helen herself, daughter of Zeus, is still discernibly divine, but her brief rebellion ends with a surrender to the dictates of patriarchy at Troy: eventually, as testified to in the *Odyssey,* she achieves a peaceful, even influential coexistence with her conquerors, remaining chthonic in her knowledge of drugs, yet having deferred finally to the hierarchy of male domination. The usurpation of the goddess/heroine and her tribal ethics of connection and care is a fait accompli in the epics, yet there are still remnants of the more ancient values, and evidence of the manipulative interpolation which patriarchal mythmakers used to crimp the ever resurging archetype of the heroine.

Eva Cantarella points to the proselytizing of Hector to his wife and Telemachus to his mother; both suggest the restricted domestic sphere in which a woman is allowed her limited power, and both emphasize the need for modesty and obedience to male figures as criteria for continued enjoyment of their limited status. These are conceptual abstractions presented as ideas of perfection, but which are rooted in a hierarchal view of society and designed to perpetuate that hierarchy by presenting paternal affection and approval as the most desired goal of female behavior. Paternal affection could be secured by cultivating the attributes of fidelity, obedience, passivity, submissiveness—all while under rather stressful conditions since the Homeric male was allowed concubines, both prisoners of war and slaves, who lived within the household, the designated sphere of the woman, and whose children were allowed some status alongside the wife's own.[15] The rebellious woman was to stifle her complaints to an absurd pliancy and see herself as unworthy if she could not.

The well-being of the married woman under the patriarchal order was dependent upon the largesse of her husband, especially if she had forsaken or lost her own tribe. This dependence was especially precarious during wartime, as revealed by the tender exchange between Andromache and Hector in Book Six of the *Iliad*. Despite recent speculation that Andromache's history reveals that she came to Troy from a matriarchal tribe,[16] she herself is immersed in the ways of patriarchy, and understands too well their implications for herself and Astyanax if the Trojans lose the war. She is a lonely figure as she appeals to Hector to consider not just his reputation but the fate that will await her and their baby son if she is widowed and Troy lost. Again there is the self-deprecation and suicidal despair expected of the Indo-European woman.

> and for me it would be far better
> to sink into the earth when I have lost you, for there
> is no other consolation for me after you have gone to your destiny—
> only grief; since I have no father, no honoured mother.
>
> [6.410–13]

Without the matriarchal tribe, she is a figure confronted by a merciless fate which she is powerless to alter, although she is certainly not without acumen and guile. After reminding Hector again that he is all she has, Andromache attempts to offer him some sound advice on military strategy, advice which might have been wisely followed had Hector been more concerned with Trojan victory than with individual performance (6.433–39). But Hector rejects the advice, fearing such a maneuver would diminish his reputation and breach the heroic code. In the end he is reluctantly committed to the patriarchal ideal of individual aggrandizement, although he too knows the consequences for his wife and baby as well as for Troy. Accepting his doom and sealing hers, he disregards her advice that he rally his men for battle under the fig tree at the weakest spot and instead goes off to face the individual contest. He sends Andromache back to the domestic sphere (6.487–93) fully aware that rape and slavery are the inevitabilities which await a hero's wife, one who, as Andromache says of herself in Euripides' *Trojan Woman*, has "cast her arrow at good repute" under the ascending patriarchal order. The scene can be read as a confrontation of masculine and feminine ethics. Andromache lobbies vainly for empathy; her suggestion for a collective military maneuver might have saved Troy and made her the heroine, but it is Hector's commitment to male individuation, however reluctant, which prevails. Cantarella points out that under this order, "The virtues woman were supposed to have were not ones that would make protagonists of them."[17]

Cantarella makes two important points which suggest within the epics the continuing process of goddess reduction. Violence is an accepted, legitimate method of suppressing the goddess. Hephaestus is thrown from Olympus for coming to his mother's defense. Hera, an ancient mother goddess tethered by a repressive and unhappy marriage to the abusive Olympian, is at one point threatened with "whip strokes," and reminded that she has been hung from the heavens by two weights for her rebellion against her husband and that it can happen again (*Iliad*, 16.16–21). The unhappy fate of this once-autonomous goddess includes threats and chronic abuse, accepted dynamics of conjugal interaction, at least on Olympus. Cantarella writes: "The Zeus-Hera relationship is one of particular conflict and violence, which certainly cannot be taken as a model marriage. Yet their marriage presents a picture of conjugal relationships that the public somehow accepted. Evidently the public was used to considering such punishments as a non-pathological aspect of the relationship—in other words, they could laugh at Zeus' excesses, but they were not shocked."[18]

Cantarella also makes note of the fact that Homeric men just do not trust women, not even the most faithful and noble of women. Furthermore, they illogically leap from the specific offense to a rash generalization about the limitations of the sex. The bitter Agamemnon complains that no woman can be trusted when he instructs Odysseus in the Underworld. He makes no connection between Clytemnestra's action and his own sacrifice of Iphigenia,[19] but instead generalizes from his own experience, suggesting to Odysseus, "Bring your ship back to your homeland secretly, not openly, since women can never be trusted" (*Odyssey*, 11.454–56). Clytemnestra and Demeter might have had some corresponding advice to offer other women about keeping children safe from their treacherous fathers had these been the epics of a matriarchal culture. Although Odysseus had been told by his own mother in Hades of the faithfulness of his wife, despite the pressures put on her by the suitors, he remains a typical Homeric man, suspicious of the most well-behaved wife, and so Penelope is the last one to whom he reveals himself. Despite his wife's nobility, Odysseus passes on to his son the standard of patriarchal distrust of women, and mimics the sentiments of Agamemnon: "For this reason do not ever be too kind to your wife, or tell her the whole of your plan, however well you know it, but tell her part of it, and leave the rest hidden" (*Odyssey*, 11.441–43).

Unlike her cousin Clytemnestra, Penelope functions appropriately within the prescribed limits of the patriarchal culture's circumscribed expectations of women, and is rewarded with her husband's approval and an immortal reputation—the ultimate achievement sought by the hero of the Heroic Age. She does this by effectively taking over the leadership of Ithaca during the Trojan War and maintaining it, albeit through devious ploy and counterploy, amidst the growing anarchy that results from Odysseus's delayed return. But in contrast to Clytemnestra, especially as she is portrayed in classical drama, Penelope does not seem to thrive on that leadership and is seen throughout as deferential to men. In the *Telemachia* she responds diffidently to the sudden and presumably unexpected assertiveness of her son, who is clearly more comfortable with ordering his mother to her room than he is with ordering the suitors to desist their depletion of his inheritance. The issue of Penelope's remarriage is a crucial one to the continuity of power on Ithaca. Although she herself is from another kingdom, the behavior of the suitors clearly implies that whichever of them is successful in his suit to marry her will gain the kingship of Ithaca. This, despite the fact that Laertes, Odysseus's father, still lives and despite the fact that no one but the young man himself, and then only in insecure moments, doubts the legitimacy of Telemachus as Odysseus's son.[20]

There are vestiges of the tradition of matrilinear descent in the epics, a pattern which certainly determined leadership in the Aegean tribes of matriarchal social organization. It may have been that the custom was passing out of widespread use, yet the epics suggest that it continued to be a powerful aspect of social organization not just in Sparta and on Ithaca, but elsewhere in the Aegean.[21]

Women did rule, but the model which the epics offer is a model in which they accept the reins of leadership only during the absence of the rightful male leader and then defer to him upon his return and to their sons and fathers during his absence. Thus Clytemnestra and Penelope, who may have begun as legendary figures from matriarchal mythology became allegorical figures in revised myth. Clytemnestra is presented as treacherous in the epics, monstrous in later times, while Penelope has been lauded for her fidelity and appropriate guile. Foley refers to this deference as "likemindedness" in accepting the separate and unequal spheres of influence allowed to men and women in the world of the epics. "Penelope's restraint in preserving Odysseus' kingship without usurping his power reveals the nature of her own important guardianship of the domestic sphere.... Odysseus and Penelope recreate a mature marriage with well-defined spheres of power and a dynamic tension between two like minded members of their sex."[22] Penelope functions as a guardian of patriarchal cultural values while using powers bequeathed to her by the matriarchal past. Foley points to her similarity to Alcinous, the king of Phaeacia, who successfully keeps discipline among the unruly young men of his kingdom, as Penelope does with the suitors in Ithaca. She, too, receives and interrogates visitors, preserving the guest-host tradition which was so vital a connector between the isolated enclaves of civilization in what was essentially a still savage world. She maintains the tribal values as well, weaving and unweaving

Laertes' shroud as she symbolically forestalls the impending disintegration of her husband's tribe, which has been shattered and wasted in the twenty years of his absence. She does seem to be connected still to mysterious chthonic powers, suspending time on Ithaca by refusing marriage, by accepting a lengthy chastity and an unnaturally prolonged grief; she uses "the weapons of Helen and Circe not to destroy but to maintain social order."[23] Yet she is not wholly admirable, there is an element of the wanton in her behavior. She has held off the suitors by capitalizing on her beauty, her sexuality, and her power in Ithaca, yet she seems unable to refuse them outright, making promises and passing notes to all 108 of them,[24] while crying herself to sleep with grief for Odysseus. They themselves complain to Telemachus at the onset of his rebellion that it is she and not they who are responsible for their prolonged dissipation of his inheritance. They insist that Telemachus force her to make a choice and do not recognize as a choice the possibility of not marrying, of the autonomy of the goddess. Beyond the resources of coquetry, she is renowned for her craft, that chthonic gift of women which links her to the sagacity of the ancient goddess, and makes her a favorite of Athena, as is her husband, but Penelope's wisdom is used in the service of male centrality. In the final analysis Penelope does preserve the social order and the rights of her son, both tribal tasks reflecting feminine ethics, but she does so by upholding patriarchal values including the deferential surrender of power to Odysseus upon his return. She is unoffended by his stubborn testing of her, another manifestation of self-deprecation, a cultural expectation of respectable women. It is as though she too accepts that women are not to be trusted, but must be repeatedly tested. In the end her deference is rewarded with a reputation for fidelity and a reduced, secondary power, like the power of Arete to intercede with her husband or the Virgin Mary to intercede with her son.

Even this secondary power is available to only a few fortunate women in the world of the epics. The main characters are the aristocratic elite. Andromache's fear of capture and enslavement is a realistic one, but the quality of her life as a slave will be dictated by her estimated value as a spoil of war, and that has already been determined by her current status in the male hierarchy as the wife of the prince of Troy. The autobiography of Briseis (*Iliad*, 19.287–300) suggests a probable scenario for Andromache and the other royal women after the defeat of Troy. Briseis and Andromache were both natives of Thebe, where Andromache's parents had ruled. It had been attacked and destroyed by Achilles and the Myrmidons on their way to Troy. Although Andromache was already in Troy at the time her city was sacked, both women were bereaved of parents and brothers by the marauding Myrmidons. Achilles, who would become her consort lord, was first known to Briseis as the murderer of her husband. Briseis goes "all unwilling" from Achilles to Agamemnon, but it is Patroclus whose death she bemoans. Patroclus, compassionate conqueror, had been her advocate after the destruction of her home and family, and had helped rebuild her life by convincing Achilles to take her as his paramour. Compassion is not a laudable attribute of men in the heroic world, especially compassion toward women. Briseis's praise of Patroclus suggests that his empathy was unexpected. Helen's praise of Hector in Book Six expresses the same surprised appreciation.

For most Achaean men, women were accoutrements which helped measure a warrior's status, mere pawns in the ever changing dynamics of the masculine power structure. Agamemnon offers Achilles seven already captured women of Lesbos, first choice of twenty Trojan women after the defeat of the city, and one of his daughters in marriage as part of his propitiation. Rape and the possession of conquered women was the prerogative of the victor whose superior strength was his license to power over weaker nations. The exchange if not the disposal of daughters was the prerogative of the father, a right bequeathed from his Paleolithic status to his subsequent membership in a military elite. A prudent woman like Andromache prepared herself for the exchange, or like Briseis, made the most of her bondage to a foreign lord, suppressing any resentment she might have toward him as the murderer of her parents and her family. As a system, this exchange undermined clan loyalty and cut cruelly into the natural feminine ethics of connection and care. Women were necessarily poised to make abrupt alterations in affection and attachment, however unwillingly or repugnant the change might be. Subsequent children fathered by men who were once their mothers' enemies engendered new loyalties and interests promoted by the primal compelling connection of a mother to her child.

There is another class of female whose situation was even grimmer than that of captive royal women. These were the women without the status of Andromache or Briseis. In the *Iliad* Peleides displays the prizes for a wrestling match, a tripod for the winner, "the worth of twelve oxen."

> But for the beaten man he sets in their midst a woman
> skilled in much work of her hands, and they rated her at four oxen.
>   [23.703–5]

The slave women of Odysseus's household, like Briseis, make the best out of the shift in the masculine power structure on Ithaca. They accommodate their new overlords, the suitors of Penelope, who are clearly in control on Ithaca. When Odysseus returns, this behavior is deemed treacherous and the women are executed in a horrible fashion. They are first compelled to drag out the bodies of their slaughtered lovers, then to clean the bloodied hall.

the women all in a huddle came out,
with terrible cries of sorrow, and the big tears falling,
First they carried away the bodies of all the dead men,
and laid them under the portico of the well-built courtyard,
stacking them on each other. Odysseus himself directed them
and hurried them on. They carried the bodies out.
They had to.

[22.446–51]

There can be no mistake as to who they cry for. Odysseus had ordered Telemachus to "hew them with the thin edge of the sword" but the boy is not satisfied that they have been punished sufficiently; so after they have cleared away the carnage, he pens them into a section of the courtyard, takes "cable of a dark-prowed ship" and hangs them from the rafters:

so their heads were all in a line, and each had her neck caught
fast in a noose, so that their death would be most pitiful.
They struggled with their feet for a little, not for very long.

[22.470–72]

An ancient analogy is used; they are snared and helpless birds. One wonders at the gratuitous brutality of it, but Richmond Lattimore points out that the violence is excused, blamed on another female, the goddess Athena, who is righteously pitiless and insists Telemachus be also.[25]

At the other end of the scale there are powerful, autonomous, chthonic goddesses still evident in the epics, especially in the *Odyssey*. In that story the hero has left the narrow masculine world of warfare and the celebration of individuation afforded by that theatre, and his encounters in the larger world include anachronistic remnants of the ancient goddess. These are powerful and magical divinities like Calypso, Circe, and the Sirens, and the occasional less significant nymph, like Ino, who assists the faltering hero in a moment of dire need. The presence of these figures suggests that the chthonic heroines still had their appeal, but their geographic and cultural isolation underscores the triumph of the religion of the northern invaders over the autochthonic goddess religion. They exist beyond the defined parameters of civilized society, and although all of the women are beneficent as well as awesome, they are sequestered in that magical sphere just beyond the enclaves of recognizable civilization, a sphere which also includes such horrible tribes as the cannibalistic Cyclopes and Laestrygons, the monstrous Scylla and Charybdis.

These nymphs, however, are not cannibals, although all have an ominous, supra–Olympian power over life and death. Thetis, the nymph who is Achilles' mother, has this same power in the *Iliad*. After his public humiliation Achilles reminds his mother that she had often boasted in Peleus's hall of how she had once saved the life of Zeus himself when the other Olympians had tried to overthrow him. Thetis, whose name suggests she may be a version of Themis, "the orderer," the ancient goddess honored at Delphi before Apollo, sent a one-hundred handed, chthonic monster who cowed the Olympians and secured Zeus's power. It is Zeus's recollection of this peculiarly unexplained debt to the sea nymph which prompts him to favor her request (*Iliad*, 1.396–407).

In the *Odyssey*, Circe, still a discernible Mistress of the Wild Things, is associated with drugs, weaving, and chthonic metamorphosis; she turns Odysseus's men to swine for the fun of it, or for the practice, or because she is annoyed at their intrustion into her private realm. She is a gorgeous, willful witch with both charming and diabolical ways. The punishment is particularly heinous because the men retain the minds of men after their transformation, but the restoration is remarkable as well, for they become "younger than they had been and taller for the eye to behold and handsomer by far." Both her pique at their intrusion and the subsequent punishment are reminiscent of the Sumerian Inanna. Like Inanna, Circe has prodigious knowledge as well as bleak magic, and it is her counsel which Odysseus must secure. It is the wisdom that will allow him to enter the Underworld, to die, and be reborn, that enigmatic ability offered by the agrarian, matriarchal religion and never fathomed by the Indo-European hunters. Circe herself is cavalier. She is impressed with the virile Odysseus, but intends to first copulate with him, then destroy him in the tradition of the immolated consort kings. Only with the intercession of the magician Hermes with his Olympian antidote, can Odysseus disarm Circe. True to the fantasy of the Indo-European conquerors, she fails to subjugate him; instead she falls madly in love with this first truly masculine lover, and so surrenders her secrets.

The relationship between Circe and Odysseus is sexual;[26] they are lovers who enjoy equal status and apparently equal pleasure. Odysseus's men must finally insist that he leave Circe's bed and return to the task of getting them home. He has lingered with her for over a year, basked in the powers and pleasures of a life where both the masculine and feminine principles are expressed and enjoyed, but which is no longer available in the mainstream of accepted civilization, and which is in fact counter to the values of the masculine hierarchy. This is the chthonic temptation, the possibility of a society without gender hierarchy, but where the feminine ethics and principle are accepted, even valued where women exercise complete control over their sexuality. Speaking of his necessary encounter with Charybdis, whom she calls an "immortal mischief," Circe advises Odysseus to circumvent rather than confront the monster, pointing out that battle is pointless with the inevitable irrational realities of life. She gives Odysseus a map to the Underworld where he must seek instruction from the blind prophet Teiresias, "to whom alone Persephone has granted intelligence even after death."[27] Circe is unlike the rash young Medea, unlike the suicidal Dido, unlike the reluctant Calypso. Circe trundles Odysseus off with a cheerful following wind, and makes no effort to delay him when they return to bury the hapless Elpenor. Remaining home, Circe remains powerful; she retains the strength which Medea and Ariadne surrender when they forsake their own homes to follow their heroes. This well-adjusted witch lets the hero come to her and then go away again. She is not tempted to patriarchy; she does not have his babies, forsake her tribe and home for his love, or dirty her hands with his blood or that of his kin; she is neither self-deprecating or deferential; she merely shares her secret and lets him go.

Calypso too is chthonic; she tempts Odysseus with the offer of immortality, and no longer urged on by his crew, Odysseus remains eight years as her lover. The two goddesses themselves, linked by both their isolation and the repetition of epic formula descriptions, are both dread goddesses, of shining tresses: both autonomous, ominous, and arrogant. Both possess the special ability to guide, which we have seen was among the last talents the goddess was allowed. In the pattern of Theseus whose heroism can only come to fruition with the assistance of Ariadne, Odysseus needs the secret wisdom and instruction of Circe, and would be stranded indefinitely on Ogygia if Zeus had not dispatched Hermes to tell the goddess to release him to return to his journey. Calypso takes the opportunity of this rare visit from an Olympian to complain about the unfairness of the double standard which limits the sexual freedom of the goddesses who wish to copulate with men.

> You are hard hearted, you gods, and jealous
> beyond all creatures
> beside, when you are resentful toward the
> goddesses for sleeping
> openly with such men as each has her true husband.

[5.118–20]

Even after his departure from Ogygia, the assistance of another goddess is needed to get the hero safely to Phaeacia. Ino appears in the ancient bird form as Odysseus falters after Posiedon's storm has shattered his raft. Motivated by compassion, the goddess materializes from nowhere, a winged gannet, and hands him her chthonic veil to protect him from the Olympian threat.

The Sirens are another, more primitive adaptation of the ancient goddess; they are Keres still, in nature and form connected to the earliest constellation of the chthonic religion. The Sirens are thought to be bird women, but they have no form in Homer, although they possess the duality which is characteristic of the enigmatic bird goddess. Like Calypso particularly, but Circe also, the Sirens combine isolation with seduction and sorrow and a chthonic promise. The Sirens promise that those who listen to their song will, leaving, "know(ing) more than ever he did."

In the vase painting images which follow Homer, the Sirens can be seen in bird form; there they are gentle snatchers, who, like the Harpies and later Nereids, were once associated with early death, and only later with malign female entrapment.[28] Harrison theorized that these ancient primitive forms—at first closely associated with birth and death within the clan—diversified with one line developing into the earth goddess of later religion. Another line resulted in the conception of the irrational entities which escape containment in Hesiod's fiction. At the time of the epics they are still both benign and malignant, offering knowledge of the irrational, but perhaps seducing the listener to an early death on the rocks. The Achaeans are resolved to sail past.

The epics aided in the inexorable movement of Western culture toward a pattern of hierarchy by insisting on the metaphoric centrality of the heroic male, with women acting as their satellites, stripped of the anchorage in matrix clans which ordinarily facilitates the expression of feminine ethics. In the world of the masculine individual, where "agon," the contest, has exaggerated value, feminine ethics are often futile, their expression fractured or ephemeral, and so feminine rectitude is redefined to facilitate the continuance of the male order. That order emphasizes differences and dominance by a few successfully aggressive males. These crucial goals leave no room for merger or amalgamation. The less physically assertive, the weak, the feminine, are by their nature ripe for violation and relegated to a secondary status which excuses that violation.

With the epics, fictional women are presented who are models of behavior according to the gender system and who begin the tradition of complicity by giving voice to the revisionist notion of women's inherent unworthiness. Such self-deprecation is surely not authentically mythic as it does not contribute to a self-affirming vision which allows for the possibility of autonomous heroism. It does, however, create an external description of enormous cultural significance, one which endorsed the gender system, including the use of women as tokens of exchange after the contest: the heroic woman was defined as one who contributed to the stardom of the hero by aiding him with her skills and wisdom and by deferring to his superiority and fame. Those few throwbacks to the great goddess/heroine, although not necessarily barbaric, are certainly not understood, and so are removed to a quarter outside civilization. In this other world they are grouped with freaks, monsters, cannibals. Because they are not clearly masculine or feminine as defined by masculine interests, they are sequestered, segregated, and suspected. The insidious self-deprecation of the women who remain within the definably civilized is proffered through the canon of mythology as a feminine ideal to be emulated, a criterion of truth.

Chapter V
The Reconstructed Divinity:
Danae, Athena, and Pandora

It was the Indo-European emphasis on male individuation which ushered in the Heroic Age celebrated in Homer's epics. The agonistic, self-absorbed individual was idealized, admired not for any mystical awareness of the continuity of life or tribal values, but for the unconquerable human spirit with which he faced his fate, and so made himself superior to it. It is an ideal of singular majesty, but for the merging tribes of the Aegean world it came into prominence only at the sacrifice of the feminine, tribal ethic which the Indo-Europeans perceived as anathema.

Achilles pleading with his chthonic goddess-mother on the beach at Troy is representative of the new ethic; he is singularly unconcerned with others; he is indifferent to the grief his actions cause his mother whose labors on her son's behalf suggest a different ethic; he is oblivious even to Patroclus, who must die before Achilles recognizes that his actions have brought his friend undue agony. Throughout the epic, Achilles remains unaffected by the fact that he is the reason for the suffering of the other Achaeans. The increasing despondency of his fellows is not a factor which influences Achilles, although it does Patroclus. Nor does it deter Achilles from stoking his personal pique. It is only when the consequences of that behavior is personal loss, when Patroclus dies, that Achilles is moved to end his dudgeon.

The survival of the tribe is not even a secondary consideration for these warriors. The women and children left back in Thessaly, in Mycenae, on Ithaca, in Sparta, and sandy Pylos are rarely mentioned. The vagaries of the ten harvests they miss do not concern them. Presumably, they are confident that those left behind can accommodate the needs of the tribe, while at the same time recognizing that it is a far finer thing which the warriors pursue in Troy. When the Achaean is inclined to discouragement, the inclination pivots on the individual warrior's perception of himself, not homesickness or loneliness. What provokes an Achaean hero to despair is an individual insult or personal problem. Achilles' concerns are utterly selfish. He begs his mother to intercede with Zeus so that the Greeks will begin losing and thus realize how essential is the individual to tribal victory. His deep depression in that scene comes from the fact that his individual worth has been devalued, his reputation sullied; he has been publicly declared second best. The consequence of that humiliation is that he must now sequester himself, reversing the ancient tribal punishment of ostracism in order to punish the tribe. But at the same time he denies himself the theatre of war, that one perfect stage for the tragic confrontation which was the primary goal of these descendants of the Paleolithic hunting tribes.

But there are aberrations to this type; Ajax is a peculiar Indo-European,[1] a male who kills himself. This action is generally reserved for women in myth and tragedy. Overwhelmed by his own irrevocable actions of the night before, and propelled by the biochemics of his hangover, he is driven to an awkward suicide. When one has sullied one's own reputation, there is no other fitting ostracism. But when Odysseus encounters him in Hades, Ajax's behavior is reminiscent of the sulking Achilles. Having forgotten his own failings, Ajax is deeply petulant.

Patroclus provides a more anachronistic kind of aberration. He is driven to his rash and suicidal heroics by a tribal spirit, his anguish at the suffering of the other Achaeans. This is a different kind of courage, a throwback to matriarchal tribal ethics. Patroclus has already demonstrated this atavism by his unusual empathy for Briseis. A less privileged son of the Achaean aristocratic order, he is without the potential to achieve the reputation of an Achilles or an Agamemnon. The irony is that his tenacious attachment to the older tribal, feminine ethics of connection and responsibility are what secure for him what was most enviable to the warrior of the Heroic Age, immortal reputation.

In his travels Odysseus comes closest to despair, not when he hears of the disruption on Ithaca or when he wearies of his many struggles, but when his men rebel against him in the episode with Aeolus, the wind god. Campbell points to this encounter as a confrontation of individual and group values: "Phrased in terms of individual psychology: while Odysseus, the governing will, slept, his men, the ungoverned faculties, opened the wallet (the One Forbidden Thing). Phrased in sociological terms: the individual achievement was undone by the collective will. Or putting the two sets of terms together: Odysseus had not yet released himself from identification with his group, group ideals, group judgements, etc. but self-divestiture means group-divestiture as well."[2] What follows, according to Campbell, is complete humiliation, which prepares the hero for his encounter with that finest representative of the chthonic feminine, Circe, who cannot be dealt with according to the Achaean tradition. Odysseus does deal with her, using her to his own ends with her cooperation, but eventually leaving her behind.

It was the urge to polarize values, with individuation and self-aggran-dizement on the ascent, which forced the group model into a less flattering position in myth and which suggests, as through these vignettes with Aeolus and later with Circe, that there can be no lasting reconciliation of the two in the emerging culture of the Aegean. As we have seen the chthonic feminine is deliberately set aside while the acceptably feminine is of artifi-cial design, a manipulative paradigm presented as the cultural ideal.

But the myth of the pre–Hellenic goddess apparently remained popu-lar. It is etched, somewhat enigmatically to be sure, in the visual art left by Crete and the pre–Hellenic mainland. Allusion to the earlier stories cling in image and symbol to artifacts produced even after the imaginative in-vaders had begun the process of revision and reinterpretation. Both Har-rison and Campbell point out the curious inconsistencies in pre–Hellenic depictions of the Judgment of Paris, and to confusing juxtapositions of im-agery in later art as well. Harrison explicates such conundrums in vase paintings and bass reliefs which others have ignored.[3] Hermes, a pre–Hellenic god, always accompanies the goddesses. The *Cypria,* a poem in which the legend first appeared, accounts for his presence as the escort of the goddesses-contestants. Curiously, Paris himself, the contest judge, is sometimes missing altogether, and is often facing the goddess trio with reluctance and trepidation. The goddess trinity is from an older stratum than the Olympian story, a stratum which called upon the young consort, the seasonal king, to make his individual sacrifice for the communal good. Yet when the three goddesses were pictured with Hermes, with or without Paris, and regardless of his obvious hesitancy, mythological redefinition tells a different story, the demeaning story of the first beauty contest. Again we see that the syncretism of the archetype was used to discredit her. For revisionists who entertained an exaggerated appreciation of the individual the cyclic nature of the goddess trinity would be somewhat obscure. Dis-torted to perpetuate cultural notions of gender, the goddess is fragmented into three separate characters who are locked in social conflict with one another.

But ancient art preserved the Cretan goddess trinity, as it did the early duo of the goddess and her daughter. The trinity was often accompanied by the chthonic Hermes, guide of souls to the Underworld, and his pres-ence, the suggestion in some pictures that he is compelling Paris, adds to the idea that Paris was not so much judging the respective loveliness of the goddesses as attempting to resolve some crisis of his own.[4] Harrison sug-gests that the trinity of goddesses is actually the Charities, the gift givers, who in procession were often accompanied by Hermes and are another of the feminine trinities who directly descended from the great goddess.[5] Whatever the derivation, a most detrimental innovation of the revising mythmakers was the infusion of this infighting, this banal competition between the goddesses, who are actually versions of the single complex goddess.

The legend of the Judgment of Paris is a quintessential example of this revision. It has already been established that this particular aspect of the legend was not part of what Homer knew or chose to tell. The *Cypria* is the first piece to tell this tale, and although the date of this is indeterminable, it is certainly post–Homeric.[6] Apollodorus in the second century B.C. embroiders the tale, but his additions were long after the definitive misogynist version was established during the reign of Peisistratus. By the time of Apollodorus the process was complete. Out of the representations of the goddess trinity in art have come new stories which deny the multiplicity of the goddess by fragmenting her powers into separate functions, each in the charge of a different Olympian goddess, who is all too often locked in permanent enmity with another. The irony, of course, is that in her archetypal form, there was a single goddess within whom was focused the diverse roles of tribal mother, chthonic sister, and emerging Kore.

Again and again the mysterious dual and triple goddess of ancient art reappeared in mythological revisions, often trailing fragments of the ancient obliterated archetype. The story of the three daughters of Pandareus, whom Penelope remembers in the *Odysseus* as she prays to the chthonic version of Artemis to take her life, carries the lingering aura of the first stratum of myth.

> ... as once the stormwinds carried away the daughters of
>   Pandareus. The gods killed their parents, and they were
>   left there
> orphaned in the palace, and radiant Aphrodite
> tended them and fed them with cheese, and sweet honey, and pleasant
> wine; and Hera granted to them, beyond all women,
> beauty and good sense, and chaste Artemis gave them stature,
> and Athene instructed them in glorious handiwork
> But when bright Aphrodite had gone up to tall Olympus
> to request for these girls the achievement of blossoming marriage,
> from Zeus who rejoices in the thunder—and he well knows
> all things, the luck and the lucklessness of mortal people—
> meanwhile the seizing stormwinds carried away these maidens
> and gave them over into the care of the hateful Furies.
>   [*Odyssey*, 20.66–78]

The goddesses working together retain the archetypal aspect; they are the Charities, the gift givers, the goddess as trinity. Despite Olympian attempts to reform them into bickering and nonnurturing competitors, they remain *Kourotrophos* (indiscriminate nurturers of all life as was the Cretan goddess). The early deaths of the sisters and their disappearance on the storm winds suggest the ancient function of the Harpies, the wind snatchers who offer the paradoxical escape of death which Penelope herself longs for.[7] Of course, the revised myth tells us that Zeus was behind the kidnapping of the goddesses' adoptive daughters and it is he who has them turned over to the Furies who will punish them for their father's sin against him.[8]

The Furies are another collective feminine entity, another trio, associated even into classical times with attempts to retain feminine power. A most tenacious chthonic remnant, they more often work against Zeus than with him. According to Harrison, they were the gradually altered Keres of ancient matriarchal tribes, specifically the spirits of victims who were unrighteously slain.[9] But these bogeys were eventually confused with the chthonic side of the goddess herself. Demeter at Thelpusa had two statues and two surnames. When angry she was Erinyes, another name for the Furies.[10] The animism of the Erinyes faded as the Northern culture delineated and concretized the mystical aspects of the goddess religion, but as Harrison wrote, "The Erinyes are from beginning to end of the old order, implacable, vindictive; they know nothing of Orphic penance and purgatory; as 'angels of torment' they go to people a Christian hell."[11]

The enigma of the chthonic side, of the goddesses' peculiar, mystical comfort with both birth and death, with the repulsive and the benignant in nature, confused the patriarchal revisionists while providing them with endless possibilities for the propagandistic fragmentation of the original archetype. The Gorgon Medusa is another example of this bastardization of the ancient trinity. Harrison points out that the Gorgon itself was a cult object, a mask used by the priestess in the rituals of the goddess, undoubtedly to avert some Ker which threatened the tribe. The misunderstood mask in combination with the goddesses' chthonic aspect became the basis for the story of the monstrous and malignant Gorgon, who was devoid of any gentler side and eventually fell to the intrepid hero, whose quest had been undertaken to aid his own mother, and in which he is assisted by his goddess-mentor Athena.

The story of Danae and Perseus is a myth which reflects the alteration of the social system, including matrilinear descent. The father of the hero is peripheral, if divine.[12] His mother, Danae, is the skeletal remnant of a pre–Achaean goddess of Argos.[13] Her chthonic counterpart Medusa is also a mother, her offspring, fathered by the pre–Hellenic Poseidon, is Pegasus. Harrison associates Medusa with the horse-head Demeter worshiped in Arcadian Phigalia.[14] Danae becomes a supporting actress in Perseus's story as the emphasis moves from the goddess as mother and maid, to the goddess and her male child, finally to the divine son with only the shadowy backdrop of his mother.

If Danae was once a great goddess, she had been effectively deactivated by the time Perseus's story is finalized. The hegemony of the king/father was threatened by Danae's offspring, a conflict reminiscent of the aging hunter's anxiety but also reflective of the social change from matrilinear descent and a corresponding fear of the power of the mother-child bond. That is the focus of the story, not the efforts of the woman to save her child from the forces which threaten him. The mother herself has been rendered static. "Danae has been systematically divested of all eroticism, and becomes a passive, colorless, and more or less virginal figure who contributes little to the story besides her son, and his spouse."[15] The story of the mother's heroism, a conflict necessarily paramount to the survival of the tribe, has been rendered culturally insignificant. Danae is denied even a prematernal existence. The story tells of her imprisonment in an underground chest until the mysterious birth of Perseus. The hero's father is reputedly divine; his mother, however, is a nonentity, buffeted about by forces beyond her control. She is mute, pliant, pitiable; the dehumanized vessel through which Zeus begets yet another son of god.

The myth does retain almost against its will the free-floating fragments of the shattered goddess mythology. Endless psychoanalytical interpretation of Medusa has led to her association with female genitalia and fear of women's generative powers, but she is also merely a prop, a reconstruction in the Indo-European mode of the necessary villainess without whom we would never have known Perseus's potential; she provides the theatre for the hero's full achievement of individuation. But it must be remembered that Perseus overthrows the ogress only as he flees her chthonic sisters and his triumph is facilitated by the goddess as foster mother and guide, a specialization also drawn from more ancient mythology. In this specialization she is the necessary inspiration and motivation of the heroes who dumbly function as subalterns, their wisdom lying in their willingness to take instruction.

But the Gorgon Medusa is in fact never fully severed from the more benign versions of mother-mentor-maid; she is never fully separated from Athena, who ever after wears Medusa's severed head upon her shield. Campbell tells us that the conquest of Medusa by Perseus is a story of the thirteenth century which testifies to "historic rupture, to sociological trauma," the conquest of a new Indo-European rule at Mycenae through the overthrow of a local goddess and the violation of her rite, one which may have included sacred marriage and regicide.[16] While the villainy of Medusa further reduced the power of the goddess, even the sanitized Athena retains anachronistic symbols of her chthonic past.

There were those who retain chthonic powers intact, but not without some sacrifices of wholeness. These are often stripped of their maternity, some are childless, and asexual, others nonnurturing or inadequate mothers. The loving intimacy of Demeter and Persephone is lost to the stories of Hera's dislike of her sons, to Apollo's patronizing assistance to his powerless mother as she is harried and persecuted by the jealous Hera,[17] and to the abominable story of Selene's demise, told by Apollodorus in the second century B.C. This is another story which pits one mother-goddess against another, which manipulates the original multiple goddess into self-destructive conflict with herself. The conflict is Hellenic in nature for it is over the attentions of the ever desirable, ever superior male. Selene is prompted by the malicious Hera to demand the impossible, that she be allowed to see her divine consort. Zeus warns her that it will be too much for her, that she should be docile and accept his nocturnal attentions without benefit of actually knowing him. But Selene, once the moon version of Hera herself, forgets that which is appropriate for the Indo-European woman; Zeus, regretfully, we are told, appears in his full divinity for their next tryst and poor, pregnant Selene is destroyed, consumed in a conflagration at the moment of sexual union. This provides her divine lover/killer the opportunity to usurp her ancient power; he seizes the embryo from her womb at the moment of her death, stitches it into his thigh and eventually gives birth to Dionysus. In a similar story Apollo saves Asclepius by cutting him from his mother's womb. In a moment of rage, Apollo had had Coronis executed for her unfaithfulness to him, although she is nowhere said to have been his wife. It is an abhorrent and fanciful reversal of the marriage of the ancient fertility goddess and the cyclic immolation of her consort.[18]

Another version of the same story is told by Hesiod of the birth of Athena. The goddess's name is pre–Hellenic, and its etymology is associated with the Cretan word which names the celebration of the feast of Ariadne.[19] This connection is underscored by their supporting roles in the stories of heroes. Both are mentors to Indo-European heroes, both are known for wisdom and guile. The likelihood is that they are versions of the same originally Cretan goddess, although according to the Pelasgians, Graves theorizes, Athena was born in Libya where she was a Mistress of the Wild Things, and Pallas, her other name, was another version of herself.[20] Her wisdom is an ancient prerogative of the Cretan goddess, as is her association with household crafts, the snake, and the bird.[21] In the epics her pre–Hellenic nature is still obvious. In the *Iliad,* in what is probably an interpolation, Athena receives Erechtheus into her temple, but in the *Odyssey* she is still a Cretan household goddess who resides in the palace of the prince.

Farnell suggests that Athena became more complex the longer she was worshiped, but there is much to suggest that from her origins as a Cretan great-goddess she was gradually stripped, first of the sources of her power, her sexuality, and fertility, and then overlaid with the wearisome, artificial burdens of patriarchy. It was only through the revamping of her entire nature, through enforced sterilization and androgenization, that she could come to share Zeus's spotlight as much as she did. In fact she participates more intimately in the lives of men than her father does, in a god-the-daughter role, yet it is understood that she goes about her father's business. She retains her chthonic sagacity only by surrendering her sexuality. As Karoly Kerenyi and Carl Gustav Jung point out, the mature Hellenic vision of divinity was Apollonian, rational, and intellectual; it had repudiated the mystical and feminine and insisted that divine wisdom was a masculine characteristic.[22]

Hesiod was helpful in facilitating this transition for it was he, grim misogynist that he was, who told the story of Metis and Zeus. Metis was the ancient goddess of wisdom, described as a Titaness, one of the first generation of divine order, and associated closely with Themis (social order) and Dike (justice), who is said to have been Themis's daughter. Metis knew more than the gods. When the Indo-European sky gods usurped the powers of the ancient goddesses, there was no longer a need for a goddess of wisdom, at least not one of the first generation, of the matriarchal occult, so Zeus raped Metis as he had so many other tribal goddesses. But the rape was not enough in the case of the ancient goddess of wisdom. There had to be a more thorough and perhaps more willing merger between the impudent, bumbling, violent Indo-European sky god and the goddess who represented the ancient sagacity and mysticism of matriarchal tribes. Since learning from a woman, especially one honored as a goddess by a conquered tribe, was a foreign or abhorrent concept to the invading tribes, Zeus swallowed Metis, so Hesiod tells us, and so benefited from her wisdom evermore because she thereafter advised him from the bowels of his gastrointestinal tract. By the act of ingesting Metis, Zeus wolfed the principle of intelligence and subsequently displayed the merger through the birth of the goddess Athena, whose sex made her no threat to him politically and whose peculiar parentage made her dependent on the male in an unprecedented way. Her birth was phrenic and androgenetic. In dispatching her, Zeus again aped the goddess's power, giving birth from his head to the new, revised, more malleable Indo-European model. Metis's daughter, once a tribal Kore, arrived fully grown, an androgynous female who would become the mouthpiece of her father's Indo-European message. Harrison called the story "a desperate theological expedient to rid her of her matriarchal conditions."[23] Graves points out that Hesiod borrowed from earlier depictions in ancient art which present the agrarian tribes' mimetic ritual of opening Mother Earth's head to release the Kore[24] and thus secure a bountiful harvest.

The myth of Athena's birth rose out of this depiction in ancient art. The *Anodos* of the Kore, the rising of the harvest maiden, left its silent testimony to a more ancient mythology of heroines, while giving rise to misogynist revision. There are various artistic renditions of this story, with the harvester summoning the harvest by assaulting the earth, and so luring forth the gift-giving maiden. The harvester used a pick or hammer to break up clods. In revised myth it became the hammer of Hephaistos. By the time of Hesiod's *Theogeny* mythopoesis had taken on a culturally dysfunctional role. A primal psychic compulsion may well have spurred the original myth of the maiden rising, but Hesiod, a relative latecomer to Aegean mythmaking, revised the story to tell of both Athena and Pandora, and to assert a status quo which was not the first but the second stratum of sociality; it reduced and ridiculed the goddess in order to affirm the superiority of omnipotent male divinity, and the corresponding authority of the human male in the tribe.

In his story of Athena'a birth, Hesiod begins the permanent association of phallic and cerebral, a juxtapositioning which may have been innovative when Hesiod composed, and was instantly popularized as a handy justification for the social hierarchy. Mythmakers of the Indo-European culture, artists, philosophers, poets, statesmen, enthusiastically endorsed and elaborated such myths as rationale for reducing the significance of both female experience and its critical nature as an element of social formation. The goddess-mother was stripped of her power and status by the ascendancy of the divine son. In contrast to Inanna or Coronis, whether goddess or human, the mother was presented as mute or appropriately deferential in this reordering. The struggle to give birth and especially the heroism of the mother who saves her child were stories counter to this interest, consequently they were diminished or revised in stories of Zeus's efforts to save his offspring from the villainy of the chronically raging Hera. The tribal Kore was disconnected from the bounty of the harvest and only vaguely retained her association with childbirth. Her new social function was to surrender her autonomy and asexual freedom to the will of the gods. By the time of Aristotle the maternal function had been thoroughly attenuated; woman was but a vessel, the provider of physical form. The seminal dyad, the mother-child bond, had been systematically devalued until it was rarely recognizable as the crux of human sociality. The female became form for ridicule, no longer the tribal mother, but a character in a farce, fatuous and laughable.

In order to reach this nadir, however, tangible motifs were woven into the revisionist myths of the Olympian stratum. A case was made against women in a moral theatre, one which perhaps began with the case against Helen of Troy in the epics, but which became more generalized with the writing of later mythologists, and was provided with a vitriolic and quantum leap with the writing of Hesiod.

Hesiod is a slippery figure; some historians place him within a generation of Homer. His technique is not the technique of the oral poet working within a fixed tradition. The dialect, meter, and vocabulary show the influence of epic, but they are used with an unpolished freedom suggestive of a less than conscious artist who only half understood the skills of oral composition and knew the epic formulae were ill-suited to his more popular and mundane subject matter. From Boeotia, he shows the influence of Ionia and the East in his writing.[25] This tincture of the East may have contributed to his misogny, for the Orient at this time viewed women as property of their husbands and kept them in seclusion and harems. Little is known of the individual Hesiod, but the biographic material which exists presents a rather miserable and narrow-minded soul. Legend has it that his misogyny brought him to a violent end. Hesiod and an Ionian traveling companion were guests in the home of a man whose young daughter they seduced or violated. The girl committed suicide. The writer and his companion were pursued and killed by her brothers.

It is this singular individual who, inspired by the goddess mythology of the *Anodos* of the Kore preserved in visual art, bastardized the existing myth with the stories of Athena's anomalous birth and Pandora's irresponsible villainy. His story of Pandora is a later cosmogonical revision. Based on the preposterous "memory" of a golden age without women, when the earth was "without evils or hard labor or grievous sickness," Hesiod took Olympian chauvinism to its ultimate delusion, the delusion not of androgenetic birth but of an epoch when birth was akin to spontaneous generation and Zeus in his wisdom generated only men. Such peculiarity may have been the result of the individual author's own bias, but some have suggested that a drastic alteration in the economic role of women had occurred just before Hesiod's time. The warriors of Homer's epics were meat eaters. The pre–Hellenic Aegean tribes were agrarian, but agrarian in an ecological environment which was rich in its offerings and did not demand hard labor to produce harvests. Hesiod, however, writes of an overworked farmer, the slave of a labor-intensive agricultural pattern. His lot may have been complicated by an increase in population, which led to the despair and resentment mirrored in the author's *Works and Days*. It also led to a reevaluation of the contributions of the sexes and to Hesiod's conclusion that women were parasitic, a view which contrasts with the grace and value put on the work of the women in the epics, where even goddesses are lovely as they work the loom.[26]

Pandora, whose name means "all-gifts," was a goddess as Kore, who offered the rich gifts of the harvest to her people. "One lovely figure in Greek mythology undoubtedly comes straight to us from the Cretan mother, that is the figure of Pandora, the All-giver. . . . In origin there is no doubt that Pandora was simply the Earth-Mother, the All-giver, but an irresponsible patriarchal mythology changed her into a fair woman dowered with all manner of gifts."[27] She is connected to her matriarchal roots even in the revision of Hesiod. Once the giver of gifts, Pandora is inverted by Hesiod to the receiver of gifts, but it is other spinoffs of the great goddess who endow her with her own graces. Aphrodite, Athena, the Graces, the Hours, and the Lady Persuasion all contribute to this "gift, a sorrow to covetous man." The sorrows which she subsequently unleashes on man are the ancient Keres, the spirits, both malignant and benign, which plague the lives of men. In Hesiod's revision they are a cruel and Gothic lot, yet the last of the sprite-like creatures to escape the box is Hope, in atavistic recollection of the earliest Keres which were to be supplicated as well as averted by the ancient matriarchal tribes.

Harrison refers to a late, red-figured krater in the British Museum which is obviously a work of art that came after Hesiod. In contrast to the artistic renditions of the *Anodos* of the Kore, which antedate Hesiod, the Pandora in this particular work is not earthbound, but fully grown. She stands awkwardly among the Olympians who have fashioned her. Yet despite revision's attempt to sever this ancient Kore from her roots in the mythology of the rising maiden, to disconnect her from the earth, "a chorus of men, disguised as goat-horned Panes, still dance their welcome."[28] Harrison writes:

> Hesiod loves the story of the *Making of Pandora;* he has shaped it to his own *bourgeois*, pessimistic ends; he tells it twice. Once in the *Theogony*, and here the new-born maiden has no name, she is just a "beautiful evil," a "crafty snare" to mortals. But in *The Works and Days* he dares to name her and yet with infinite skill to wrest her glory into shame. . . .
>
> Through all the magic of a poet, caught and enchanted himself by the vision of a lovely woman, there gleams an ugly malice of theological animus. Zeus the father will have no great Earth-goddess, Mother and Maid in one, in his man-fashioned Olympus but her figure *is* from the beginning, so he remakes it; woman, who was the inspirer, becomes the temptress; she who made all things, gods and mortals alike, is become their plaything, their slave, dowered only with physical beauty, and with a slave's tricks and blandishments. To Zeus, the archpatriarchal *bourgeois*, the birth of the first woman is but a huge Olympian jest.
>
> He spoke and the Sire of men and of gods immortal laughed.[29]

Stripped of her archetypal accoutrements, the goddess is presented in her Olympian manifestation as idle, superfluous, mischievous, laughable. Pandora contributes nothing of worth. She is a necessary evil, human only in form and completely without ethics, either feminine or masculine. Like Athena, she is stripped of the roots which gave women power, the chthonic, the maternal, the tribal, and then presented to be judged in a moral theatre where calumny obscures perspective and she is allowed no voice with which to defend or explain herself.

Again something must be said of Edith Hamilton's perpetuation of this bias into modern times. Although she must have read Harrison, she cites no possible alternative theory of Pandora's inception, but relies completely on Hesiod, who although crude, is for her "the principal authority for the myths about the beginning of everything,"[30] and faithfully renders his Golden Age story, that there was once a time when men existed blissfully without women, until Zeus created women to punish them.[31] She calls Pandora "this beautiful disaster" and continues without hesitation: "From her, the first woman, comes the race of women, who are an evil to men, with a nature to do evil." This is a leap even from Hesiod, though one which reveals philhellenism made insidious by the influence of Biblical exegesis and the unquestioning acceptance of women's guilt as a tenacious or necessary component of intellectual formalism.

At the other extreme, the redefinition, the sanitization of the feminine divine is made clear with the evolving characterization of Athena. Later overlays in the characterization of this goddess continue the insidious process by which the feminine was realigned in the interest of prescribing gender. Virginity is imposed on her, although she retains her original maternity by being foster mother to Erechtheus (or Erichtonius). Graves assiduously analyzes the reordering: "The Athenians made their goddess's maidenhood symbolic of the city's invincibility; and therefore disguised early myths of her outrage by Poseidon, and Boreas; and denied that Erichthonius, Apollo, and Lychnus ('lamp') were her sons by Hephaestus. They derived 'Erichthonius' from either *erion,* 'wool' or *eris,* 'strife,' and *chthonos,* 'earth,' and invented the myth of his birth to explain the presence, in archaic pictures, of a serpent-child peeping from the goddess's aegis."[32] Her wisdom and her skill as well as her maternity came from her Cretan origins and were no longer allowable when she became the patron goddess of Classical Athens. In revision she is the voice of wisdom which inspires the heroes, as Ariadne had been. Her foster son, Erechtheus, founded the city of Athens and, in a curious revision, Erechtheus's three daughters—remnants of the triple goddess preserved in pictorial art—become the self-sacrificing Athenian virgins who are sacrificed to Athena, and die willingly.[33]

The first legendary king of Athens was Cecrops, a relative of Erechtheus (or Erichtonius), perhaps his father. Closely associated with the worship of Athena, he is the figure who is said to have introduced monogamy, and it was during his reign that Athena came with the gift of an olive tree for Athens, which was then a city controlled by Poseidon. Their subsequent dispute over possession of the city was arbitrated by the gods. They voted along lines of sex and so the city became Athena's.[34] But patriarchal values had already become primary so there was a necessary price to appease the wrath of the god. Graves records that "the women of Athens were deprived of their vote, and men forbidden to bear their mothers' names hitherto."[35] Pomeroy cites a variation on this story as justification for the repression of women in the classical period:

The introduction of monogamous marriage was considered a civilizing step in the progress of humanity. According to a myth known only through post–Classical sources, the Athenians attributed this institution to their legendary first king Cecrops. During his reign, when Athena and Poseidon contested the patronage of Athens, the women, who were more numerous, voted for Athena while the men voted for Poseidon. In revenge, the men took away the vote from women and declared that no longer would children be known by their mother's name. Formerly, sexual intercourse had been promiscuous, and children did not know their fathers. Hence, marriage was instituted by men as a punishment for women, simultaneous with the loss of women's political equality and sexual freedom.[36]

Why Hesiod and the mythologists who followed him right down through the classical period engaged in such vituperative bastardization of the original archetypes of the feminine can only be speculated upon. The inherent desire of the dominant Indo-European culture toward dialectics of polarity and hierarchy certainly contributed, as did alterations in social institutions like the shift from matrilinear descent to patrilinear descent and the related need to crimp women's sexual freedom. The focus of social organization became connected to the authority of the male, and precipitated the emergence of the patriarchal nuclear family, often with the wife a token of exchange from outside the attenuated tribe, in function a foreigner who would never become a member of the privileged subgroup. Lerner points out that because the archaic state from its onset recognized its dependence on the social hierarchy of the patriarchal family, including the men's control of women's sexual practices, laws were made to perpetuate that control.[37] Economic factors and an increase in population may have drastically altered life, as some have suggested, but whatever the constellation of factors which precipitated the change, the change itself is obvious and grim. Women were perceived as making little or no valid contribution to society. In story, the feminine character was presented as precarious, unruly, suspect, and this fictional type operated to validate the male as the appropriate governing force.

Thus new types of the feminine appeared in myth which were fashioned in the second stratum of social development. They have certain vague atavistic connections to the archetypal goddess, but are more truly the forced refashioning of revisionist mythmakers bent on preserving male status. Whether threatened by the generative and social powers of women or merely bent on organizing experience in a way which preserved the hierarchic dominance of male elites, the rewriters of myth facilitated the abrogation of natural feminine ethics and helped foist on Western culture conceptions of the feminine which were not authentic or mythic but allegorical and relentless disparaging, culminating in the utter banalization of the goddess myth in corruptions like the story of the Judgment of Paris or

Pandora's Box. Although as fictional representations such stories are essentially alien to adult female experience, they have had a powerful imaginative influence and operated to inculcate both men and women into skewed notions of what determines appropriate authority relationships, of who can be heroic and who may be saved, of who can hear the voice of god within and who must be dogmatically instructed in what that voice communicates. That women allowed such fictional bastardization or came to accept them as valid is further testimony to their position emphatically outside the machinations of the intellectual elite.

Chapter VI

The Feminine Principle in Classical Athens: Cultural Imprimatur of Second Stratum Archetypes

The point at which the evolving mythology of Greece became a permanent, recorded collection of verbal constructions having that peculiar power to stand apart and above the human beings who composed and revised them is of particular concern to this study. We have seen that that ancient tribe's drive for life prompted its first rituals, its initial divinity, and subsequently its myths. Ecological factors affected the composition from its onset, with social anxieties entering the process in revisions. For the tribe myth was blindly egocentric even as social anxieties influenced composition. The ancient Hebrews worked out an exclusive relationship with a god who did not at first aspire to be the only god, but did from the first assure the nomads that they were his chosen people and that his gift to them would be land. Even in adversity, myth is grandiose. When the Egyptian pharaoh was antagonistic, it was the Hebrew god who "hardened Pharaoh's heart," not some interest or malice of his own.

The nature of mythology for the individual is no less self-affirming. To believe in the possibility of your own heroism by having conceived imaginative scenarios of such behavior or by having heard stories of such heroism by your own kind in the mythology of your culture is to make appropriate psychic advancement toward that end. "Myth redeems," Frye tells us, pointing to its use by later, seemingly unrelated people like the American slave who reached into the Western tradition to compose the analogous spiritual "Go Down, Moses."[1] Yet despite her tenacious spirit, there are no stories left in mythology which support the vision of an autonomous heroine. There are instead only allegories of directed revision which tacitly instruct women to forsake archetypal self-affirmation for the approval of pleasing patriarchy, for the heroism of Penelope.

Considering the legacy of the goddess myth, that this bastardization was possible is remarkable without a sense of the cultural and political forces at work in the process. At work in the process also and most significantly was the dynamic of group behavior and group interaction which spawned the first conceptions of divinity—that ethnocentric immanence spontaneously generated by the ancient tribe. By the time of classical Athens, the ancient tribes had merged into the first hieratic cities, but the process of separating and stratifying groups, of alluring that which benefited the group and averting that which threatened it, continued in a different pattern. This ancient, archetypal, social dynamic, this striving by man for what is larger than himself became more vertical, more internal than in ancient times. The newly sanctified group was the empowered male elite and its desire to retain that hallowed sense of itself was a factor in the shaping of mores, law, and art. Such psychic satisfaction elevated the primitive will to dominate to an irrefutable imperative and linked it to the conception of divinity which had come to be seen more and more as an exclusively masculine sphere.

At a specific historic junction—the fifth and sixth centuries in Athens—the previously organic stories of mythology were pinned down as Peisistratus and Solon concerned themselves with compiling *official* versions of the ancient epics and stories. A review of the political fortunes of women during those two centuries of the classical period suggest it was the most unfortunate of times for women, with those in authority including the intellectual and governing elites passionately commited to insulating themselves and their claim to authority by perpetuating the notion of the moral correctness and civilizing necessity of the gender system.

The legacy of classical Athens is prodigious. It is a watershed in the intellectual development of Western culture, its impact on so many different disciplines an inexplicable phenomenon; one which continues to occupy a place in dialectics. The enigmatic social status of women during that epoch has been debated since 1923 when Frederick Adam Wright's book, *Feminism in Greek Literature,* first appeared with its strong polemical position. "The fact is—and it is well to state it plainly—that the Greek world perished from one main cause, a low ideal of womenhood and a degradation of women which found expression both in literature and in social life. The position of women and the position of slaves—for the two classes went together—were the canker-spots which, left unhealed, brought about the decay first of Athens and then of Greece."[2] From that point on the status of women has been a source of scholarly debate, with classical scholars of subsequent generations influenced by both their own ideas of what is appropriate for women, and by the traditional, somewhat sacrosanct regard with which Western civilization has long honored its intellectual parent, classical Athens.

Pomeroy has reviewed the general trends of this debate in *Goddesses, Whores, Wives, and Slaves: Women in Classical Antiquity,* and concluded that the "wide divergence of scholarly opinion is puzzling, and cannot be attributed to sexist bias—for male partiality can be detected on both sides of the argument."[3] Her conclusion is that the confusion comes from the evidence used to draw inferences. A. W. Gomme and his followers, who rejected Wright's view, turned exclusively to classical tragedy to opine that the strong characterizations of heroines in tragedy reflected the status of women in history. Contemporary scholarship, both feminist and otherwise, has suggested that such a narrow focus can give only an attenuated vision of women in classical Athens. Pomeroy points to the continuing evidence that the conception of the feminine ideal continued to develop in a way which gave legal sanction to the evolving hierarchy and which kept women fragmented, often in social conflict with one another. "Behavior appropriate to one group of women detracted from the status of another group, and this distinction was confirmed by the law attributed to Solon."[4]

The fact that the women of Athens were thoroughly compartmentalized, repressed, sequestered, and exploited has only recently been something which scholars have ceased to debate. How that repression contributed or detracted from the intellectual output of the era remains at issue. But the fact is that the symbols and images, the motifs and archetypes of Western literature were not conceived in a vacuum, spontaneous products of phylogenetic psychic imperatives deserving of enshrinement. Revision of mythology included the elimination and reinterpretation of certain symbols and motifs, specifically the chthonic aspect of the mother-goddess, the goddess as trinity, the autonomy of the Mistress of the Wild Things, the *Anodos* of the Kore, the bird, tree, and snake associations of the goddess. The pattern of that revision was woven into Western literature over a long period of time but in a way indicative of an ongoing social anxiety.

In Greece this was finalized at a time when the lot of real women was horribly repressive and when the state was concerned with making laws which legalized social stratification by gender and class. By the time of Aeschylus, Sophocles, and Euripides, the social position of women in Athens had reached its nadir. Respectable women, the mothers of Athenian citizens, lived in Oriental seclusion. They were allowed only limited social interaction, and had few legal or political rights. Instead they were laden with political duties, the principal one being the production of legitimate heirs. They were married prematurely into patriarchal families to husbands twice their age, cut off from their own kin, and subject to a system in which they could visit relatives only when veiled, could not remain in the main room of the house when their husbands entertained other men, could not even appear in the windows of their own homes. Within this circumscribed condition a wife's individual value was measured first in terms of the number of sons she produced, then in terms of her menial domestic utility. In the tradition of Hesiod and Semonides, women continued to be seen as parasitic, a conceptual innovation of gender.[5]

Woman's self-worth was necessarily constricted by this system. In the Indo-European tradition, lengthy affiliative relationships including the elemental bond between a mother and her children, which we have seen as the probable root of inherently feminine heroism, had been utterly devalued by the time of the playwrights. A woman produced children as a civic duty to be members of her husband's family, a group to which she herself was not so much a member as a sojourner. She might well be a sojourner in successive families. Originally female children lived in seclusion with mothers and sisters and female slaves, but this initial association was shortlived and often precarious. The young Athenian girl was subject to laws which allowed her father to sell her, although after Solon's reforms, only for engaging in premarital sex.[6] At fourteen her more virtuous sister was transferred out of the family of origin according to the whim of her father. She left behind her dolls in a ritual of surrender to Artemis and went to produce legitimate heirs for a first husband whom she had never met. But this was not likely to be a permanent home either. Because the wife was so young, the desire for legitimate citizens so acute, and the legal possibilities so myriad, a woman could expect to be a wife in successive marriages, with her dying husband sometimes arranging for her next marriage. The successive contributions which she was expected to make were in the form of legitimate male heirs who were then left behind as she was dispatched to the next marriage. In the case of divorce or separation, even when such action was initiated by the wife because of the husband's cruelty, children remained with their father. One cannot help but feel the silent poignance of these historic women, a poignance which had been eloquently expressed for them by Breisis and Andromache, legendary spoils in a war from a more "primitive" period. What progress civilization had made in the hundreds of years which separated the legendary Trojan War from the classical era could not be measured in the fortunes of women.

Such a system was antithetical to the ancient tribal formation which had been the incitement to the conception of the feminine divine. Such a system sorely eroded feminine ethics. The consequences can only be speculated upon, but it is reasonable to assume that the majority of citizen women in Athens led unhappy, frustrated lives. They did not produce art which was preserved; and they did not participate in the ongoing aggregation of cultural symbols or the interpretation of those symbols.

Philip Slater, in his interesting book, *The Glory of Hera*, has speculated upon the effects of such a unique familial constellation on the psychic development of men, women, and children in Periclean Athens. He believes that social position and psychological influence are quite different matters in ontological development, and that a wary misogyny was the natural outgrowth of a social situation where the male imprisoned the female and took himself to the marketplace. The female's power within the home existed without balance and the effect on the mother-son relationship was the fostering of a hopeless misogyny, the child's exaggerated fear of his repressed mother, and the lingering image upon culture of the menacing mother whose needy, agonized presence haunted one's boyhood; Slater suggests that this conflict led into the dramatic characterization of women by classical tragedians. The mother-daughter relationship was also hopeless, but for the impossibility of its fulfillment and sustenance within the social repressions of Periclean Athens.[7] He writes:

> The male child was thus of vital importance to the wife—her principal source of prestige and validation. Yet how much she must secretly have resented the callous and disparaging male attitude toward female children, who were an economic liability, a social burden (i.e. guarding their chastity), and of no redeeming religious significance to the house, of which they were, in any case, only a temporary member. The mother-daughter bond seems nonetheless to have been the closest, most affectionate and least conflicted of all familial dyadic relationships, as is true in most sex segregated societies.[8]

In fact, young girls had only their mothers. In the family of origin they had limited contact with males; their fathers were elsewhere; their brothers left the gynaeceum at an early age to join the other men for life in the agora. This segregation continued even after marriage. Because they were outsiders in the patriarchal family, women's loyalty was suspect even as their maternal role was undervalued. Athenian women were not even valued among themselves. Divided into separate, segregated classes, slave, hetaera, and citizen, all were deliberately uneducated in the richest of intellectual environs, and only little and sporadic attention was shown to their physical development. Reputed to be sexually insatiable, the daughter of a citizen was married at a point too early to fully enjoy sexuality, and then was denied that possibility as she grew older because her husband was encouraged to satisfy his sexual needs with professional prostitutes and to have intercourse with his wife only for the purpose of procreation. Birth control in classical Athens seems to have been a consequence of the sexual repression of respectable women. And all these measures were sanctioned by law, that peculiar urban entity which was the direct descendant of the tribal taboo.

The first lawmaker to begin the legalization of the repression of women in Athens was Solon in the sixth century. His reforms, long lauded as seminal contributions to the development of a civilized society, were the first legal inroads taken out of the dark ages toward the Utopian possibility of democracy. But they also shackled the women of the sixth century and ushered in the dystopian misery suffered by women of the fifth century. Under Solon's laws the descendants of the great goddess, the once-honored tribal mothers, became the chattel of their fathers, husbands, and sons.[9] Women became subject to the ubiquitous dominance of male guardians so that every vestige of legal clout associated with matrilineal descent was obliterated. Dowries controlled by men determined the marriageability of women. Even the laws which ostensibly protected women were written in terms of the effects which breaking them had upon men whose vision of appropriate relations included male control of female sexuality. The penalty for rape was a fine of one hundred drachmas. Seduction was considered a more serious crime since it threatened authentic paternity, and the husband was allowed to execute the man found committing adultery with his wife. The husband of the raped or seduced woman was legally bound to divorce her; burdening the victim had an ancient sanction, as is evident from the stories of Kores like Callisto, who is raped by Zeus and then punished by Artemis in one version, Hera in another. Solon was the innovative legislator who abolished a father's right to sell his children for any reason, except in the case of a lascivious daughter. So intrusive was he in his desire to structure and limit the lives of Athenian women that he attempted to legislate a limit on the number of garments which a woman could own. Conversely, he refused to legislate against bachelors, claiming, in the tradition of Hesiod and Semonides, that "a wife was a heavy load."[10] Such laws had replaced the taboos of the tribe and were clearly influential in structuring societal prohibitions so as to place women in a secondary social position and an arrested state of development, thus increasing their separation from the process of formalizing and interpreting mythology. It was a social system which perpetuated ideas of sexual polarity: the male was realized, perfected, appropriately dominant, the female unformed, imperfect, appropriately recessive.

In this most enlightened of times laws were written which further eroded the power and ethics of the adult woman. Under them women were afforded no education, allowed no ambition, permitted no growth, and acknowledged little status—a situation which fed the popular belief in women's inherent intellectual inadequacy. A childlike underdevelopment was fashionable even in adult women, as the common practice of pubic hair depilation suggests. There is evidence of this prodigious travesty in the popular theory that the woman had no generative function in the conception of her child. The discernible ejaculation of the male was thought to contain the seed which then grew in the nurturing womb, but without a generative contribution from the mother. The patriarchal state approved the view, as did the reconstructed patron-goddess Athena. Speaking through the vehicle of drama, words written by Aeschylus (525–456 B.C.), Athena articulates the city's revised evaluation of motherhood:

> She who is called the child's mother is not its begetter, but nurse of the newly sown conception. The begetter is the male, and she is stranger for a stranger preserves the offspring, if no God blight its birth.
>
> [*Eumenides,* 658–61]

This absurd theory that the mother is no parent to the child was voiced in *The Oresteia* (produced in 458 B.C.), as divine justification for Orestes' acquittal of the murder of his mother. With it literature endorsed the new civil law by metaphorically negating maternal affiliations, a bias which would hold sway in classical dialectics for a remarkably long time. Eventually Aristotle (384– 22 B.C.) would use this specious Attic mythos as a rationale for his "scientific" theories about women. His theory that the female did not possess the capacity for a fully actualized "rational soul"[11] precluded her participation in his conception of divinity and contributed mightily to the elimination of the feminine divine as an acknowledgeable component in Western consciousness. The development of aesthetics and philosophy on the one hand and law and custom on the other, from Solon and Peisistratus in the fifth century through Pericles and the playwrights and philosophers in the sixth century up until the time of Aristotle, was pivotal in cementing cultural prescriptions for gender.

Athens forthrightly demanded that the needs of its women be inconsequential as a function of their patriotic duty. The famous funeral oration of Pericles, a bombastic study of patriotic complacence, exalts its men:

> We are lovers of beauty without extravagance, and lovers of wisdom without unmanliness.... Great, indeed, are the symbols and witnesses of our supremacy, at which posterity as all mankind today will be astonished.[12]

In contrast, his admonitions to the widows of the fallen soldiers underscores public acceptance of the inherent inferiority of women while presenting a scenario of appropriate behavior for a woman coveting honor:

> Not to be worse than your natural condition, such as it is, that is your great glory, and greatest is the reputation of that woman about whom there is least talk among men, whether in praise or in censure.[13]

Sophocles echoes the sentiment in *Ajax,* "Silence is woman's glory" (1.293). It was a cultural directive for arresting both the development and the expression of the feminine in cultural life. With it the chance to organize a mythos of feminine development was restricted and the silence and cultural insignificance of Danae was approved. With it Pericles presents a formula for perpetuating a society of exclusively patriarchal focus,[14] but also

evidence of a society in which language itself has been relegated to an exclusively male voice.

Eva C. Keuls, in *The Reign of the Phallus,* has focused on the glorifica-
tion of sexual violence, an aspect of sixth-century Athenian life evident
from the art it bequeathed and expressive of a vital component which
shaped the mores of the sixth century, particularly which shaped the mores
of the sixth century, particularly those which led to the legal repression of
women. Her view, supported by the imagery presented on vase paintings,
is that a cult of male aggressiveness had hold of Attic society, fostered in
part by the mythological tradition of gods raping goddesses to initiate them
into the accepted hierarchy of Indo-European marriage which we have
already seen was a fictional device inserted to expedite notions of male
authority.[15] This cult engendered a cavalier attitude toward the value of
female life, an attitude accepted as an aspect of the ideal feminine and included the willing sacrifice of the fictional virgin for the good of the city,
as with the mythological tales of the self-sacrificing Aglauros and Iphigenia.
This ideal of submission and self-sacrifice as aspects of the feminine is emphasized throughout the revision of myth. We have seen it in the self-
deprecation voiced by the speaking women of epic, in the imposed silence
of the goddess remnants in myth, in the cavalier use of rape as symbolic of
the abrupt subjugation of unwilling, once-autonomous goddesses. Eventually the ideal is internalized in aesthetic models, and martyrdom and
suicide would take their place as common and appropriate twists of plot by
which to dispatch the recalcitrant or atavistic heroine.

Keuls suggests that the prospect of death in childbirth, a very likely
possibility for primaparas who were married at fourteen, was deliberately
glorified by the Attic culture as analogous to the male citizen's heroic death
on the battlefield and was accepted as a necessary risk of marriage. She
notes wryly that the scientifically minded Athenians were apparently none
too anxious to unravel the medical mysteries of childbearing, leaving it to
uneducated midwives, and very likely consoling themselves with their attenuated view of the mother's significance in procreation.[16]

The conceptual achievement of the misogynist Attic tradition was this
idea that man was the only true parent, woman a mere incubator. It is the
culmination of a long struggle evident in myth to denigrate the ageless
power of the mother who, in giving birth, transcends death. Zeus's awkward usurpations in myth preceded its emergence as a scientific theory.
Aristotle was so enamoured of this asinine hypothesis as to attempt to fuse
it into the philosophic and epistemological traditions of the West. Such a
scientific misconception testifies to the separation of women from any influence or significance in intellectual quarters. Yet it also testifies to an intellectual elite willing to entertain any absurdity which supported man as
the social and authoritative apex. That men, through both myth and force

of will, could arrogate to themselves so thoroughly the procreative function, despite the empirical evidence of bonding offered by their own
mothers and the mothers of their children, bespeaks an almost unfathomable bias. It is also symbolic of the completion of the cycle away from the
goddess religion, a cycle propelled by "enantiodromia," that process of
psychological, historical, and cosmogonic reversal and overbalancing
which was first identified by Heracleitus in the sixth century and which
Campbell cites as a characteristic of mythopoesis.[17]

That there was public attention to sexual matters including the element of sexual antagonism is evident in aesthetics. Rape and homosexual
violation are not just themes in myth but are also depicted in the fine arts,
such as on vase paintings and symposium cups. Keuls notes that images
which told of the rape of goddesses by gods were popular on vase paintings
of the fifth century, but those same couples were represented as harmon-
iously wed by the time they appeared on fourth-century vases.[18] The
popularity of maenad and satyr conflict as well as the recurring story of
Athenian heroes defeating Amazons contribute to this testimony in aesthetics of "rituals of violence, lust and antagonism."[19] Vase paintings also
suggest that violence was an accepted part of the sexual activities of the
symposium.[20] History testifies that public abuse of adulterous wives was
encouraged, and vase painting again and again presents men battering
prostitutes.[21] The sexual antagonism and violence of artistic imagery was
clearly a part of real life as well.

According to Keuls's theory, sexual practices in the Archaic period
were used as a means of social control. She disagrees with other scholars
that classical Athens gloried in homosexuality as an alternative to hetero-
sexual relationships because they sought to avoid the despised female.[22]
Keuls believes that homosexuality was on the wane in classical Athens after
having flourished in the Archaic period. Even in that earlier epoch, the
Greeks had not practiced true homosexuality, between consenting male
adults, but instead favored pederastic homoerotica suggestive of rites of
passage traditions in other cultures and associated with hierarchical social
orders.[23] Classical Athens had begun to be uncomfortable with such practice, which easily developed into patterns of adult homosexuality and
homosexual prostitution, patterns which undermined the social order. Her
conclusion is that the Archaic period had bequeathed such homoerotica
and that Classical Athens attempted to actively censure its consequences,
as well as adult homosexuality and homosexual prostitution. Keuls addresses only peripherally the fact that social sanctioning of pederasty in the
Archaic period imposed an artificial pair bonding, between older men and
young boys, a dyad which has parental overtones and which may actually
have been an attempt to substitute for the threatening mother-child dyad
which the ascending male-centered culture sought to diminish.

Ideas of likeness and difference, of analogy and polarity, are discernible patterns of prelogical mentality in both ontogenetic and phylogenetic development. As mankind became more cognitively sophisticated, more able to entertain abstractions and make choices about what he wished to be, he revised his mythological heroes to reflect the change. This is evident from the documented process of imposing the urbane and cerebral Athenian hero Theseus over the more primitive Pelasgian Hercules.[24] The urbanization of tribes called for a new type of hero, one more egalitarian and less disposed to heroic individuation at the expense of others within his own group, yet bent on defeating what was symbolically oppositional, those uncivilized elements which remained outside the interests of the polis. So Theseus was presented in perpetually victorious combat with the Amazons and Centaurs, in fourth- and fifth-century vase painting, temple metopes, and eventually, on the walls of the Parthenon. Symbolic of the mysterious, indigenous Aegean tribes, these anomalies were adopted by the citified Athenians to represent that which was outside their urbanized culture, specifically the barbarian and the aggressive woman; both entities perceived to be counter to the city's interests. Athens leaned toward prescriptive allegory in aesthetic depiction; the mythic Theseus is presented as a romantic representative inevitably defeating all which was not Athenian.[25]

Within the enlarged, urban tribe, great numbers of men interacted, somewhat warily no doubt, in a system which continued to include the exchange of women. The ideal of one man in single combat with his enemy, indifferent to the needs of his fellows as he pursued immortality, Achilles' fashion, was not a model which served the communal need of the city. The hero had to be redesigned for utility in the polis, but resigned without devaluing individuation or challenging the metaphoric centrality of the empowered subgroup. Demarcations necessarily shifted; otherness polarized into contrasts of men and women, human and animal, Greek and barbarian. Patriarchal marriage, in Athens an endogamy practiced among patrilineal families and orchestrated by fathers, provided a workable system which unified and reinforced the power system.[26] The continued practice of pederasty, the exchange of sons for purposes of sexual and societal initiation, provided yet another component which contributed to the hierarchic nature of the man-centered society. The emphasis on polarization divided culture and discourse into doublets which excluded each other but which contributed to the status of the male elite: "In the classical period, the juxtaposition and subsequent analogy served to supply a definition of *man*— the Greek male—as the sole significant figure of culture. It is he, not female, not animal, not barbarian, who is the subject of endogamous marriage and thus of culture itself."[27]

Even after the accumulation of an approved mythology, addenda to these stories continued to serve as a vital tool in the organizing and evaluating of cultural experience. Since the archetypal goddess continued to reappear, fictions continued to be concerned with categorizing her. Antigone, who is true to her connate ethics, is admirable if circumscribed in her ability to make a lasting impact on her culture. Ultimately, she is dispatched to martyrdom and suicide. Clytemnestra, who will not yield, becomes a vehicle by which reflective, metaphysical thinkers continue the aesthetic tradition which skewered and devalued motherhood and attachment patterns by judging her without regard for her maternal ethics and then couching their judgment in notions of necessity. The presentation of such prescriptive allegory in the public theatre of Athens could only have increased women's alienation from the remnants of the self-affirming goddess myth and perpetuated its underbelly the acceptance by women themselves of the secondary nature of their status, their subjugation to a patriarchal order, their internalization of the conceptual abstraction of the redesigned ideal feminine, one who seeks patriarchal approval within the gender system and gains cultural affirmation thereby.

The playwrights, Aeschylus, Sophocles, and Euripides, provide invaluable clues to tracing the developing consciousness of Western man. The conflicts developed in their dramaturgy offers the earliest articulations of the individual in personal and metaphysical conflict; no longer is it the gods, or the event which has primacy in this literature, but the individual who is mortal, who may be cursed, but who may also choose, may also be heroic. The characterizations, motifs, and themes of their plays have been hallowed; lauded as invaluable revelations into the "universal" event, into that which is always happening. But they also provide a window through which to see how continued revision of myth by male writers who were the products of their own strange times contributed to the systematic obliteration of the archetype of the feminine divine and consequently the abrogation of the authentic heroine.

Aeschylus was a visionary who asks universal questions: why does a good man suffer, how does a man reconcile free will with fate, how is a moral order imposed? In addition, he dispelled select superstitions. Refusing to accept the idea that suffering comes when the gods are jealous of man's prosperity, he instead accepted the vision of the Levant, that suffering is the result of sin. He infused the concept with a difficult optimism: wisdom can be learned through suffering; expiation is

> God, whose law it is that he who learns must suffer and even in our sleep pain that cannot forget falls drop by drop upon the heart, and in our own despite, against our will, comes wisdom to us by the awful grace of God.

Aeschylus yearns for a moral universe and grapples with the possibility of compelling one, despite the frailties of man. Toward this ideal he seeks to

fuse divinity and law. The playwright was a thinking man, capable of
elegant metaphysical flights, yet not free of the biases of Athenian culture,
the tendency to polarize, to identify through differences and stratifications,
and where he confronts the injustices of the state he revises and pontificates
in favor of the status quo, offering the "yoke of necessity" for those who
have made the wrong choices but also for those who have not been born
into the ascendant tribe.

The dramatist has been seen as both religious conservative and radical.[28] Driven to push aside the trappings of myth and ritual, he searches into
the thing itself. But his reach is toward an irrefutable schema, an authoritative monotheism; he would convince that there is one who hears on high
and governs consequences,

> Some Pan or Zeus some seer Apollo
> And sendth down for the law transgressed
> the wrath of feet that follow.

His search conjures up a paternal figure, one whose edicts are the stuff of
both religion and the law, a fusion welded in his own unquestioning acceptance of "the fixed foundation of Right." A historic framework shaped this
literary imagination. Around him Aeschylus saw nothing of the order of the
ancient tribe, of the feminine ethics of attachment and care. From his own
experience and the fragments of already revised myth there was little of the
older order, so he yearned not for the tribal mother goddess who gives life
and death and solace in her syncretism, but toward "Law that is Fate and
the Father." It is a conception of divinity which is from the second stratum
of religion in the Aegean, one artificially wed to the newly sanctified, prac-
tically misogynist, self-serving entity that was Athenian civil law.

The Oresteia, Aeschylus's last work, serves the male-centered polis while
paradoxically exposing the awful injustices that urban society perpetuated
on those it deemed "other" and lesser in degree. In it he struggles with the
problem of his times, how to adjust the urban conception of justice with
the ancient chthonic imperative to avenge the deaths of kin. His view of
civilization itself was that it was the result of forces in conflict.[29] Patriarchal
endogamy was a compromise between oppositional forces, one which came
with the blessing of the state. Athens sought to impose it as a stronger bond
than that between blood ties, and so to preserve itself against the risk of
women's rebellion within the repressive system. The ancient tribal bonds,
of mother and child, of blood to blood, had to be kept down along with
originative feminine ethics. The playwright contributes by domesticating
the chthonic Furies, by promoting the androgeneous characterization of
Athena, both fictional representations which reflect the conviction that the
advancement of civilization was a process of rejecting one oppositional

force for another, deemed superior by prevailing authority.[30] The motivation is cultural necessity, the evaluation that such measures are progressive.

The dramatist's conception of a "fixed foundation of Right" is clear in the second choral ode of *Agamemnon;* it has been called Aeschylus's vision of a moral universe[31] and it intricately entwines the ideas of sin and crime. Troy falls because Paris broke the most ancient tentacle of civilized interaction, the guest-host tradition. He betrayed his host's good will, took away with him the host's wife, and in the spirit of both ancient and reconsidered justice, Troy falls as a fitting consequence of its prince's crime against civilized behavior.

> Such was the sin of Paris, who came to that house of the Atridae and dishonored the hospitable board by theft of the wife. Leaving to her countrymen the din of shield and spear and the arming of fleets, and bringing to Illium ruin for her dowry, she had passed with light step, careless of sin through the gates. And oft they sighed, the interpreters of the home, as they said, "Ah for the home! Aha, for the home! Aha, and ah, for the princes thereof, for the husband's bed yet printed with her embrace.

Helen, not fully separate from her sin, had not broken the guest-host tradition, but defiled the sanctity of patriarchal marriage—an institution of parallel concern to the integrity of the evolving civilization. Whether willingly seduced or violently abducted, Helen's culpability is in having been absent from her rightful place in "the husband's bed." Aeschylus is not without a healthy compassion for the women in his tales, but Helen, once a Pelasgian tribal goddess, whose husband inherited his kingship through marriage to her, has become in his hands a shadowy symbol of erring woman, much more the descendants of the revisionist Hesiod's Pandora than of the ancient distaff goddess which was her archetype.

Although concerned with the wedding of divine and civil justice, Aeschylus is conscious of the flaws inherent in such a union. His chorus paints a grim picture of Agamemnon's brutal sacrifice of Iphigenia, "a little maid who danced at her father's board," yet this is to contribute to the characterization of Agamemnon, whose hubris and impiety justify his death. The playwright is less concerned with fostering empathy for Clytemnestra, this "woman with a man's will," than he is in presenting her husband as a man who thinks himself above the law, unable to accept necessary limitations. Having raped Cassandra, whom Apollo had left to her virginity, he allows his wife to goad him into walking on the purple cloth of gods before he has been purified. Agamemnon is a monster in Aeschylus's vision, a man unable to surrender the compulsion for self-aggrandizement to the justice and holy powers that have evolved to order the world.

Rooted in the chthonic religion like her sister Helen, the legendary Clytemnestra is a powerful figure. The daughter of Leda, another name for the ancient goddess Leto, she remains associated with chthonic ethics, with feminine power and the ancient tribal justice of revenge. In her earliest appearance in extant literature, she is not depicted as a bloodthirsty murderess. Zeus blames the murder of Agamemnon on Aegisthus, without mentioning Clytemnestra (*Odyssey*, 1.35), and when wise Nestor tells Telemachus of the murder he implies that Clytemnestra had been duped into the scheme by Aegisthus, "for her own nature was honest" (*Odyssey*, 3.265–66). Nor do the epics allude to Orestes' matricide, which was apparently a complication added by Aeschylus. In the *Odyssey*, Orestes is praiseworthy, having taken a righteous revenge upon the treacherous Aegisthus. Only Agamemnon in the underworld maligns his wife, and with the bigot's inverted syllogism rushs to a general condemnation:

> ...she with thoughts surpassingly grisly
> splashed the shame on herself and the rest of her sex, on women
> still to come, even on the one whose acts are virtuous.
>
> [11.433–35]

Although Homer does not know of the sacrifice of Iphigenia, the legend as it is told by Aeschylus is reminiscent of the abduction of Persephone in the Homeric hymn. Like Zeus, Agamemnon is heedless of the cries of his daughter and sacrifices her to an artificial convenant, a bond between men. Clytemnestra, like Demeter, takes power from the elemental sanctity of the connection between herself and her daughter and exercises a righteous and powerful rage like that of Inanna or Demeter. Through Aeschylus, the state condemns her and the ancient ethic she embodies.

In *Eumenides*, libations are offered to the ancient gods as well as to the Olympians and to Zeus, Aeschylus's savior God, testimony to the playwright's leaning toward the Levant. This middle play of the trilogy is historic drama, propaganda as well; it tells of the reestablishment of the Council of Areopagus as Athens's high court after it had been stripped of its powers for a three-year period because of its aristocratic connection. Expedient compromise, including the myths that tell of the rapes and forced marriages of the Kores, had allowed the chthonic and Olympian religions to exist side by side into classical times, but that was no longer possible. The rise of Athens had brought with it the man-centered state. The rites celebrated by chthonic ethics and tribal and feminine considerations needed to be clearly restructured in the service of new values.

Chthonic principles conceived of a simple justice connected to tribal bonds and blood vengeance. The Furies, embodiments of the Keres, were bound to the ancient task of averting whatever threatened tribal unity, beginning with its most internally destructive crimes, crimes of blood. Grafted on to this was the upholding of the guest-host tradition, a primitive sanction necessary from the oldest days of tribal interaction. In Hesiod's cosmogony the Furies are "childless children of Night," sisters of the Fates, another powerful chthonic trio. But Aeschylus would have them seen as irrational and base:

> rampart witches ... abhorred hags, children of ancient birth: with whom no god consorts, nor any mortal, nor even beast, at any time. It was on account of foul deeds that came they into existence.

He aligns them with cruelty and an inability to fathom mitigating circumstances, elements of primitive justice which the new polis was rightly forsaking. They appear

> ...where there are punishments of striking off heads and scooping-out eyes and the cutting of throats, and by the destroying of the seed the vigor of boys is impaired, and mutilation of extremities and deaths by stoning, and where men moan forth their horrid misery impaled below the backbone.

Yet he cannot forsake them utterly, for they have their role as instillers of the fear that moves men toward morality.

Harrison points out that Aeschylus is the first to give these forces shape, and that he knew their chthonic roots since he has them identify themselves with curses and "haunts below the earth." He gives them Gorgon-Harpy monster form, "Black robed with tangled tentacles entwined of frequent snakes." But their forms are horrible though the ancient snake was not; it is this author's rendering which has them vile. Before Aeschylus they had no artistic manifestation, not even in pictorial art.[32]

Within the social infrastructure of Athens, the empowered had needs which were diametrically opposed to ancient tribal needs. Civil law, a flawed and factitious creation at best, needed to be sanctified in order to consecrate the empowered who were solely male. The intermingling of law and religion is an important enigma here as is their joint interest in presenting marriage customs as intricate to both. Law had always been an aspect of religion, an outgrowth of group needs, as was religion itself. The sixth-century lawgivers coordinated the holy codes *thesmoi* and they became *nomoi*, or man-made laws. But at the same time, the lawgivers, the codifiers themselves, were concerned with creating a legal system which would repress the chthonic religion and sanctify the gender system. Toward this goal the Furies were assigned a new function—protection of the state-sanctified marriage. Aeschylus grapples with the conflicts between patriarchal law and chthonic justice and presents the problem symbolically through the agony of Orestes. Orestes, much more a static character than either his father or his mother, becomes a pawn pulled by oppositional responsibilities, but his ultimate acquittal for matricide can be seen as Aeschylus's conservative endorsement of the lopsided civil law. Apollo through the Delphic Code had circumscribed the endless feuds which were the bleakest outgrowth of tribal vengeance, and offered the possibility of purification for the avenger, so the bloodshed might end. At the same time he denies the elemental tentacle of tribal affiliations, the mother's relationship to her child. He employs the Furies to goad Orestes on, yet coolly condemns them as repugnant. Apollo and the Furies are polar visions of law, both essential aspects of justice and divinity, yet seemingly irreconcilable and juxtaposed; they represent the crucial conundrum of urban Athens.

The solution comes through the intervention of the anomalous Athena, whose only chthonic remnant is the Gorgon on her shield. She placates the Furies as a "reasonable spirit of accommodation" and introduces a religious festival—the Panathenaic Festival—to quiet them. In contrast to Clytemnestra, maligned mother and murderous wife, Athena forsakes paradox for polarity, condemning the tribal feminine principles and giving her divine endorsement to the factitious law of the polis.

> Tis my part now to decide the suit by the remaining vote; and I shall give this ballot to Orestes: for there is no mother who gave me birth, and I approve of the male side—except that I do not marry—in all respects with my whole heart, and am entirely in favor of the father's cause. Thus I shall not pay undue regard to the death of a wife who slew her husband.

It is an absurd speech even for a deliberately recrafted goddess. Once Kore, in Attic drama Athena has become the advocate of civil law, a goddess who would not only subsume but negate the mother-child bond, who endorses violence,[33] repudiates the feminine for the masculine, the occult for the absurd.

The development of cultural consciousness, a cognitive process by which men sought to organize and interpret as well as understand experience reached a vital juncture in the fifth century with the tragedians. The Athenian impact on that process was to lead it toward *logos,* a masculine force associated with the Olympian religion, with civil law, with what could be understood as rational and analytic. Frye links the concept to language and the ability of myth to compel, leading to the conception of a "unity of consciousness."[34] Concurrently, the concept of *eros* was feminine, connective, but also mysterious, threatening, and deemed repellent.[35] With the emerging of *logos* as a dominant idea, the genital aspects of male sexuality were downplayed in favor of loftier phrenic activities.[36] Inherent in this process was the idea of accepting civilizing limitations, as

Agamemnon could not, but Prometheus learned to do. Inherent also was the illogic of denying the mother's connection to her child and imposing on women a behavioral model by which they could accept that and patriarchal marriage customs as necessary.

With Sophocles, younger than Aeschylus by twenty years, the concept of acceptance had taken on the nimbus of both civil law and *logos*. Hamilton wrote of Sophocles, "Athens was to him the city which has 'the perfect fear of heaven in Righteous laws.'."[37] The poet himself reached toward a code which recognized and accepted the limitations of life, including those of law and the state, but did so without allowing the crutch of ignorance or blind conformity.

> Sophocles was conservative, the upholder of an established order.... He took contentedly the orthodox view of the hierarchy of Olympus, but a mind and a spirit such as his could not rest there. His beatific vision has nothing to do with the fancies and fables of a childish mythology. The word forever on lips is law and when he searched the heavens seeking to understand, what he found was, "Laws of purity and reverence which no forgetfulness shall ever put to sleep, and God through them is great and grows not old."[38]

In his version of Orestes' story, *Electra*, the character no longer wrestles with conflicting responsibilities to his mother and his father. He asks the oracle not whether or not he should kill his mother, but how to do it most expeditiously. When the deed is done he is neither distaught nor repentant, but self-righteous and complacent. "All in the house is well," he announces. The patriarchal order is validated.

Electra herself laments ubiquitously, clinging to grief which is all she has of stimulation; she has utterly repudiated her mother and invested herself in her brother and his trials in a variation of the pieta motif, which Keuls has pointed to as the only acceptable type of motherhood sanctioned by Periclean Athens, that of the powerless, grieving mother, a neutralized revision of the Demeter myth.[39] Although Electra is rebellious, and Chrysothemis echoes Ismene in her affirmation of the rebelliousness,

> Nevertheless, right is on your choice, not of that which I advise; but if am to live in freedom our rulers must be obeyed in all things...

Electra's adherence is to the patriarchal imperative; freedom for women pivoted upon their compliance with gender restriction. The absence of chthonic overtones guarantees that Electra's dramatic persona will be acceptable and not necessitate the suicide which dispatches Antigone. In the end, despite her assertiveness, Electra is a type which the city would allow. In debate with her mother she defends her father and Artemis in the sacrifice of her sister; she denies and undermines the validity of the concept of tribal justice which has no formal sanction. Electra cautions women like her mother to desist their efforts in its name.

> But grant—for I will take your own pleas—grant that the motive of his deed was to benefit his brother: was that a reason for his dying by your hand? Under what law? See that in making such a law for men you do not make trouble and remorse for yourself. If we are to take blood for blood you would be the first to die if you meet with your dessert.

Electra however is a variation of Antigone. She struggles against Chryso-themis's prudent conservatism as Antigone does against Ismene's. But Electra's resolution is against feminine ethics; she declares nebulous the pull of unsanctioned chthonic law. It is unrecognized by man-centered civilization. It is, in fact, an endorsement of the formalism celebrated by Sophocles: "By ever-virgin Artemis, I will not stoop to fear women, stay-at-homes, vain burdens of the ground," she swears. Like Semonides' bee woman, she has placed herself outside and apart from other women, for whom she expresses scorn. By having internalized these vital components of the gender system, she is spared the despair of Antigone. She lives to marry Pylades.

Antigone's belief in her own powerfulness, in her freedom to reach into the well of ancient chthonic rites and reorder the universe made her death inevitable in Sophocles' schema. A revolutionary anarchist, Antigone is committed to laws which she perceives as higher than those of the state. She allies herself with the Furies, her connection to the responsibilities of blood ties. An avatar, she collides purposefully with patriarchal law propelled not by the rage of Demeter but by the sense, long lost to women, that she may listen to the voice of divinity within even when it conflicts with the restrictions imposed by patriarchy. Antigone advocates the seamless continuity of the human community, in accordance with laws which she, unlike Electra and the lawmakers, does not see as at all nebulous. Campbell has suggested that the dichotomy of male and female conceptions of the "virtue of heroism" can be seen as contradictory approaches to the nature of the universe, with the male will toward reformation and the female toward affirmation.[40] In his characterization of Antigone, this most conservative of Athenians has created an authentically archetypal heroine, but one fettered with the unfeminine complications of revision. Hers is a masculine hubris; she fails to be deferential. However disquieting her ethics, ultimately she is like Agamemnon, destroyed because she could not conform to civilizing necessity.

Endlessly analyzed by modern critics in "numerous and contradictory attempts to characterize and categorize the figure of Antigone," there remains "something enigmatic in her, something beyond comprehension—and not only to Creon."[41] Sophocles himself may have found his avatar inscrutable; he certainly presents her so. He seems not to have been concerned with elucidating her motives so much as her joyless, regretful end: he did not present her to his audience as a woman to be emulated. Bertolt Brecht has pointed out that she has been much more admired in later times for "the ancient play, being so distant in time, did not invite identification with its heroine."[42]

In *Oedipus at Colonous,* where she first appears, Antigone lobbies to have her father see Polyneices, whom he is initially reluctant to see. Antigone lobbies Polyneices to act out against the cure of Oedipus and refuse to do battle with Eteocles. Despite Antigone's sensible prodding, Polyneices perceives himself as a powerless pawn, as in *Antigone* their sister Ismene perceives herself as powerless, a submissive woman in the Periclean mode. But Antigone has the persistent nagging power of conscience. She appeals to Theseus to allow the expression of feminine ethics. She demands the right to interfere in the affair of war with her irrational, impossible faith:

> Send us back then, to ancient Thebes,
> And we may stop the bloody war
> from coming between our brothers.

There is a mystical compulsion to her actions which foreshadows Joan of Arc's voices. Antigone is a throwback to the mystery of the chthonic past but, consequently, she is stripped of personal appeal, presented as the puzzling, impassioned apostate. She absolutely courts martyrdom when she repeats the burial ritual, but her conservative creator has her go to her death regretful, bemoaning the fact that she dies childless and unmarried—the fact that she falls short of the Athenian ideal. Sophocles has made her lackluster, bitterly unable to accept the limitations which had brought down Aeschylus's Agamemnon, but deserving of only grudging admiration. Any subsequent emulation of her is complicated by her martyrdom and her own respect.

Hamilton juxtaposes the whining Antigone of Sophocles, who faces death

> Unwept, unfriended, without marriage song
> I pass on my last journey to my grave.
> Behold me, what I suffer and from whom,
> Because I have upheld that which is high.

with Aeschylus's less renowned version of the same character whose motivation has Promethian stature:

No one shall ever thus decree for me.
I am woman and yet will I make
a grave, a burying for him.... With my own hands!
Courage! For I will find the power to act.
Speak not to stay me.[43]

Although true to feminine ethics, indeed a model of a prevailing feminine archetype, Sophocles' Antigone does not learn the wisdom of Prometheus in submission. Her motives are implacable, yet she dies lamenting her failure to fulfill the reconstructed, unattainable ideal imposed by the dysfunctional authority of culture. Søren Kirkegaard viewed Antigone's despair as existential, rooted in her connection to her father's guilt.[44] Yet there is another possible analysis. Accepting that hers is an existential despair, however, enigmatic, one may see it as less connected to her father than to the literary tradition of revisionist mythopoesis which called for the implosion of authentically feminine heroism.

In Deianeira Sophocles presents another fragment of the archetypically feminine. This heroine, who has such strong roots in chthonic myth, has been manipulatively reconstructed as a woman aspiring to the patriarchal ideal of female, and then killing herself when she inadvertently wields chthonic power.

Deianeira is from the order of Amazons. She drove a chariot and carried arms into battle. Graves links her to Ishtar and aligns Gilgamesh and Hercules, who are both undone because of their love for a chthonic goddess.[45] But Deianeira drives no chariot in Sophocles' drama. She is instead the subservient minister, who does not crave or even consider autonomy, but rejoices in her marriage to Hercules as the least offensive alternative. Achelous, the river god who also courted her, could change his shape at will, a mysterious ancient art alien and terrifying to the reconstructed Periclean woman.

> I, as I sat there, was distaught with dread lest
> beauty should bring me sorrow in the end.

So Deianeira watches the glorious Hercules, son of Zeus, defeat her river god suitor in individual combat. What follows is a marriage of the Periclean mode, with children and an absent husband. The maiden becomes wife, "finds her portion of anxious thoughts in the night, brooding on danger to husband or to children." Deianeira, no longer akin to Amazons or Atalanta, has embraced the pieta motif as appropriate for woman.

Expressing maternal compassion for the captive maidens including her rival Iole, she exhibits none of Clytemnestra's resentment of Cassandra. She is long-suffering, submissive, self-deprecating, but empathetic for Iole "whose beauty has wrecked her life and she, luckless girl, all innocent, has brought her fatherland to ruin and to bondage." Though she refuses to be angry with Hercules, she knows she cannot tolerate sharing him with the lovely young concubine. In desperation she turns to chthonic powers, the magic of the barbarian, of the Centaur Nessus, the magic of Medea. But Deianeira is not as passionately enraged or diabolical as Medea. Deianeira claims no rage, and when she inadvertently kills Hercules, she turns on herself. The chorus expresses astonishment that a woman "could do such deeds." Hercules' suffering is exacerbated by the fact that a woman's trickery has vanquished him; he who subdued chthonic monsters has come to his end by the irrepressible feminine. The dying Hercules is unmoved by Hyllus's defense of his mother. Instead, he reaffirms the system of exchange which founded the polis, insisting that Hyllus take Iole as his wife. Hyllus is initially horrified at the idea, but allows himself to be pressed by his father. The chthonic feminine is again rejected. The exchange of women ends the play, and even the reluctant Hyllus affirms its correctness: "In all this there is naught but Zeus."

Sophocles celebrated the ascendant tribe. Athens at its zenith was the quintessential expression of the agonistic mode of behavior.[46] The subjugation of the weak, of otherness, of woman, and of barbarian was accepted, even idealized. Part of guaranteeing its continuance was the enculturation of women into roles as meek and suffering subservients who accept that all women are stigmatized and vulnerable to gender injustice and who, perceiving themselves as without recourse to power or rage, turn on themselves rather than to rebellion.

Chapter VII
Euripides

That there might be some unwelcome consequences to this polarized view of gender, that as a cultural premise such a view might well be a metaphysical mistake, seems first to have occurred to Euripides. The last of the trio of icons, Euripides grew up amid the wilting of Athens when the crucible of civil war tested its self-canonization and men of reflection saw that their civilization was not blessed. Allegory was no longer the appropriate or accepted function of storytelling. The playwright and his audience had come to question the absolutes which authority had previously touted.

If a general statement can be made about the imaginations of the three tragedians, it is that they no longer saw mankind as the pawns of mercurial deities. They expressed through the development of dramatic form this alteration in human consciousness. Evolving from the dance, drama was originally a group exercise, an outgrowth of religious ritual. With Aeschylus it developed into a dialogue between the individual and the group. In the epic tradition the event was paramount and, while the individual was the focus, he was buffeted about by the event, which was orchestrated by benign or malevolent deities. Tragedy introduced a conception of the universe which included individual choice against a backdrop of manipulative deities and the complications of cataclysmic events, but reflecting an essentially new conception of man: alone in existential conflict, capable of error and culpability, as well as of magnificent rebellion.[1]

Venus stops Aeneas from killing Helen when he encounters her cowering beside the temple, as Troy falls around him.

> It is not the hateful
> Beauty of Spartan Helen you must blame,
> Nor even Paris—it is the gods—the implacable
> Enmity of the gods that is wrecking Troy
> and hurling her empire down to utter ruin.[2]

She goes on to "peel off all the glaucous mist that dulls the vision of mortals" and reveals to her son Neptune "prodding the walls down with his mighty trident and undermining the city's deep foundations," his fellow Olympians' labor behind every aspect of the destruction. Minerva and Juno oversee the fighting. Zeus goads the Greeks to new courage: "rousing the very forces of heavens against the Trojans."[3]

This is the Homeric world view. By the time of Socrates the conception of divinity and the individual had altered; the thinking man had begun to conceive of divinity as connected to the individual, as "the divine faculty of which the internal oracle is the source."[4]

The primacy of event in the epic narrative is replaced by the primacy of individual conflict in Attic drama, but there is evident in both Aeschylus and Sophocles the dissolving of this vision of the controlling deities into a faith in the despotic righteousness of Periclean Athens. Through religious adherence to the new tribal constructs, civil law, and social necessity, man submitted to a new orchestration, but by this exercised a modicum of free will while yet holding off the awful realization of the self alone against the pitiless world. Through such rituals he might lure what benefited, avert what threatened, and enjoy his portion of divinity.

It was a faith which narrowed the vision of these playwrights in a way which was no longer true for Euripides. As dramatic form evolved through Aeschylus to Sophocles to Euripides, so did the scope and imagination of the playwright. Perhaps as a result also of the political decline of the polis, perhaps merely as a result of the author's more critical intellect, Euripides saw the individual as sometimes the innocent victim of events, saw events as controlled not only by the gods but by those in power. His ability to see behind the self-sanctification of Athens, to recognize machinations of his own civilization as imperfect, gave Euripides a more sweeping vision than his predecessors and resulted in an art which was more complex and subtle, one which introduced the vehicles of stereotype and dramatic irony. He departed from the classical tradition of man courting tragedy in illustration of some metaphysical abstraction, his sufferings an exaltation of humanity at its most complex and lofty. To Euripides, mankind was of two sexes and many castes, and was essentially pitiable. Euripides departed also from the Classical tradition of uncritical endorsement of social paradigms as necessary aspects of an imperfect civilization, and articulated through art an ability to distinguish between the individual in conflict with the inexorable forces of nature and his fate and the individual in conflict with the abominable conventions of a constricting social order.

This break with tradition gained Euripides the criticism of conservatives including Aristotle who, in *Poetics*, deems Euripides "the most tragic" yet the most flawed for his reliance on special effects, the deus ex machina, whose use bespoke the irrational component of chance in human life, the improbable, which others had sought to banish to the uncivilized past. "Within the action there must be nothing irrational," Aristotle wrote,

"If the irrational cannot be excluded, it should be outside the scope of tragedy. Such as the irrational element in the *Oedipus* of Sophocles." But Euripides felt the presence of the irrational in human intercourse and tacitly refused to use his drama as civil allegory. His social conscience did not reduce his art or render it inherently greater than the achievement of his predecessors. Instead, it is suggestive of a much more contemporary world view, privy to the angst of the moderns, which cannot be dispelled by god or governance. Such ruthless vision resulted in authentic presentation of what was by then almost buried, the archetypal feminine. More significant and perhaps more chilling, it offers a clear articulate voice for the tragedy of the goddess.

Hamilton called Euripides the first iconoclast of Western literature.[5] Wright pointed out that his use of irony has made him an enigma, historically misinterpreted. Well it might. As an element of fiction, irony is a complex and difficult filter; understanding it is among the last and most sophisticated skills mastered by the individual in developmental reading. First used as a pedagogic tool by Socrates, it contributed to the suspicion and misunderstanding aroused by his teaching. It is intricately dependent on tone, an aspect of language easily confused by translation and the whim of bias of interpretation. Reputedly an intimate of Socrates, Euripides seems to have taken to heart the philosopher's challenge, that "a life unscrutinized is unworthy of man." The playwright sought to bring that admonition to a national level. With devastating insight he probed to the heart of the self-serving conventions of Athenian society, particularly the idea that this just and civilized polis was inherently righteous. Both philosopher and playwright suffered censure and virulent criticism for making the accepted appear ridiculous or questionable, for making the "worse appear the better cause."

Moreover, the complexity of Euripides' irony is heightened by the years that separate him from those who struggle to fathom his art. There are modern critics who, despite the aid of interim interpretations, see Euripides as the misogynist Aristophanes mocked him for and use his deliberately static, two-dimensional characterizations, such as the laughable Hippolytus and the bigoted Jason, as a basis of their view.[6]

But Euripides recognized the possibilities inherent in legend and characterization, and was the first artist to concern himself with the question of what really motivated women. Euripides created authentic women by taking tragedy a step further than his predecessors. They had focused on the individual man as the protagonist, his conflict existential, his agony expressible through tragedy. Euripides focused on women through the same lens and recognized that much of the existential conflict inherent in their lives came from the oppression of a society which celebrated male citizens by demanding self-destructive obeisance from women. In retelling the story of Agamemnon's death, Aeschylus makes the wife the villain of the legend, yet in his hands she never offers a credible explanation for her act. Sophocles' Antigone, while functioning to uphold feminine ethics, remains enigmatic. These characterizations are flat: there is no clear expression of what moves them to action. This is Euripides' achievement. Even though Medea murders her children, one empathizes with her rage and the desperation that leads her to such singular atrocity.

Like Clytemnestra, Medea is a figure who has been thoroughly condemned as the most heinous of creatures—a mother who killed her own children. No omniscient goddess appeared to justify her action in terms of the newly sanctified needs of the polis, as Athena had for Orestes. Yet as maligned as she has been, Medea is an arresting figure in literature, much more so than Orestes, whose act overshadowed the actor. Medea is logical, articulate, and fascinating, a complex heroine who remains a powerful, disquieting force. She has the lasting magnitude of Inanna or of the early Demeter.

Medea retains the powers of the first stratum of society, the goddess's power of fertility, or seminal tribal associations of life and death. She possesses the constellation of attributes associated with the ancient goddess. Legend places her with both divinities and nymphs. Aeetes, her father in the Golden Fleece story, was said to have descended from Helios, the sun god, and Euripides picks up on this to orchestrate Medea's escape. Another version of her legend claims that she was the daughter of Hecate, whom Medea repeatedly invokes in Euripides' drama. Wilamowitz-Moellendorff, the authority on classical philology, considered Medea an Underworld goddess herself, possessing chthonic powers.[7] Graves called Medea the priestess of Hecate and connected her to the matriarchal Aegean tradition by pointing out that Colchians had buried only females.[8] Apollodorus connects her to Circe, supposedly her aunt, who helped to purify her and Jason after they had killed her brother.

According to later myth, the germ of her later ruthlessness was in this gruesome act. Legend claimed that Medea delayed her father's pursuit by committing fratricide, chopping her brother to bits and dropping the pieces overboard. It was necessary for her father to gather up the individual pieces in order to bury his son. Although this aspect of her legend was emphasized by later writers, even Apollodorus (1.9.24) includes this detail. In Euripides' embellishment Medea herself connects her downfall to this earlier sin. She calls upon her lost tribe: "In what dishonour I left you, killing my own brother for it."

What is clear is that Medea provided for Jason the same service which Ariadne had for Theseus; in the tradition of the great goddess she was mentor and guide to the hero. She possessed the necessary sagacity, later misnamed magic, which the hero himself did not. But the goddess's sagacity had been devalued and discredited in the context of the altered needs of the polis. Intelligence in women was undesirable, awesome, a reason for criticism and stricture. The intelligent woman, after all, is not powerless, nor does she readily comply with the gender system. Creon points out that the clever woman is "versed in evil arts," and Medea herself claims that because she has been "considered clever," she has "suffered much."

Unlike Ariadne, Medea remained a figure of the ancient mode. She was not inverted to suit the Attic schema, as Sophocles had inverted the chthonic Deianeira. Instead, Euripides leaves her an awesome figure, possessing passion and intelligence and having no desire to follow the Athenian ideal of the feminine, an ideal which served men and the state but which had brought about her isolation and left her vulnerable to disaster. By leaving her chthonic nature intact, Euripides attempts through characterization and plot to explicate her motives.

The chorus first expects Medea to turn on herself, as the Athenian woman was expected to, as Deianeira did when she inadvertently discovered herself in possession of power, but Medea is a foreigner, atypical, "a strange woman." Only her first instinct is self-destructive:

> Oh, what use have I now for life?
> I would find my release in death
> And leave hateful existence behind me.

But despair fuels her rage, and her sense of her own power mitigates it. Her anger prevails, against Jason specifically, but also against the society which has fostered this complacent, thankless hero, lauded his sex and type while isolating and disparaging women like herself.

Medea is an articulate, logical social critic. She offers an organized and valid assessment of the plight of women in Periclean Athens, citing the social ills perpetrated on women who must "buy a husband and take for our bodies a master; for not to take one is even worse." Once married, "she arrives among new modes of behavior and manners, and needs prophetic power, unless she has learnt at home, how best to manage him who shares the bed with her." She bemoans the loneliness of a woman's sequestered life, the friendliness if her husband prefers the agora, the agony of childbirth with little medical intervention: "I would very much rather stand three times in the front of battle than bear one child." Medea's poignant articulation of what was reality for women in classical Athens must have disquieted Euripides' audience, and it certainly contributed to the fact that he received far fewer dramatic awards than did his less iconoclastic fellows.

Medea's intelligence is her real flaw. According to Creon, anything is preferable to an intelligent, educated woman. When Medea begs to be allowed to remain in Corinth, swearing obeisance to the men who rule her, Creon cannot allow it:

> Still in my heart
> I greatly dread that you are plotting some evil
> and therefore I trust you less than before.
> A sharp-tempered woman, or for that matter a man,
> Is easier to deal with than the clever type
> Who holds her tongue.

Again Medea is different, a barbarian. Unlike the reshaped feminine ideal, she does not commit suicide; instead, praying to Artemis and Hecate, she plots to murder, to leave no enemy laughing at her fate. First she resolves to kill Creon, his daughter, and Jason, but she wants Jason to suffer. Cunning as well as astute, she seizes on what she has just learned from Aegeus of the pain of a childless father. She struggles with Jason to force him to commit himself to caring for his children, but although he loves them, he shunts the daily responsibility of their care to Medea. He himself will marry Creusa and enhance the social standing of his children by giving them royal siblings.

The age of Euripides was an age in which men controlled the lives of children, where infanticide was still practiced at the determination of fathers. Medea takes upon herself this paternal right. She kills her children to make Jason suffer, but also to keep them from the life of insults which would await them should they remain with their father in Corinth. In this ruthless act she breaks the most ancient of tribal bonds, yet with it she refuses the new feminine ideal of powerlessness and despair.

> Let no one think me a weak one, feeble-spirited,
> A stay at home, but rather just the opposite,
> One who can hurt my enemies and help my friends;
> For the lives of such persons are most remembered.

She chooses murder as the only act of power left her, but it is no easy thing. Euripides' Medea may have been overlaid onto an age which thought mothers merely incubators of their children, but Medea does not break her bonds with them easily. Her agony is palpable, "but stronger than all my after thoughts is my fury, Fury that brings upon mortals the greatest evil."

Her preposterous escape and her magic murder are both rooted in chthonic traditions; Helios appears with his chariot to spirit her away, wordless and unjudging. In helping Jason in Colchis she had repudiated her matriarchal roots, broken faith with tribal connections. Although she blames and scorns Jason, because of this first sin Medea accepts responsibility for her own downfall. With Medea Euripides speculates on the psychology of the woman who could not accept the redefinition of the feminine. He presents in this powerful archetypal figure the goddess who would not despair, who refused to be mortised with patriarchal overlay. Explosion is the result, but not the now traditional implosion of the goddess, not suicide. Instead, Medea's vengeance goes to the heart of what is built through feminine ethics. In killing her children she repudiates the rootlet of society, the mother-child bond; Medea is the goddess who exercises her chthonic rage, opting for anarchy. She inverts the central connection of society as Inanna had when her son did not properly acknowledge her heroism. Medea's ominous blow is to the infrastructure of society, the very crux of human sociability.

With his strange and disquieting characterization, Euripides challenged Attic modes of conception, of definition through contrast and isolation. Medea is everything that is completely excluded from the dominant tribe of classical Athens. A foreigner, she is also a female of the old order, matriarchal and chthonic. As a force she is nebulous, threatening and labile, in opposition to *autarkeia,* the ideal of male self-sufficiency introduced by Hesiod and wistfully longed for by Jason. But she is irrepressible and uncowed. For a society like Jason's, which nostalgically fantasized about a mythical time when women were not a necessary part of human culture, she was quintessentially antithetical. A great intellectual force, Medea courts anarchy because there is no redress for her wrongs; alone, she refuses the redefinition of the feminine and challenges the complacent pride of Athens and the self-proclaimed beneficence of man-governed civilization.

Euripides offers in her story a "continuing discourse about the problems of differences" and speculates that, without release or reordering, the repression of the archetypal feminine could result in societal anarchy, the repudiation of the most profound of connections, the connection of mother to children.[9] The play makes clear Euripides' belief that there is no clear link between divinity and human order, between maleness and righteousness. It is a plea for the acknowledgment of chthonic female: "Flow back to your sources, sacred rivers, And let the world's great order be reversed."

The play also suggests some of the discernible imperatives at work in the formation of the polis civilization which also contributed to its decline.

> By the very fact of her presence in the city, by her violence, her female, bestial, barbarian nature, Medea exemplifies the eruption of difference within the family, with the *polis,* among the Hellenes. Difference is represented by Euripides as *internal* rather than external, omnipresent in the body of the Greeks. The other, bestial, foreign, most of all female, is

for Euripides a marginalized marked figure who is nonetheless at the center of the tragic drama. Her difference results from internal conflict, from forces, within the *oikos* and the *polis* which do battle with one another.[10]

It is tragedy on more than one level. Medea and Jason are individuals in conflict over gender and worth, over power and the appropriate use of it, as Demeter and Zeus had been in the earlier myth of the abduction of Persephone.

In his *Hecuba* and *The Trojan Women*, Euripides chose yet another woman, also barbarian and by the time of this story a slave, the conquered queen of Troy. In the earlier play Hecuba is much like Medea in her bleak, compelling nature. Polydorus, the youngest of her sons, has been murdered by the man to whom his parents sent him for sanctuary; after the fall of Troy, Polymestor, a vile political opportunist, killed the boy despite his oath to protect him. Polydorus had called up "the gods below" to allow his body to be returned to his mother for burial. Hecuba, though conquered and awaiting slavery, is unable to accept herself as the plaything of the Fates, unable to accept the Attic ideal of feminine behavior or repudiate ethics of attachment and responsibility. Like Medea, she has nothing to gain by catering to the patriarchal ideal. Despite multiple losses, she rejects the pieta motif, and restlessly prays to the goddess Earth to beat back the dreams she has of her dead children, to limit the debility of her grief. The discovery of her son's corpse releases an elemental passion not unlike Medea's, the passion of unredressible wrongs.

> The fiend, the fury,
> singing, wailing in me now,
> shrieking madness!

Not even the handmaiden who accompanies her understands, "What fury?"

She calls on Agamemnon to help her avenge her child's murder, reminding him that hers is a cause of more primacy then any created by man-made liaisons.

> I am a slave, I know
> and slaves are weak, But the gods are
> strong and over them
> there stands some absolute, some moral order
> or principle of law more final still.
> Upon this moral law the world depends;
> through it the gods exist; by it we live
> defying good and evil
> Apply that law

> to me. For if you flout it now, and those
> who murder in cold blood or defy the gods
> go unpunished, then human justice withers,
> corrupted at its source.

Something of this mystical appeal touches Agamemnon, stodgy as he is, but he is committed to political connections between men, ties of artificial significance but a more tangible hold than those which Hecuba has to Polydorus:

> This is my dilemma. The army
> thinks of Polymestor as its friend
> this boy as its enemy. You love your son
> but what do your affections matter to the
> Greeks?
> Put yourself in my position.

But her appeal has rattled him. He understands that the "common interests of states and individuals alike demand that good and evil receive their just rewards," yet he is a relentlessly practical man. He agrees finally to give her no resistance, comfortably skeptical that a woman can exert any power over a man.

Hecuba, however, is absolutely confident of power:

> Why?
> Women killed Aegyptus's sons. Women emptied Lemnos
> of its males; we murdered everyone.

The vengeance which Hecuba visits upon Polymestor is perfectly fitting. His own sons are killed, he himself blinded and transformed into a bellowing animal. It is the vengeance of a Circe, the chthonic vengeance of a woman who never doubts her power of righteousness, but instead reaches beyond delicacy to a primal act of hedonic aggression, one which is more just than civilized.

I suggest that Hecuba is not horrible, any more than is Medea, and that it is an ancient bias born in Attic tradition which insists that she is. Generations of critics have seen Hecuba as demonic, "a kind of Hell-hound with fiery eyes, whom sailors saw at night prowling round the hill where she was stoned" and turned instead to Euripides' characterization of Polyxena, the willing virgin martyr, as "the only light that shines through the dark fury of the *Hecuba.*"[11] What also shines through is the dark, lost power of the goddess, ever Mistress of the Wild Things, ever guardian of the elemental tentacles of society, the connections between mother and children.

Euripides' characterization of Hecuba in *The Trojan Women* is more acceptable to Western sensibilities. In this later play the old queen projects the Athenian model of the suffering mother who exerts only the passive power of influence through persuasion and relationship. Certainly a more resigned and therefore more justifiable woman to Athenian audiences, this Hecuba has been admired by Western culture and "remains with Leah the tenderest study in literature of desolate old age."[12]

She first appears onstage prostrate outside Agamemnon's tent. Despite destitution and bereavement, she drags herself to her feet, propelled by ethics of attachment and responsibility. No concern for the opinions of men or for preservation of her status in society enters into her motivations as she takes up leadership of the royal women now captives who wait to be meted out to the conquerors.

> And I, as among winged birds
> the other, lead out
> the clashing cry, the song: not that song
> wherein once long ago,
> when I held the scepter of Priam.
>
> [145–50]

But it is futile, powerless leadership which she exercises. This is not the chthonic Hecuba who plots to blind Polymestor, but instead a tractable Attic version, one who recognizes that she must "hold not life's prow on the course against wave beat and accident," one who counsels against contumacy. It is through this central focus that Euripides orchestrates the play's progress as it stops momentarily to pity one Trojan princess after another in her new role as slave and concubine.

In aspect these are acquiescent Attic women. Only Cassandra, ancient priestess of the goddess, is reminiscent of the archetype of the great goddess, and she is quite mad now. Having been raped by Ajax at the altar where she served, she is now sentenced to become Agamemnon's concubine and is fully aware of the violent deaths that await them both. In her Euripides has presented a remnant of the archetypal goddess as exegetical revision would have her, powerless and raving. She is without even the allowable power of the restructured feminine, the power to influence; Cassandra's bleak curse, sent to her from Apollo, was that she be prescient yet unbelieved. Neither her mother nor the other women believe her to be anything but mad, her incontinence is their last great shame before the Greeks. She is symbolic of the goddess's alienation and not even her own mother recognizes her truth as she foretells the bloody vengeance Clytemnestra will wreak for Troy by murdering Agamemnon in fury over the barbarian princess he has yoked to his side.

In her powerlessness Cassandra is enigmatic and contrary. She embraces despair, invites her own death while mouthing the outworn epithets of the heroic notion, the hollow conviction that despite Troy's destruction, some greater good was served by the war which, along with carnage and misery, guaranteed immortal reputation for fallen Trojan warriors. Without the arrival of the Greeks they would never have known the bravery of Hector. Cassandra claims the subsequent perdition is justifiable according to that agonistic ideal; she futilely decries the pathos in that paradox.

Through Cassandra, Hecuba repudiates the optimism of Aeschylus, that in suffering men learn wisdom "through the awful grace of god." "You move so wildly," she tells Cassandra as she takes the torch from her, "your sufferings, my child, have never taught you wisdom."[13] It is more than the iconoclast's nihilism; it is a scenario in which the ancient goddess's power has been confounded.

Yet the attempt has not been successful. Cassandra, though unbelieved, though apparently powerless, remains symbolic of the irrepressible chthonic feminine. Despite the efforts of the culture to defuse her, it is this goddess remnant who achieves a vengeance for her tribe. It is not just to the god Hymen who prays, but also to Hecate as she makes the promise her mother cannot fathom:

> If God still lives, my marriage
> shall be bloodier than Helen's. Agamemnon the great,
> the glorious lord of Greece. I shall kill him, Mother,
> make him pay for all he made my father suffer, brothers and...
>
> [401–5]*

It is in Andromache that Euripides presents the quintessentially Attic feminine. Her legend goes back to the *Iliad* where she was the daughter of a matriarchal tribe, her mother the ransomed leader of Asian Thebe. But by the time she reappears in Euripides' embellishment, she is a perfect model of the restructured feminine; having embraced the redefinition, she disciplined herself to fit it and strove with single-minded self-deprecation to be that which others had defined as appropriate:

> I aimed my shaft at good repute. I gained full measure and missed happiness. For all that is called virtuous in a woman, I strove for and I won. In Hector's house knew well in what I should rule him and when give him obedience. Silence, a tranquil eye I brought my husband....'. And this report of me came to the Greeks for my destruction.*[14]
>
> [645–50]

Having achieved reputation in this fashion, she is the most desirable plunder, and even before the awful ripping away of Astyanax, she longs for death, aching for the peace Polyxena's martyrdom has brought her.

She has died her death. And happier by far than I.

[630]

Mother, hear a truer word. To die is only not to be,
and rather death than life with bitter grief.
She is dead, your daughter. To her the same as had
she never been born. She does not know the wickedness that killed her.*

[636–40]

Andromache has been allotted to Pyrrhus, the son of Achilles, who had
killed Andromache's father on his way to Troy, according to her own testimony in the *Iliad*. In addition, according to Aeneas's rendition of the fall
of the city, Pyrrhus had murdered Priam at the altar where he and his queen
had gone for sanctuary. With Hecuba as witness, Pyrrhus slaughtered her
son, then dragged her ancient husband, slipping and sliding in his son's
blood, to his own execution. Yet in the grim daylight Hecuba admonishes
her daughter-in-law to cleave to the ways of Attic womanhood, and with
her voice gives some understanding of why women complied. She advises
quiescence and obsequiousness, for therein there may be the hope of the
resurrection of their city:

Let Hector be, and let be what has become of him.
Your tears will never bring him back.
Give honor now to him who is your master.
Your sweet ways, use them to allure him. So doing
you will bring hope to your friends. Perhaps this child, my own
child's son, you may rear to manhood and great aid for Troy
And if ever you should have more children,
they might raise her again.... Troy once more be a city.*

[696–705]

Yet what follows is the nadir of despair. An old woman, alone with the
corpse of her last progeny, still adheres to the Attic ideal of the feminine;
she turns not on the ways of men, on war, or the conventions that have
made women chattel, she turns instead to blame another woman. "Now
cursed Helen has robbed you of it, robbed you and destroyed your life, and
ruined utterly your whole house."

The characterization of Helen in *The Trojan Women* is of an utterly
depraved, self-serving vamp. Hecuba's last struggle to exercise power is in
her futile efforts to prosecute Helen, addressing the need for a loftier imperative than that which is served by Menelaus's lust. But *The Trojan
Women* presents a world where the only remnant of the chthonic feminine,
Cassandra, has been raped, driven mad, and led off to her execution. What
prevails is the Attic feminine, a characterization of women enslaved not

only by their tragic political position, but by their deafness to Cassandra, their complicity in the revised ideal. Consistent with this, they blame Helen and her untoward passion for a war in which noble Trojans "perished in their thousands," and left them in slavery. Consistent with this, they accept that they are powerless, even to save their own children: "God hath undone me, and I cannot lift one hand, one hand, to save my child from death," Andromache laments as she surrenders her son. Consistent with this also is the sequence in which Hecuba lobbies futilely for the execution of Helen, demanding recognition of a higher justice than that created by the factitious will of men. In the revised ideal the syncretic goddess is fractured, cleft into attenuated subordinates, each sharply circumscribed in power and often in conflict with herself, either through self-deprecation or as one woman pitted against another. Blind to their chthonic heritage, women saw the cause of their grievances as men did, not in male governance with its adherence to agonistic modes of behavior, its construction of laws and conventions which served the dynamic of a man-centered civilization, but in one another. Helen alone triumphs in this play, and in this characterization she is a distaff viper in the tradition of Hesiod and Semonides. But she is no longer just the curse of the individual man. Her malice has become a leviathan. Once the underpinning of social systems, the tribal mother in the Attic revision, she fells nations at her evil whim and leaves enslaved women and broken children in her wake.

But Euripides knew the myriad possibilities inherent in legend and characterization, and while Helen is a vile figure in *The Trojan Women,* he breaks with the tradition of maligning her in *Helen.* In her own play she is innocent of the crimes ascribed to her and is, in Lattimore's assessment, closer to her characterization in Homer. Lattimore sees the iconoclastic playwright striving toward optimism with this romantic comedy and presenting themes of paradox, illusion, and surprise. "Triumphantly the heroine emerges with all the attributes Homer gave her—the charm, the wit, the self-importance, and self-pity—above all the inescapable loveliness . . . but adding to all these, in perfect harmony, the virtues of Penelope."[15] Euripides' was the ever inquiring mind. He capably presented women as cultural stereotypes, the legitimate prey of powerful men and gods, as with Creusa in *Ion.*[16] He exacerbated the Hesiod tradition with the Helen of *The Trojan Women.* She is heinously manipulative, whereas Pandora had been merely inept. Yet with the Helen of this romance, he has conjured yet another possibility. Reaching into the syncretistic nature of the original goddess and taking from that rich archetype, he produced an enchanting character who is the polar opposite of the execrable Helen of *The Trojan Women.*

Despite the prodigious influence of the epic tradition, there persisted that ancient variant on the legendary Helen which suggests an earlier reverence for this "daughter of Zeus." The epithet itself, so common to mythological heroes, clings to Helen from the earlier stratum when she was the Kore/heroine, daughter of thee goddess made daughter of the god yet retaining this lingual status despite revision. Hesiod, in a lost work, seems to have referred to this older tradition which claimed that the Spartan tree-cult goddess had never gone to Troy. One cannot doubt but that Hesiod was skeptical about this version of the legend which downplays the culpability of the woman while presenting men in their vanity pursuing a phantom and bringing on their own destruction. Stesichorus, a sixth-century poet, had supposedly lost his sight for having composed lyrics which blamed the Trojan War on Helen's infidelity. Herodotus, whose work appeared contemporaneously with Euripides', claimed to have had the ancient legend validated by the priests of Egypt, who were apparently less dedicated to imbuing cultural tradition with the fiction of women's guilt.[17]

The character who emerges has spent seventeen years in Egypt, virginally awaiting Menelaus. This is in stark contrast to the Helen of epic who, following Paris's death, became the wife of successive Trojan princes. There are various tentacles of the chthonic tradition in this presentation, including a female prophetess who is both believed and respected. This is the royal princess, Theonoe, daughter of Proteus, who functions as a balance to her agonic brother, Theoclymenus, a ruler in the Athenian mode.

From the onset there is clear juxtapositioning of the chthonic and the Attic feminine. Helen discovers that Leda, her mother and an ancient goddess in the Pelasgian religion, has killed herself, and some say Castor and Polydeuces have as well. Helen's is clearly a family of the matriarchal tribes. Mortised into their story are the revisions of the later tradition. There is repeated suggestion that Zeus was Helen's father, with little attention to the possibility that either Leda or Helen herself are divine. Helen's prayers, however, are to chthonic female deities, to the Siren and Persephone. This Helen has embraced much of the reconstructed ideal but her chthonic roots shoot forth almost against her will. She contemplates suicide, embraces guilt, spouts the Attic model as though attesting to higher truths:

> I know there is no good in learning, but when
> you love you feel a fascination in even the sorrows
> of those you love.
>
> [763–65]

Yet she is inherently sagacious. While Menelaus struggles with his ego, ruminating over how to die with honor, Helen plots a strategy of escape. First securing the complicity of the prophetess, Helen next arranges a ruse in which she will claim Menelaus is dead and ask for a ship so as to bury him in effigy at sea. But there is no praise for her ingenuity: instead her task is complicated by the need to coax a reluctant Menelaus, which she does with Attic self-deprecation:

> I know! Even a woman might have one clever thought,
> Are you willing, though not dead, to be reported dead?

Menelaus is only cajoled into accepting her plan when he realizes that after securing the ship there will be fighting: "man to man, sword against sword." In Helen's efforts to persuade the unyielding hero to constructive action there is suggestion of the untold stories of Ariadne, Medea, Hera, and Athena.

Throughout the play runs the motif of the ancient goddess worship. The Chorus tells of the half-remembered story of this lost syncretic deity, who was mother and Kore, empowered by her connection to earth and motherhood, later disempowered by the sky god invaders who prevailed through confrontation and conquest:

> Long ago, the Mountain Mother
> of all the gods, on flashing feet,
> ran down the wooded clefts
> of the hills, crossed stream-waters in spate
> and the sea's thunderous surf beat
> in wild desire for the lost girl
> not to be named, her daughter,
> and the cry of her voice keened high to break
> through mutter of drums and rattles.
> And as the goddess harnessed
> wild beasts to draw her chariot
> in search of the daughter torn away
> from the circling pattern of dance where she
> and her maidens moved, storm-footed beside
> the mother, Artemis with her bow,
> stark eyed, spear-handed Athene
> attended. But Zeus from his high place
> in the upper sky shining ordained
> a different course to follow.

[1301–18]

The story tells of a goddess made cruel by grief, unmoved by the Graces and the Muses whom Zeus sent to placate her, and eventually ignored, replaced by the vacuous Olympian Aphrodite. But the Chorus warns that usurpation is not resolution, that the chthonic deity still smolders and is worshiped still in the Mysteries and the rites of Dionysus, that latecomer to Olympus who brought with him an impassioned mysticism as alternative to the Apollonian religion of conquest and rational thought. The Chorus addresses Aphrodite:

> You had no right in this. The flames you lit
> in your chambers were without sanction.
> You showed, child, no due reverence
> for this goddess' sacrifice.
> You won the great mother's anger.
> The dappled dress in the deer skin
> is a great matter, and the wound
> green on the sacred hollow reed
> has power; so also the shaken,
> the high, the whirled course of the wheel
> in the air; so also the dances,
> the wild hair shaken for Bromius,
> the goddess' nightlong vigils.
> It is well that by daylight
> the moon obscures her.
> All your claim was your beauty.
>
> [1352–68]

Lattimore claims the play is Euripides' "escape from his own conscience," in which "he indulges himself in an illusion of optimism,[18] yet it is just as possible to see this lighthearted rendition of the long-maligned Spartan woman as yet another of Euripides' relentless stabs at the lingering complacence of his society and to articulate through Helen the voice of the reduced goddess as mentor, her own heroism subsumed to the allegedly universal story of the hero.

I do not suggest as Wright did that Euripides was a deliberate feminist, merely an iconoclast who questioned everything and was capable of deviating from the tradition by giving authentic, not deferential, voice to women's experience while simultaneously refusing to allegorize. His Medea was not the madwoman that history has insisted upon. She was a mother who killed her children, taking upon herself the right to exercise a power which was regularly exercised by fathers in a society which tacitly allowed exposure. The Hecuba of *Hecuba* was, according to Lattimore, "the *mater dolorosa* of Troy transformed by suffering into the 'bitch of Cynossema,' and survives in classical imagination as a supreme example of the severest degradation the reversal of human fortune can inflict."[19] Yet he goes on to point out that despite early popularity the play fell out of favor in the nineteenth century partially because Euripides himself failed to conform to a narrow reading of Aristotle's formula for ideal tragic structure, the consequence of which was to "snarl Euripides's meaning by hopelessly disfiguring his form."[20] That his message with either Medea or the Hecuba of this play is that women are fraught with the potential to destroy civilization is a misogynist interpretation, one which tolerated only the defused and derential goddess. Rather, that both women batter bleakly against the conventions of men which reduce them, that they refuse to deny or internalize their rage, a stricture at the crux of the gender system, but instead turn to violence toward others in their rebellion; all these make them authentically chthonic in their ethic and motivation. Traditional literary criticism has viewed these women as monsters, made inhuman by their suffering, madwomen who are ever linked to the Gorgon Medusa, and the bad mother who haunts the nightmares of the Athenian youth. They have also failed to see them as desperate rebels faithful to an earlier social order who strive against a despotic and corrupt civilization which sought to alienate women from the divinity within and insisted that docility, isolation, and self-deprecation were natural and appropriate feminine characteristics, aspects of that essential "necessity" which Aeschylus had taught that civilized mankind must learn. In the tradition of establishing polarity, they are the epitome of women in conflict with the social righteousness of man-governance, antithetical to the Attic conception of civilization.

Such an ordering of experience defines these women in terms of second stratum archetypes. They are figures of the Gorgon mode, degenerate forces who threaten the social order, disintegrative forces who threaten psychic order. They are judged heinous in a moral theatre which has itself been conceptualized to keep civilization a man-centered entity. Because they are unsoftened or unweakened by motherhood, because they reject sorrow for rage, they do not serve the interests of the dominant tribe. That they both adhere to a justice, the *thesmoi* which is beyond manmade law and beyond political self-interest, remains the enigma which this playwright would not allow his culture to ignore. In a different ordering of experience they might well have been viewed as rebels of Promethian stature.

Whether Euripides was the conscious fomenter of such an iconoclastic challenge to the self-sanctification which marred Attic civilization and which persists as an aspect of Western consciousness, or whether, like the artists of Socrates' survey, he was merely a diviner who transcribed divine truths without understanding them, will remain forever unresolved. While his iconoclasm functioned as a cultural conscience, he was outside the mainstream. A generation later Aristotle deemed him flawed and defined god in Durant's summary as "pure thought, rational soul, contemplating itself in the eternal forms that constitute at once the essence of the world and God."[21] It was the divinity of the tribe of the male philosopher, of which women had no ken.

Part Three

Reemergence of the Lost Archetype

Chapter VIII
Merging Traditions of Goddess Deprecation: The Heroism of Eve

What is clear from this directed review of the mythopoesis of ancient Greece is that there was a substratum to the mythology that has been presented to us as the hallowed wellspring of irrevocable archetypes and universals, including the conception of heroism. This near-lost substratum in the Aegean suggests the possibility of another pattern of heroism stemming from original tribal myths in which the feminine principle was revered spontaneously because of its connection to the drive toward life. It was manifest in woman's ability to give birth and so defy mankind's most ancient fear and was associated with the mystery and spontaneity of life. This was conceptualized not only in the goddess of the autochthonic Aegean tribes but also in the cult of Asherah and Baal which thrived in Canaan long after the composition of the Pentateuch had begun. The tribal goddess was honored long before tribes merged into hieratic cities or conceived of the idea of "civilization" as something which was organized around the irrefutable premise of an elite male tribe and characterized by a compulsory hierarchic ordering of human beings according to a cross-disciplinary fiction of "natural" superiority. Subsequent mythology, controlled by those in authority—including the first artists and literary critics and concerned with what they thought people needed to know—gradually stripped women of an archetypal and self-affirming mythology by deposing the goddess, obscuring her motives and rendering culturally insignificanat the primary motif of her myth, the mother's heroism in birth and in the saving of her child. Such a conflict, connected as it is to the drive for life which prompted the first tribal myths, was necessarily an aspect of the first myths and remains a primal aspect of women's experience, yet there is almost no evidence of this left in mythology.

The concept of heroism itself is a way of organizing experience, one which the revisionist has insisted is a tough job, best filled by a virile male.

The long history of Western literature from epic to modern times has leaned toward this bias and but for the lingering remnants of the goddess myth in the language and visual aesthetics of Greece, we would have irrevocably lost the vision of the powerful chthonic goddess as trinity and her matriarchal ethics. Accepting this bastardization, we can begin to comprehend the elemental distortion of our cultural conceptualization of what was and is heroic for women and why women studying literature have had to adopt a kind of pragmatic detachment in reading about themselves in literary criticism.[1] Why, as one critic writes, "Women cannot comprehend male books, men cannot tolerate female books. The working rule is simple, basic: there must always be two literatures like two public toilets, one for Men and one for Women."[2]

Even Joseph Campbell, who elsewhere in his writing regretfully deplores the relentless dissemination of the feminine principle in Western culture, structures his analysis of the hero in *Hero with a Thousand Faces* around the metaphoric centrality of the male and the shoring up of this cultural fallacy through the vehicle of psychoanalytical criticism. He uses Daphne, the Kore who escaped being raped by Apollo by use of her ancient powers of metamorphosis, as an example of one who refuses the call to heroism, as one who has lost the power of "significant affirmative action and become[s] a victim to be saved."[3] In the righteous evolution of a patriarchal civilization in which women were domesticated into matrimony through rape, Daphne's successful rebellion needed to be categorized.

> The girl had retreated to the image of her parent and there found protection. . . .
> The literature of psychoanalysis abounds in examples of such desperate fixations. What they represent is an impotence to put off the infantile ego, with its sphere of emotional relationships and ideals. One is bound in by the walls of childhood; the father and mother stand as threshold guardians, and the timorous soul, fearful of some punishment, fails to make the passage through the door and come to birth in the world without.[4]

Campbell goes on to associate Daphne's unwillingness with "neurosis, psychosis: the plight of spellbound Daphne."[5] But this is just one way of explicating this story of the goddess' metamorphosis, although obviously the one consistent with traditional analysis. To that interpretation, the hero is autonomous, mature and male, a champion of his own rational mature civilization. Heroism is only incidentally accomplished by a female, and then only of an approved pattern devoid of autonomy and disconnected from tribal or maternal concerns. "When the child outgrows the popular idyl of the mother breast and turns to face the world of specialized adult action, it passes spiritually, into the sphere of the father—who becomes, for his son, the sign of the future task and for the daughter of the future husband."[6] Again there is the relentless imposition of patriarchal marriage as the first imperative in feminine behavior. But Daphne was also the goddess/Kore, her "virginity" was once autonomy and untethered freedom. Her "refusal" can also be seen as a heroic resistance to subjugation through rape. To an untutored analysis, Daphne's story was of a heroic escape from an evil force through the timely intervention of a benign supernatural force not the river god that revision had made her father, but the mother-goddess who is a version of herself. But to the tutored patriarchal view such a powerful and successful rebellion would be culturally threatening, absolutely unacceptable, and therefore Daphne is categorized: unheroic, immature, psychotic. If the goddess is crazy or chronically misunderstood, as was Cassandra, her power is dismissible.

The myth most frequently used to delineate patterns of appropriately feminine heroism is the late Latin myth of Cupid and Psyche which was told by Apuleius in the second century A.D., long after the goddess mythology had been revised. As a model it has been used again and again to validate as "archetypal" a pattern of behavior for the heroine in Western culture that is intricately interwoven with her acceptance as *necessary* even the most bizarre patriarchal marriage. For her acquiescence, for her blind faith in a system which is alien to her inherent ethics and her natural desire to know, a system which demands her surrender to the superiority of physical might, she is offered a sop, the romantic fantasy of the frog/prince (and spared the grim punishment Selene received for her hubris). If the heroine willingly gambles she may well discover the "divinity within," which Campbell correctly identifies as the objective of heroism.[7] This divinity, however, will not be within herself, but within her husband, as the male became the single absolute repository of divinity allowable in Western thought. "And when the adventurer, in this context, is not a youth but a maid, she is one who by her qualities, her beauty, or her yearning, is fit to become the consort of the immortal. Then the heavenly husband descends to her and conducts her to his bed—whether she will or no. And if she has shunned him, the scales fall from her eyes; if she has sought him, her desire finds its peace."[8]

The goddess does feature in Campbell's scheme but only as a manifestation of the supernatural endorsement afforded the hero. The figure is a second stratum fragment of the goddess; it is Ariadne, who supports Theseus's heroics, or Danae, who although also entombed, becomes in myth merely the incubator/protectress of her hero-son. "What such a figure represents is the benign, protecting power of destiny. The fantasy is a reassurance—a promise that the peace of Paradise, which was known first within the mother's womb, is not to be lost," Campbell writes,[9] seemingly oblivious to the fact that either Ariadne or Danae might have articulated an alternative point of view on these adventures. But such categorizing generates from and serves to insulate the tradition of the male as appropriate protagonist in Western literature. The male hero must be bolstered with "all the forces of the unconscious on his side. Mother Nature herself supports the mighty task."[10] The goddess, whether as Kore or mother or crone, and often retaining remnants of her original powers, has been relegated to an immutable position in literary criticism; she is the essential backdrop against which to better focus on the remarkable feats of the ubiquitous male hero. "Woman, in the picture language of mythology represents the totality of what can be known. The hero is the one who comes to know. As he progresses in the slow initiation which is life, the form of the goddess undergoes for him a series of transformations: she can never be greater than himself, though she can always promise more than he is yet capable of comprehending."[11] It is a perspective riveted to the absurdly simple ideal that the only possible formula for heroism in Western thought is in a young boy's titanic struggle to break away from his mother's dominance and subsequently express his "maturity" by denigrating or patronizing her influence in his early life.[12] His mother, his wife, his female mentor can be nothing but accoutrements in his quintessential experience. So the hierarchic ordering by gender continues into aesthetics, a psychological mutation of the stubborn archetypal exercise of ethnic conflict.

This relentless reduction of the archetypally feminine appears to have been a ruthlessly cataclysmic imperative for the ancient Hebrews as well, one which even more irrevocably shaped the ideology of women.[13] Justified by nebulous considerations of necessity to the rational civilization of the Greeks, in the Hebraic tradition it was validated by the sacral evidence of Scripture, that uniquely hallowed myth, understood only by the male priesthood, which allowed the goddess no quarter. In her place we have Eve, still associated with both tree and serpent, but whose "story begins with her death as a goddess and her rebirth as the first and representative woman."[14] Yet Genesis was clearly the work of multiple authors and in fact juxtaposes two different stories of creation, the one which appears first (1:26–28) describes the simultaneous creation of the sexes without overtones of gender hierarchy or polarity. Yet the story which has compelled the imagination of the culture is the anthropomorphic fable of Adam and Eve (2:5™3:24). The woman in this story was undoubtedly a remnant of the Near Eastern primordial goddess emphatically reduced Pandora-like to the bane of man, the saboteur of paradise, coconspirator of the serpent. As cultural prototype Eve is closer to the devil than to the divine, she gains power through trickery and hubris and lures Adam to sin with her sexuality or her guile. As with Pandora and Helen, Eve's single action brings down anarchy and untoward destruction. In a tale with four characters, Eve has been traditionally identified as the enemy of God and the foil of the ingenuous male protagonist. To another analysis she might have been the goddess mentor leading the hero out of the confines of his innocence, an Ariadne, or the temple priestess sent by Ishtar to tame the wild man Ennkidu. But tradition has allowed only one interpretation of Eve's function in myth.

The divinity in her story is authoritative and masculine; omnipotent, omniscient, self-contained, judgmental. He is easily and righteously enraged. There are some striking similarities between Yahweh and Zeus, in character and mythic function. Both are shapers of the social order in civilized life, both reign through the prerogative of an ominous and summary anger, an attribute once associated with the ancient goddess. The angry god remains appropriate and intact. The goddess's once-righteous wrath, however, has been banalized, preserved only in the harried cruelty of Hera to Zeus's Kore victims, in textbook references to Inanna's "terrible temper."

The omnipotence and omniscience of the Hebrew God establishes an immutable pinnacle to the divinely designed hierarchy of being, a hierarchy which is developed further with the story of Eve's creation as an outgrowth of Adam. A commodity specifically designed for his benefit, she is to be his solace and his subaltern. This plot embellishment renders the role of Ariadne an aspect of Eve's inception rather than her demotion. The Creator Himself is a force of amorphous language who activates generation through speech. He is not a part of mankind, is absolutely not human, but unchanging, separate, and above. Any attempt to locate in him a feminine side is not only futile but apostatic. He does not procreate as the tribal mother did, is not rooted in nature, as she is, does not love his creations with the indiscriminate and unconditional regard characteristic of the earth goddess (some of whose children are monsters). Instead, this God creates by edict, conjuring life from nothingness with the power of His word. Philips sees Him as the divinity, as artificer, but He is unlike the sweating craftman Hephaestus, the impassioned artist Prometheus, or the ingenious inventor Daedalus. Instead he is the necromancer God, more magician than artisan, and the magic formulas he uses are in the language of technological innovation.[15] He is the architect of civilization, "the source of creativity," Lerner points out, "the invisible ineffable God."[16] Designing by divine decree, he fashions a perfectly synthetic, hierarchic society, kept in place by the ubiquitous threat of his violence and the irrefutable arcanum of his priests. He creates Eve to mitigate Adam's loneliness and in a grand gesture initiates the cruel illogic by which one woman is accused and fault becomes a characteristic of her sex. Thus is man given mythic justification for his desire to maintain himself as the elite subgroup, to see himself as divinely appointed to control the sexual practices of women and also to interpret for them their once-removed relationship with the divine. One cannot help but suspect it was more a prescriptive parable than a descriptive one. Like so many other women in mythology, Eve herself is rendered silent, the interpretive inference is that she accepts the judgment of her culpability in mankind's fall.

Yet archaeology testifies to the simultaneous presence of the cult of Asherah, the tree and fertility goddess, who also makes her appearance in Scripture. There she is the minor enigmatic enemy of the Hebrew god, yet another false god appropriately belittled. In Jeremiah (44:15ff.) however, she is yearned as the Queen of Heaven; for a moment, the Hebrew women express their archetypal need to worship her, to participate in the essential conception of divinity. But already the terms of interpretation are in backdrop not merely literary and intellectual as with the Greeks, but hallowed and immutable, from the one true God. By daring to articulate such a need these women feed the bias, confirming for cultural analysis their connection to the sinfulness of Eve, reiterating yet again women's inherent tendency to rebellion against the just and prevailing divinity. By his decree a moral paradigm was erected in terms of violent, authoritative necessity and culpability, particularly women's culpability; thus her subjugation and denigration by the priesthood was elevated to a clear and sacred imperative. Lerner writes: "Whatever the causes, the Old Testament male priesthood represented a radical break with millennia of tradition and with the practices of neighboring peoples. This new order under the all-powerful God proclaimed to Hebrews and to all those who took the Bible as their moral and religious guide that women cannot speak to God."[17]

An alternative explanation of the Eden myth has threaded itself elliptically through the more orthodox tradition. During the Enlightenment, J. C. F. von Schiller in his *Thalia* introduced a rogue explanation for Eve's actions, one which viewed her as a character of Promethean proportions, who coveted the wisdom of Yahweh as Prometheus had coveted the fire of Zeus. Such a reading accepts the view that the Eden myth tells mythically of that juncture in the history of human consciousness when mankind veered away from the instinctual imperatives of his primate ancestors and instead chose to order his own experience through the filter of rational thought. But in this interpretation Eve is heroic because, through her curiosity, her spontaneous courage, her instinctive yearning to know,[18] she led mankind to a higher, albeit more complex and sorrowful consciousness. This contrasted with the rigid intellectual tyranny which demanded that the myth of Eden was a man's story of betrayal by a woman, that Eve was the villainness for her hubris, because by standing "alone before God . . . [she] violate[d]" divine order.[19] Yet in challenging God she is clearly Promethian, at least in her ambition to secure a boon for man, and that boon is knowledge, ancient accoutrement of the goddess. The key to the unpopularity of this alternative explication of the Eden myth is in the fact that in order to allow Eve that heroism, Western man would have had to question if not repudiate the divine ordination of a social system based on hierarchy, of civilization as a code by which to return man to Paradise. "To civilize is to be in need of salvation (or sublimate), and to be in need is to be religious (or neurotic). History is a nightmare, and primitive comfort, the womb, with Mother Nature at the beginning and end of history, is what humanity longs for. Civilization is a kind of *coitus interruptus* for the sake of getting the work done."[20]

And there is also Lillith, the legendary Hebrew goddess, once the chthonic side of Eve as tribal goddess. Lillith's story is of a renegade power, one which could not be suppressed or subjugated to the male, and since she fled Eden before the fall, one which cannot die. Lillith was the first wife of Adam, ascribed to the first story of Genesis in which man and woman were created simultaneously and as equals. According to the legend, Adam attempted to force her to submit to frontal copulation but she found the position demeaning and unacceptable and so rebelled, forsaking Eden and its restrictive civilization as Huck Finn would when he "set out for the Territory ahead of the rest." There she defiantly remained, impervious and implacable, although there were apparently divine attempts to persuade her to return. Like Calypso on her remote island, Lillith protested the rules of the male-governed universe, but unlike Calypso, Lillith would not circumscribe her sexuality to the dictates of male gods, and since she was quite incorrigible, she was rejected, judged promiscuous in a patriarchal moral theater, and banished from myth.[21] A more willingly submissive and self-deprecating wife was found for Adam's story. In the second version Adam even gives Eve her name, a lingual function which underlined her subjugation and is analogous to the process by which the Indo-Europeans named the goddesses.[22]

Philips points out that the Adam and Eve story was much more crucial to Christianity than to Judaism, and that the former clung to it as divine justification for sexism as an element of religious and social order.[23] Campbell, as mythologist, expresses incredulity that this story could be accepted by the Western world as "an absolutely dependable account of an event that was supposed to have taken place about a fortnight after the creation of the universe, [and] poses forcefully the highly interesting question of the influence of conspicuously contrived counterfeit mythologies and the inflections of mythology upon the structure of human belief and the consequent course of civilization."[24]

Literal adherence to Scripture sanctified the continuation of the dominance of the ruling fathers. In fact, their determination to perceive Eve, and therefore her daughters, as the treacherous saboteur of Eden led them to enthusiastically accept and circulate the Pandora story when they encountered the Aegean myth, while simultaneously stomping out remnant pockets of goddess worship in the Aegean. "It is clear that the fathers did not dismiss the story of Pandora in favor of Scriptures; instead they preserved it as a completion of, and commentary on, the story of Eve," concludes Philips.[25] Nor would Hamilton; two millennia later she would parrot seemingly without irony: "From her, the first woman, comes the race of women who are an evil to men, with a nature to do evil."[26]

Theological scholars have labored in vain to find some way to circumvent the Biblical endorsement of sexism and misogyny. Even those enlightened scholars who later suggested that the Genesis myth implies an inherent equality between these first parents were eternally bogged down by their reluctance to abandon the righteousness of the sociopolitical hierarchy which seemingly originated with the will of God and was mimicked throughout the history of Western culture in the conventional form of the patriarchal family. Eve's complicity with the serpent was necessity to sustaining this dynamic. She was allowed to recover the possibility of salvation through domestic servitude to a patriarchal civilization; piety became a mandatory component of appropriate feminine behavior.[27] It is by its nature a hopeless piety, however, as women have been effectively denied access or participation in the conception of divinity. But Eve was in fact another version of the lost goddess, her hubris her desire to know, a uniquely human quality. To an untutored critic, Eve might well be seen as the heroine of her story, a heroine in the tradition of Prometheus, but also in the tradition of the tribal mother, who wished to lead her children out of the darkness of their primate past, to a more tragic, more fully realized human consciousness. A heroine, who "like Prometheus, simply darted to his goal [by violence, quick device or luck] and plucked the boon for the world that he intended, then the powers that he has unbalanced may react so sharply that he will be blasted from within and without—crucified like Prometheus, on the rock of his own violated conscious."[28]

It is traditional interpretation which has brought about the most insidious bastardization of feminine consciousness. Just as the untutored critic finds evidence of the goddess's heroism in Eve, there is also something of her truncated ethics and her deliberate revision in the stories of the other women of Genesis. At the heart of their stories is the same belabored strain of vituperative competition which we have seen was imposed upon the Aegean goddesses. This was apparently a vital principle to revision, useful because it fragments both tribal connections and the powerful conception of the goddess as trinity.

The women of Genesis are also pictured in perpetual conflict, disconnected or at odds with their distaff affiliations, and set in unending competition with one another. They are fixated on men as the foci of civilized society. The contest between Sarah and Hagar, perhaps more aptly called a rout, is reiterated in the lengthy competition between Rachael and the hapless Leah, explicated as a folktale explaining the origin of the twelve tribes of Israel. Sarah and Hagar were women of different classes, with Sarah capitalizing on her own right to control the sexual practices of women with less social standing than her own. By this custom she could compel her slave to copulate with her husband and subsequently claim the infant as her own. Within that class context Sarah's fear that the older Ishmael, who enjoys his father's open affection, might threaten Isaac's right of inheritance and her subsequent request for their dispatchment has a certain cruel logic. But what of the long, sad competition between Leah and Rachael who are sisters, whose children are each other's neice and nephews, yet who are etched in literature as indefatigable enemies, obsessively directed toward pleasing and securing the pleasure of Jacob? This goal is apparently so tenacious and consuming that it utterly obliterates any sisterly or tribal affinity they may have experienced. Without insisting that such rivalry is completely anomalous to adult female experience, we can see the myth as more likely prescriptive than descriptive of relationships between men and women and especially of what motivates women in relationships with one another. It is a story which perpetuates patriarchal ideas of gender, of appropriate behavior for women, of men's notions of what moves women to action.

Like many mythological women, these sisters have been assigned motives by the preservers of their story. The plot presents nothing of the recurring and inherent appeal which has always tempted women to become mothers, an appeal which has much to do with the phylogenetic drive for life but comes also with a certain onotogenetic satisfaction that is a part of the attachment between mother and infant. The relationship is a goal in itself, one which is often intensified by the primal pleasure of the bonding experience. Yet Leah and her sister wish to bear children to please Jacob and for the social status motherhood afforded. There is little of the deeply personal despair that often afflicts women who find themselves unable to conceive; Rachael's sense that she has been forsaken by God is mitigated by Leah's repeated and futile desire to ingratiate herself with Jacob. Nor does Leah give evidence of the maternal satisfaction that often prompts mothers to want and have more children. Everything which befalls the sisters, everything which they labor to bring about happens because of their competing desire to please patriarchy. Like the goddess trinity of Aegean myth, the sisters have been split apart and then frozen in literature as eternal contestants, utterly without tribal affections or compassion for one another; they compete as righteous women must, their goal the exclusive favor of the patriarchal matrix.

And what of Hagar, Sarah's Egyptian bondswoman? Like Danae in the Aegean, Hagar bears a child who threatens the power system, consequently she is banished from the protection of civilization and forced to fare for herself and her toddler in the wilderness of Beersheba. Like Danae she is innocent, yet her maternity threatens patriarchal constructs. The Hebrew god endorses the hierarchic ascendancy by instructing Abraham to suppress his initial hesitancy and not let the plan be "grievous in thy sight because of the lad and because of thy bondwoman." Like Danae's father, who feared his daughter's child but dared not kill them, Abraham sets Hagar and Ishmael alone in the desert with limited supplies.

The story of Hagar's ordeal in the wilderness, like Danae's in her chest on the sea, has been reduced to a nonstory. The single detail of Hagar's skeletal tale is compelling testimony to her helplessness. Accepting the pieta motif and her own powerlessness, she puts her son behind a bush because she cannot bear to watch him die. Thus the story renders Hagar a victim, weeping until an angel sent by the very god who condemned her in verse 12, inexplicably saves her in verse 18. Her passive complicity with the vision of herself as a victim to be saved leads to her rescue and her subsequent triumph through her son's ascendancy.

Like Danae, Hagar has no voice in extant literature, yet events suggest that this character comes close to Campbell's formula for mythic heroism. First banished from society, she endures an ordeal in the region of danger where her difficulties are complicated by the need to protect her infant. There she is assisted by some supernatural power. She brings herself and the child out and away from danger, which is in fact the threat of extinction. Preserving this rootlet of the tribe, she survives to become the mother "of great nations" as the angel prophesized for Ishmael. But Hagar's version of events is not told, her mythology of herself which undoubtedly facilitates her heroic accomplishment is not available to us; it is culturally insignificant, lost in the service of another focus.

The story of Jacob's ascendancy is another which, to a different exegesis, suggests remnants of the great goddess story. Rebecca too suffers and in her suffering is visited by the supernatural, an angel we are told, whose prophesy prompts her to favor the interests of Jacob over Esau. What follows is a story in the tradition of the goddess as mentor with the revised goddess willingly facilitating through her superior acuity the heroism of her son. Rebecca's elaborate efforts on Jacob's behalf are reminiscent of Ariadne's or Medea's and are essential to the hero's triumph. Then, like Leto or Themis or Earth, Rebecca steps aside deferentially, a silent and willing backdrop in the story of the heroism of her son.

Such stories present righteous women struggling valiantly to gain patriarchal approval and secondarily to advance the interests of their children. These are conflicts which present women in competition with one another and with children in their efforts to live up to patriarchal ideas of appropriate feminine behavior. The behavior model is essentially immature, without autonomous ethical motivation or "significant affirmative action" as Campbell described Daphne's. To allegorical interpretation, the goddess who was once powerful enough to save herself and others has become a girl-child fleeing adult responsibility. By the time of Ovid her flight is from husband to father, a powerful river god who activates the metamorphosis and Daphne herself is presented as wide-eyed and helpless, victimized not by rape but by her own immaturity. In revision, the once powerful Aegean goddess trinity become schoolgirls who bribe and cheat to secure the accolades of the vapid Paris. In the Bible, admirable women like the sisters Rachael and Leah are seen as never outgrowing their sibling rivalry or taking on adult preoccupations; instead, even their maternal experience is rendered an aspect of their futile competition to gain favor with Jacob.

Yet we have seen that beneath the surface of these plots there are other sketetal or revised stories having more connection to feminine experience, stories of the ethical rage of the tribal goddess, of the mother goddess giving birth or saving a version of herself, stories of the chthonic goddess welcoming and consoling the dead, succoring the vulnerable and forsaken, of the goddess as trinity, generous cooperative nurturers, stories of the autonomous Kores who escape violation into the patriarchal order, of the solitary goddess who remains on the periphery of man-governed civilization comfortably juxtaposed with the irrational and possessing a power and wisdom which includes knowledge of the irrational. Finally and most significant to the survival of the species, there are the stories of the mother heroine who saves her child. Such stories have been downplayed or obscured by allegorical revision, by the gender bias of interpretation and by the sacrosanct entitlement of the Bible. Efforts to flesh out or explain female characterization in myth, other than those which explicate Western literature as a story of a male hero and his relationship to a male divinity, have been tantamount to blasphemy and likely to result in the marginalization of the aberrant critic by the intellectual if not the sacral elite. The vision of an empowered adult goddess who is not merely the silent and suffering mother, be she Asherah or Circe or Medea, has been irrevocably exorcised through connotation. Labeled diabolical and pagan, when she is allowed an unrevised existence in fiction, she is enemy of Western man's one true God, outside the confines of his ordered, rational civilization, that which is there for the hero to overcome. Thus the prodigious forces which converged to obscure authentic feminine archetypes in storytelling were eventually elevated by the irrefutable premise of male monotheism, and metamorphosed into the most ungiving authority of all, tradition.

Chapter IX
Rediscovering the Goddess

The social anxiety which prompted a nomadic tribe to chart its geographic ascendancy by telling in story of how it negotiated with god for the land it claimed or that which prompted a later urbanized elite to rationalize its political ascendancy by telling a story of gods depriving women of the vote are outgrowths of the same powerful anxiety. Spawned by every incipient matriarchal grouping, it is that which we have called the drive for life. This peculiar and unique psychological urgency was collective and archetypal and carried with it the inestimable satisfaction of participation in divinity, a satisfaction which was by its nature exclusionary and parsimonious.

As tribes conquered and urbanized, the drive refocused from more ancient concerns. The history of language through myth tracks the development of mankind's consciousness as it grappled with one abstraction after another. Questions about natural phenomenon and human mortality preoccupy the bulk of the first myths, but as ecological and social concerns come to the fore, the plot of mythology turns to the heroic event and the individual's relationship to it, eventually to epic sagas of civilizations being born. The hero and his tribe wrench order out of the chaotic and irrational while peripherially destroying the Kikonian cities and enslaving their women, while massacring the Hittites and offering their own daughters for rape or sacrifice. The hero/god and heroine/goddess of myth give way to the nearly mortal heroine, to Persephone how, though daughter of the goddess, could also die, and to the nearly mortal hero, Prometheus, who though Titan could suffer and long to die. Eventually the hero becomes Theseus or Perseus, called "son[s] of Zeus." There may once have been stories of heroic women like Helen who remained in language if not feat, "daughter of Zeus," but there is no evidence of this. Some heroes, specifically Achilles and Aeneas, remain sons not of the god but of goddesses. But by the time mythology took its permanent recorded form, the collective imperative to associate divinity with the tribe had contorted and internalized to eliminate women. The stories themselves testify to this mutation.

It would be contrary to the nature or function of myth for the storyteller to be engaged too intimately with the experience or concerns of the Hittite or the Canaanite, the Minoan or the Trojan. Now and then he does recognize a shared humanity, especially in the manifestation of a common value: Hector's heroism is akin to the Greek model, the pharoah who honors Joseph may have leaned toward monotheism or the notion of a spirit god, Achilles, dim and self-absorbed as he so often is, surrenders to Priam the corpse of his son in recognition of their mutual humanity through the experience of bereavement. This kind of momentary epiphany sometimes transcends sexual polarity, as when Sophocles presents Deianeira's compassion for Iole or when Euripides portrays with such vivid empathy the anguish of Andromache, Hecuba, or Medea. But the function of myth is to increase the imaginative potential of the author tribe, to validate its notion of itself as chosen, as ever righteous and worthy of further affirmation, elitism, and divinely ordained social dominion. So Agamemnon can make only vague concessions to the logic and passion of Hecuba's plea to revenge her young son's murder. Like Zeus he is deaf to his own daughter's pleas for her life, the factitious covenant between men of authority having become a more compelling connection. Those who fail to subscribe to this new ethic, cleaving instead to the primacy of the tribal bond, are denigrated or ostracized.

At this point the continuum of myth and literature is artifically interrupted. Issues of authority and internal stratifications, of dominion and ascendancy were paramount societal concerns. In both the Aegean and the Levant, man yearned toward a social order which would guarantee the gains of his own situation and provide a buffer between him and the pitiless workings of chance. He conceived an imaginative model, a divinely ordained hierarchy of authority, the chain of being, which rationalized certain political tyrannies, including men's control of the sexual practices of women of their own class as well as of enslaved classes. This synthetic conception of order was identified with "logos" and labeled "natural." At the apothesis of this self-serving construct was the single transcendant male god, an image which was neither universal nor archetypal. Rather it was a dramatic distortion of inherent human values, ancient and ongoing, and necessitated the symbolic deprecation of feminine experience to bring it about. Again, this was done through the powerful medium of story, made more powerful as it was recorded in written language. The Bible begins with the culpability of Eve and tolerates no alternative exegesis. Throughout it speaks to the "sons of God" who instruct and marry the "daughters of men." In the Aegean, original myths of the goddess were revised as allegories for the gender system and the notion of the goddess/heroine atrophied along with the imaginative possibilities of women. The imaginative universe of Western mankind was crimped, imagination itself espaliered.

That this took place at a specific historic junction, one which covered hundreds of years, but which included the evolution from metaphoric to metonyic language and the onset of recorded literature, permanently eskewed the continuum of myth by permanently exaggerating the imaginative significance of the hero. Because the author tribe was solely male, it no longer matters that popular religions and stories of the goddess flourished alongside the cults of Zeus or Yahweh. Within the enclaves of power, where history was finalized and formalized and endorsed through recorded story, the overriding concern was with validating authority, with establishing an irrefutable and sacrosanct model. Unfortunately, at this juncture that included an assumed need, the limitation of women's autonomy. Effected through revision of the goddess myth, the cultural consequence of this was to take from subsequent generations of women the essential and innately affirming function of myth itself.

Even contemporary women, who are the products as well as the critics of this obstinate tradition, are uncomfortable with the idea that they have some claim to divinity, to a latent goddess heritage. Nowhere is the goddess presented as both accessible and acceptable; everywhere revisions have rendered her as victim or ogre. Only arcane scholarship provides intimation of anything more and even there she is enigmatic, peculiar, if not grotesque. Originally condemned as pagan, the idea of a powerful goddess is now ludicrous. Serious intellectual discussion emanates from students introduced to the idea that God is dead, yet to suggest the deity is a goddess—is at least in part feminine and maternal—elicits their laughter. When pressed, young women will admit furtively or passionately to having balked—as women of reflection have always balked—at the awful irreconcilability of Eve's guilt and their own inherent goodness, at Ariadne's victimization and their own heroic potential, at the deadening reality of having no alternative transcendent models, no imaginative possibilities beyond the allegorical. Edith Hamilton's *Mythology,* that careful interweaving of layer upon layer of patriarchal revision, each confirming and clarifying the earlier stratum, is familiar to every schoolchild, while Elizabeth Cady Stanton's *The Women's Bible,* publicly disowned even by the suffrage movement at its publication, continues to be categorized as a feminist tract.

Yet in academic study literature presents itself as the imaginative universe, encompassing every aspect of what it means to be human. The allusive nature of the study itself obliquely perpetuates the bastardization of heroism and divinity as does the inflexibility of critical theory. Defining itself in terms of itself, literature claims a structure which refers back to itself, which clarifies with its own form, repeating and echoing the cycle of motifs which were immutably revealed in the first stories which focus on the evolving hero. The Bible and Greco-Roman mythology are looked to as containing the irrevocable core of human experience, that which

Aristotle first called the "universal event." Beyond them there is nothing new in literature.

Myth obviously does provide clues to what is permanent and universal in human nature, but the mythology first recorded by Western man was a biased and revised mythology which at least in the Aegean recorded the relentless subjugation of the hedonic, feminine values of the goddess's tribes by the agonistic, patriarchal invaders and testifies more to the time-lessness of ethnic strife than to anything resembling the archetypally feminine. Going back to these patriarchal revisions for revelation in the collective feminine psyche has been an error; feminist critics of Jungian analysis have presented the convincing premise that, in its efforts to locate feminine archetypes, it just did not go back far enough.[1]

In teaching students to understand literature we teach them that the protagonist of a story is the main character, that character whom the author has presented for the reader to primarily identify with. While the primary protagonist in Western mythology is the hero and explication of his story has limited the universal event to a male experience, it is arguable that there is another component to human experience, another aspect to heroism. This other pattern of heroism, though obscured by an exegesis which insisted upon its cultural insignificance, is connected at one end to the defunct archetype of the goddess and at the other to the ongoing experience of women. Therefore, it remains of interest especially when it can be separated from that which literary allegory has delivered.

Whatever the spontaneous goddess/heroine was like before her revision could hardly matter less to the self-contained entity which is extant literature. Yet there is evidence enough in the potsherds and remnants of aesthetics to reconstruct this other discrete divinity, an image who was honored in the imaginative world for millennia before her revision was enacted, before her denigration and disempowerment became an essential subplot of the covert political agenda of those in authority. As an authentic archetype reflective of universal feminine experience she must exist outside mythology as well, in fact, must be a reoccurring characterization of literature. Theoretically, since literature does repeat and cycle back on itself, it should be possible to enter the continuum at a point other than the traditional beginning of extant literature and find evidence of a heroine whose characterization has not been distorted or labeled pagan and whose heroism may flesh out the skeletal figure of the mythological goddess. To do this let us first focus on an unbiased assessment of the goddess's attributes as they can be inferred from mythology and then turn elsewhere in the continuum to fictions composed without allegorical concerns, as Euripides' were, when both author and reader have come to question absolutes, particularly the assumption that civilization has been morally progressive and that patriarchal models of authority are of indisputable merit.

To this end we will turn somewhat arbitrarily to American fiction, particularly that written in the twentieth century.

But first let us review the goddess as she appears in mythology, but separating her from both her role as supporting actress in the hero's rise and from the allegorical connotations which have made her alien.

From the evidence culled from revision we can speculate that the original goddess was both syncretistic and mysterious. The matrix of clans, she was emphatically isolated for intervals. Protean and akin to the insubstantial Keres and the irrational entities of the earliest myths, she was sometimes virginal, sometimes maternal, even androgynous, although created in the image of woman. The rising Kore in spring, she fostered young life without discrimination as Harvest Maiden and Mistress of the Wild Things. She ran wild and alone in the forest, fearless and without protection, independent in her virginity, a metaphor which originally meant "not tied by any bond to a male who must be acknowledged as master."[2] Hers was the power of spontaneous life; she was nymph and sylph, river and echo. But with the passing of the season, the Kore died or merged or was reborn as her own mother, who was the embodiment of another season of life. This tribal creatrix was seductive and fertile, joyous and unjudging in the nurturing of her brood, the embryonic tribe of mother and her children. Yet she would die too, of grief perhaps, for sorrow was intricate to her wisdom, and in dying she would become the Underworld goddess, the tribal ancestress who welcomed the bodies of the dead and fertilized the future with her body and with theirs. As trinity she reigned in that nether region beyond man's ken, ominous, impervious, inexorable, yet rising again as Kore, her metaphoric virginity renewed in a primordial rhythm of change and fusion that is unaffected by the synthetic coding of men.

This divinity has no connection to sin. There are no moral theatres in her schema, no drive for identifying evil, for labeling restrictions, for the expiation of guilt through suffering. Her goodness is in her ancient tribe, toward facilitating the mysterious spontaneity of all life. Her wisdom is from her unquestioning acceptance of the irrational, of suffering as a cycle of life which is unrelated to sin, but inherent to the ebb and flow of natural seasons. She is an embodiment of blind human passions, of grief and bleak depression, of love and ecstatic freedom. She would not have fit well into Plato's Academy or been excited by the logical symmetry of the Apollonian world view. Far from Aristotle's conception of god, she is more numen than idea, representative of "the liminal, intermediate regions, and energies which cannot be contained or made certain or secure ... she symbolizes consciousness of transitions and borders, places of intersection and crossing over that imply creativity and change and all the joys and doubts that go with a human consciousness that is flexible, playful, never certain for long."[3]

This goddess as heroine has little interest in personal aggrandizement. She is most certainly a figure outside of or in rebellion against the conventions and restrictions of male society, at least passively in opposition to man-governance and perhaps also the metaphoric centrality of the male in society, but she is not evil so much as unmovable. The boons she offers man are unsolicited, but representative of her primary ethics, the ethics of eros and empathy. She is not the wife of a traditional marriage, permanently subject to a male overlord, although she is often a mother. The key to this figure is her syncretism, her flexibility, her inherent ability to alter and so avoid the defeat of a secondary status in a goal-oriented civilization. Although rooted in community, in the ethics of responsibility and care, this heroine changes, accepting seasons of isolation and return. She functions beyond the restrictions of civilization, instead adhering to a more primal, less factitious code. What she offers mankind is her ability to recognize and be at peace with the irrational, to give the sapient guidance of a Circe, an Ariadne, a Medea. But she is more Circe and Lillith than Medea or Eve because she does not surrender herself fully or permanently to the restrictions of man governance, of civilization. Nor does she "will the self through violence," as Judi Roller wrote,[4] and even when violated, she continues, shunning self-deprecation, instead changing but remaining spiritually untethered. She does not implode, although there is often an externalization of justifiable rage. This heroine survives.

Connected to Circe, Lillith, Atalanta, Britomartis, and Daphne, all mythic heroines who escape the juggernaut of the agonistic, male-dominated civilization, the goddess/heroine often avoided marriage, and definitely did not "live happily ever after" or submit to the chronic torture that was Hera's unhappy lot or the chronic immaturity that was Psyche's, Rachael's, or Leah's. Escaping also rape and the questionable privileges of civilization, this figure was often dismissed or downplayed by the storytellers of Western culture but she does exist and survive. She does not commit suicide, that traditional fictional dispatchment of culturally undesirable women. Instead, she prevails, however elliptically, and so offers a thread back to the goddess, back to authentic manifestations of an autonomous feminine divine.

When we turn to the traditional novel, we find again and again women replaying the goddess's cycle in myth. As Kore she comes up against the expectation of patriarchal civilization, is duly subjugated through rape and/or marriage. From there she surrenders her wisdom and talents to facilitate the heroism of a man, or the best interests of the man-centered society. She may be satisfied with this compromise, ostensibly rewarded for her surrender by the ascendancy of her sons, or by the "socially sanctioned existential cowardice" allowed her in a conventional marriage.[5] On the other hand she may fail to thrive, may rebel even. If so, she is disposed of through suicide, or condemnation and ostracism by a disapproving mainstream. When it is women writers who tell her story she is often empathetic and tragic, an Edna Pointeller or Lilly Bart, her loss a reason to mourn patriarchy's blindness. But in the main society rationalizes such loss by focusing on her husband, her sons, by affirming the "necessity" of this arrangement to the larger goal of the advancement of a God-fearing civilization.

Carolyn Heilbrun, in *Toward a Recognition of Androgyny,* defines the hero of a work as "the central character who undergoes the major action." But she borrows from Kenneth Burke's definition to suggest that the hero begins with a "purpose he believes himself sufficiently in control of circumstances to carry out," and it is in that that the heroine is often least centered. But Heilbrun continues on the hero's limitations and achievements:

> . . . to be human is to act on partial knowledge; and so events he could not foresee, the past which he has forgotten, rise up to thwart him. He undergoes a passion, is acted upon, he suffers. He emerges from his suffering with a new perception of what the forces are which govern his world. We all know, or soon learn, what it is to think that we can plan the future, what it is to suffer as these plans go awry, what it is to learn at last what past acts—our own and other people's—were at work to render impossible our illusion of being in control of destiny. This action—purpose through passion to perception—which the hero undergoes is a universal, perhaps an archetypal action. It is at least of sufficient universality to all of us, as we say to "identify" with the hero, regardless of our age or sex or particular experiences.[6]

Heilbrun lauds the achievements in characterization of certain male writers, including Richardson, Ibsen, and James who presented female protagonists with whom the reader can identify. She suggests that the woman as hero was born "at the same moment" in the conceptions of Ibsen and James some time around 1880. But she bemoans her rapid demise; "By the end of the Second World War, however, the wench was dead. Women characters had become, as they largely still are, events in the lives of men."[7]

Yet there remains just outside the central focus of the novel, or just outside the mainstream novel, the persistent figure of a woman not specifically proffered as a protagonist, not immediately identified with because she is an outsider, yet who, to a different view of experience, presents the recurring heroism of the archetypal goddess. Simone de Beauvoir first wrote of the "unacknowledged function of the female outsider," who is a mature woman, and as such has "become" in a fully feminine sense, which is to say in a more internalized way. This feminine "becoming" is self-contained, and involves integration and development of mental breadth, complexity, coherence, and a widening and deepening of perception and feeling which are less common to masculine maturation. The fullest actualization of this kind of becoming is in the dowager, one who is no longer distracted or absorbed by the task of rendering service to patriarchal society, and thus facilitated in her function as an essential voice of moral social criticism.[8]

This mature, fully developed woman is not a terribly common character in fiction, particularly that coming out of American culture with its distressing preoccupation with pubescence, and its early emphasis on America as a pre-lapsarian Eden. Even de Beauvoir had but a grudging appreciation of this dowager's "irony and often spicy cynicism. She is one who declines to be fooled by man's mystifications" and so presents an unbiased evaluation of his society.[9] It is Dinnerstein who, in reviewing de Beauvoir's assessment, suggests a different way of looking at this woman and her invaluable function in society. She may be perceived as a more mature and less despairing Antigone, one who prevails with heroic fortitude, a Hester Prynne perhaps.

The myth of a divinely ordained hierarchy had tenacious imaginative influence which would come into play as Western Europe transplanted itself in America. Here it was employed not just as religious imperative in family life and therefore larger societal models of authority, but also as it had been a millennium earlier by the ancient Hebrews in Canaan as mythic justification for geographic imperialism. The concept of a "New Eden," was woven into a new stratum of mythology with the onset of American literature. Once again the protagonist was decidedly male. The women of American story sometimes inspired, sometimes tempted, sometimes advised, but all were essentially props in the triumph of hero. Leslie Fiedler has pointed out that American women characters are remarkably immature, that American male writers seemed to shy away from the mature woman as a character in literature.[10] It was the goddess as Kore that found her place in this new mythology and then only in her shadowy form. As an aesthetic bias, this hallowed formula had religious and philosophic underpinnings. It was an inflexible, immutable fact that whether in America or Mesopotamia, Eden was the setting of Adam's story, not Eve's.

The Eden myth has been so vital to the critical evaluation of the early American novel, with its hero clinging tenaciously to his innocence as a cultural rite and often favoring a complete repudiation of women as in the Leatherstocking schema, that it did not seem likely much evidence of the archetypal goddess would appear before the altered political climate of postmodern times allowed American women writers to rediscover her in their fiction. Linda Ray Pratt in her essay "The Abuse of Eve by the New World Adam," has pointed out that the cultural pursuit of innocence obviated the presence of the humanizing, postlapsarian Eve in this revision of the Eden myth in which the male protagonist attaches himself to "moral infancy" to avert the fall.[11] But, despite his "anti-life values of war, isolation, and sexual denial" as "elements of the definition of ultimate manhood," it is in the earliest of American fiction that the archetypal goddess first appears quite graphically. She is evident in the characterization of Hawthorne's Hester Prynne.

When Hester first makes her appearance, she is midway through the goddess cycle, having already completed her first season as Kore, she has just completed the first of her chthonic retreats. Hawthorne establishes her from the onset as a figure outside society, both paradox and rebel, who is symbolized by the wild rose bush blooming by the prison door. In the tradition of Atalanta, Britomartis, Daphne, and Lillith, Hester has already come up against the gods who would have domesticated her through marriage and self-deprecation, but she has not succumbed. Instead, she has metamorphosed out of the confrontation, descended into the chthonic region during the ellipsis of her imprisonment,[12] and emerged, a stronger figure now, a mother now, determinedly arrogant, determinedly unwilling to throw herself on the mercy of the punitive society which has condemned and labeled her. When she appears at the prison door, she is repelling the gesture of the town beadle, who would have emphasized her lowly status as offender of the godly order by shoving her into the abuse of the restive townspeople. But "she repelled him, by an action marked with natural dignity and force of character and stepped into the open air, as if by her own free will." She emerges with "a burning blush, and yet a haughty smile, and a glance that would not be abashed." The scarlet letter on her breast is arrayed in elaborate and aesthetically pleasing embroidery, and with this display she has gracefully if flagrantly accepted her place as an outsider in this narrow society. Hester is not so ostentatious with her remorse and there is no evidence of self-deprecation.

Because he had seen through the clearing lens of history that the Puritan theocracy of Hester's day was a most imperfect society, Hawthorne was as generous to this criminal as were the goddesses to Pandora. He has given her great beauty, wisdom, elegance, and grace; furthermore, he implies that there is about Hester an aura of aristocracy, which makes her the superior of the other women of her time. None of these attributes are dimmed or obscured by either her sin or her imprisonment. In the tradition of the fallen woman, she might have been expected to grovel before the worthy, to beg for her living at the doors of the more orthodox goodwives who rapaciously wait to revile her. Her situation is in fact so desperate and isolated that some form of psychotic break would not have been an inappropriate twist to the plot, especially a romance. Instead, Hawthorne allows Hester to prevail and gives some insight into her ability to do this in his description of her internal process during her hours on the scaffold. She survives by an act of will, by a retreat into herself, by reviewing and reflecting on the necessary losses which have complicated her own becoming, but also by continuing to refuse to fulfill the expectations which patriarchal society now has for her.

In contrast to the obsequious penitence which might have been expected of her, Hester adheres to her own unconventional morality, knowing, as a Stendhal heroine does, as Antigone and Hecuba did, that the "source of true values is not in external things but in human hearts."[13] Not to the public demand of the magistrates or to the private demand of Chillingworth (to whom she recognizes a certain debt) does Hester waver in her resolve to keep the secret of Pearl's paternity. The fact that it occurs to her that she has the *choice* to counter the command of these grim theocrats is remarkable, despite her sex, her destitute social position, her crime, and her own very real penitence. She prevails in this initial contest with the male powers. It is they who capitulate as they eventually cease to ask her the question. Like Antigone, Hester is inexorably committed to a loftier morality, to the voice of divinity within herself, that had urged her to the life-affirming act which had "a sanctity of its own." But unlike Antigone, she is not destroyed by her own act of fearlessness; instead she changes, perseveres, continues to become. Alone, apart, she accepts herself as a living critic of the society which sought to subjugate her.

There is no "socially sanctioned existential cowardice" for Hester, nor is there the more likely route of assuming a penitent victim's role and throwing herself on the largesse of the godly society; she is not self-destructive. Instead she becomes autonomous, "virginal" in the original sense of the word. She becomes Demeter, giving herself to seasons of grief and shame, to seasons of pleasure and pride in her relationship with her daughter, remaining protean while accepting herself as other, apart, as peripheral to the life of the community while not in radical opposition to it.

She is resourceful and pragmatic; an artist, she becomes a successful entrepreneur. Whether the viewpoint is Freudian or Jungian, these qualities are not naturally dominant in women, yet she is certainly not striving to be male, as Freud would suggest, not animus-identified as Jung might evaluate. Hawthorne himself admires her resilience. Her embroidery becomes the vogue, and although she is never fully approved of, she gradually comes to perform a part in the life of the community.

> Every gesture, every word, and even the silence of those she came in contact with, implied and often expressed that she was banished, and as much alone as if she inhabited another sphere, or communicated with the common nature by other organs and senses than the rest of humankind.

She stood apart from mortal interests, yet close beside them, like a ghost that revisits a familiar fireside, and can no longer make itself seen or felt; no more smile with the household joy, nor mourn with the kindred sorrow; or should it succeed in manifesting its forbidden sympathy, awakening only terror and horrible repugnance. These emotions, in fact, and its bitterest scorn besides, seemed the sole portion that she retained of the universal heart.[14]

In contrast to her interim role in the novel as catalyst to the public exhortations of the Puritans, Hester eventually emerges in yet another manifestation in chapter thirteen, "Another View of Hester." Here Hawthorne tells the reader that, "a species of general regard had ultimately grown up in reference to Hester Prynne"; for while deliberately remaining aloof from society Hester had become the ministering angel to it, giving her superfluous income to the poor, and visiting the sick, until "many people refused to interpret the scarlet A by its original significance. They said it meant Able, so strong was Hester Prynne, with a woman's strength." The community has come to forgive her past frailty, to see her now as the celibate nun whose service to the community has expiated her sin. Seeing her transformation as a personification of its own faith in the expiation of guilt through suffering, they have come to court her.

Hester, herself, however, has remained essentially socially unrepentant and aloof. Adhering to her own unorthodox internal code, she is able to metamorphose yet again, this time into the passionate, sexual self she once was, now enhanced by nurturing and autonomy, to allow her to save Dimmesdale and repudiate her vow to Chillingworth. "Think for me, Hester! Thou art strong," Dimmesdale begs her in language more common to docile wives, "Resolve for me." And so she does, taking on the man's role, making decisions, organizing, preparing to transport her family to a more life-affirming future.

With Hawthorne's approval, plans go awry and Hester's purpose is foiled, yet she prevails and metamorphoses yet again before the romance ends. There is another ellipsis which follows the deaths of Dimmesdale and Chillingworth and Pearl's inheritance. This is another of the mysterious chthonic retreats of the goddess cycle, and when Hester reappears in the remote cottage outside Boston, she is mother no longer, but alone, dowager and sage now, and acknowledged as such by both Hawthorne and her own community. She still wears the scarlet letter, according to the dictates of her own unconventional morality, "for not the sternest magistrate of that iron period would have imposed it." Yet she is certainly no longer the embodiment of sin. Nor is she the enigmatic mother who lived alone with Pearl on the edge of the forest. Instead, she has another function in the community, one which continues her prevailing "otherness," as well as her commitment to the voice of divinity within herself.

Her creator was most certainly not a writer known for his affinity with the cause of women's rights, yet in his last description of Hester, now quite firmly entrenched as a cynosure in the community, he suggests she was an early and respected feminist:

> And, as Hester Prynne had no selfish ends, nor lived in any measure for her own profit and enjoyment, people brought all their sorrows and perplexities, and besought her counsel, as one who had herself gone through a mighty trouble. Women, more especially,—in the continually recurring trials of wounded, wasted, wronged, misplaced, or erring and sinful passion—or with the dreary burden of a heart unyielded, because unvalued and unsought—came to Hester's cottage, demanding why they were so wretched, and what the remedy! Hester comforted and counseled them, as best she might. She assured them, too, of her firm belief, that, at some brighter period, when the world should have grown ripe for it, in Heaven's own time, a new truth would be revealed, in order to establish the whole relation between man and woman on a surer ground of mutual happiness.[15]

Certainly she has passed from "purpose through passion to perception," has accepted in her own peculiar way "the hero's solemn task . . . to return to us, transfigured, and teach the lessons of life renewed."[16] Outlaw, enigma, survivor, she suggests that patterns may well exist for archetypal feminine heroism which, under certain circumstances, are observable and spontaneously revealed even by male authors who may remain completely baffled by the chthonic aspect of this archetype, the syncretism of this figure, but who inadvertently allow a voice to the deeply buried divinity of the goddess.

Chapter X

The Chthonic Aspect as a Source of Strength in Twentieth-Century American Heroines

Feminist scholars who have challenged psychoanalytical theories of femininity have reevaluated those psychic conceits in terms of their negative impact on women, but such rebellion has been difficult. As cultural canons archetypes were quickly lauded as sacrosanct, immutable revelations of gender as a component in phylogenetic and ontogenetic coding. Women, ignorant of their great goddess heritage and saddled with a patriarchal symbol system that chronically diminishes feminine experience, grappled with the enhancement implicit in the interpretative language of archetypes and with the ill-fitting notion of a "collective" unconscious. Baffled, frustrated, they were often mute. Archetypal theory in its larger sense is intellectually persuasive, it is only in its application to women that it is flawed. That problem, rooted as it is to the previously unexplored nature of revised mythology and the loss of the original goddess's myth, rendered archetypes of the feminine utterly alien to women themselves. "Archetypes exist outside of time, unconcerned with the realities of a woman's life or her needs," writes Bolen in *Goddesses in Everywoman.* [1] They do however, inarguably serve the self-perpetuating bias of a male intellectual elite and function to support its sole and traditional interpretation of what is significant, irrefutable, and universal in Western consciousness. Although archetypes belong to the realm of literature and modern psychology they remain closely linked in effect to Western culture's ongoing religious imperatives. Perhaps because of this association, archetypal theory has provided yet another prodigious forum, another stratum in which men repeat the exercise of mythological revision by first announcing what is inherently and appropriately feminine behavior and then insisting that it is so.

But women have begun to enter into the interpretative process and to introduce new methods of explicating or employing mythology. Scholars like Sylvia Brinton Perera *(Descent to the Goddess: A Way of Initiation for Women)*, Jean Shinoda Bolen *(Goddesses in Everywoman: A New Psychology of Women)*, and Christine Dowling (in *The Book of the Goddess, Past and Present*, edited by Carl Olson) have all suggested new ways of using the great goddess archetype and her second stratum spinoffs within the realm of modern psychology. Both Bolen and Dowling are limited by their dependence on the second stratum spinoffs, however. They accept the reconstructed characterizations of the repressed Olympians while neglecting their autonomous origins, as well as the chthonic side of the original syncretistic goddess. Perera differs in this.

Perera is particularly interesting in her use of a first stratum goddess himself; she employs the myth of Inanna-Ishtar and Ereshkigal and concentrates on the descent of the goddess into chthonic depths and out again as a significant event which may offer a paradigm for viewing withdrawals into irrational modes as the catalysts of transformations. This model stems from an alternative view of consciousness rather than the "cerebral-intellectual-Apollonian, left-brain consciousness, with its ethical and conceptual discriminations,"[2] which came to predominate after the dethroning of the goddess. That prevailing conception allows no healthful quarter for the irrational and has concentrated on maturation of the individual as personal enlargement, while disparaging his participation in the ebb and flow of all life. It is goal oriented, and impacted by its own insistence on factitious restrictions to perpetuate civilization; the result is an intellectual tyranny which attempts to obviate the irrational and, as a by-product, has contributed to the obfuscation of the archetypal feminine.

In contrast, Perera's model would have attention paid to the irrational, those "archaic depths that are embodied, ecstatic, and transformative."[3] This is the chthonic segment of the goddess cycle; in story it is Inanna's cycle into rage, Demeter's retreat into grief, or Hester's retreat into emotional upheaval. A willingness to participate in this chthonic segment of the goddess cycle leads to an authentic, validated, balanced ego which the heroine needs in order to survive patriarchal civilization intact. "In those depths we are given a sense of the one cosmic power; there we are moved, and taught through the intensity of our affects that there is a living balance process. On those levels the conscious ego is overwhelmed by passion and numinous images. And, though shaken, even destroyed as we knew ourselves, we are recoalesced in a new pattern and spewed back into ordinary life."[4] The heroine who accepts the lessons of chthonic retreat ensures her own syncretism, that lost quality of the goddess archetype.

In revision, the chthonic segment of the goddess cycle has been invariably split off and left unexplained. Inanna's chthonic self was Ereshkigal, Demeter's was Hecate-Persephone. Revised myth does not recognize them to be facets of a single figure. The splitting off evolved because the

unabated, protean nature of the goddess defies differentiation in patriarchal modality and is therefore threatening. Traditionally placed outside the
parameters of what was accepted as civilization, the chthonic version of the
goddess was ruthlessly and relentlessly diminished in myth, eventually becoming but a shadowy remnant of a lost mythology, as with Hecate, or a
raging anathema, as with Medusa.

In fact, the chthonic was merely a facet of the goddess, not a discrete
figure. Perera calls her "the primal matrix,"[5] and sees her as symbolic of
human connections to impersonal, immutative transformative energy, the
energy of decay and gestation. The chthonic element is not overtly goal
oriented, certainly not civilization bound, but rooted in seasonal rhythms,
and connected to life and death of the harvest and in the wild as well as in
the tribe. The chthonic element is connected to natural law which is
"preethical, often fearsome, always preceding the superego judgments of
the patriarchy."[6] An unclear sense of it may well have led men away from
comprehending the divinity within woman, may have led Freud to see
woman as having poorly developed superegos, as being deficient in conscience.[7] As a component in ethical motivation it is beyond the structured,
self-serving superego of patriarchal law, yet it did propel the outrage of
Antigone, as well as of Medea, Clytemnestra, and Hecuba.

Perera develops a vision of the chthonic in personal growth by con-
necting it to the cruel, elemental demands of preverbal chaos, emotional
upheaval, and depressions, and insists that patriarchy has misjudged the
chthonic and, while recognizing its preponderance in women, has wrongly
seen her as the enemy of civilization. The chthonic defies differentiated
consciousness, and its dominion is "irrational, primordial, and totally un-
caring, even destructive to the individual."[8] Yet it is implacably demanding
and claims the submission of the individual, as the pregnant woman submits to a process which has no respect for her individuality, as she learns
in the act of giving birth the awesome insignificance of the individual self
in the unbending agenda of nature. The knowledge of this irrational aspect
of life, which is the knowledge of Circe, is repugnant to the heroic ideals
of male heroism. Rational, man-centered culture has attempted to deny it.
It is intellectually painful, even unendurable; the individual ego cannot
confront it without recognizing his own primal insignificance, and the in-
evitability of his death. The male protagonist turns from this knowledge,
labels it, demeans it, associates it with woman and the mastery of woman
with the suppression of this "unresolved carnal ambivalence," as Dinnerstein calls it in elaborating on de Beauvoir's original theory.[9]

The female protagonist, the heroine, when she is not merely a fragmented, two-dimensional mutation of the goddess but is the syncretistic
archetype, makes use of her chthonic experiences with their inherent suffering toward a different end. Perera points out that "knowing this basic

reality permits a woman to give up trying to be agreeable to parental and animus imperatives and ideals. It is like hitting rock bottom, from where they are irrelevant. It relativizes all principles, and opened a woman to the paradoxes involved in living with the Self."[10] Change and pain are inevitable and linked. The heroine who accepts her chthonic retreats does not avoid suffering but, in being wounded, is also transformed. Accepting this as a season of life, as Hester does, as Demeter and Inanna do, allows the continuation of the goddess cycle toward wholeness; it diverts the heroine who has been reared as a daughter of patriarchy from the self-destructive despair of Antigone or Deianeira.

Ereshkigal has been called Inanna's sister, Persephone, Demeter's daughter but the original goddess, was more than the bipolar figure Perera points to.[11] She was protean and syncretistic, beginning as a Kore, but changing and growing according to her own necessities. The seasons of her life included the autonomy/virginity of the Kore, the motherhood or surrogate motherhood of *Koupotpoos* and *Kourotrophos,* and interspersed between the ongoing transformations were the chthonic interludes when the goddess is dark, awesome, irrational. Perera writes that some women "may have to 'descend' temporarily from their accepted patterns of behavior into a period of introversion (or actual pregnancy or depression), in order to continue the process of realizing their potential wholeness."[12] The descents, so long misunderstood by patriarchal exegesis, are clearly made in the service of life.[13]

As I see it, it is in this that the archetypal heroine gains her sustaining strength. Hester Prynne as Kore came up against the demands of the patriarchal system, was dispossessed, perhaps lost briefly both self-affirmation and self-acceptance, yet something transpired to renew her ego during the prison ellipsis. No longer supported by the social system which had given early meaning to her life, she still emerges unbroken, resilient. Having repudiated the superego ideals of her society, she has been reborn with a carapacing of sustaining arrogance. Unlike Antigone, Hester suppresses the animus-ego complex nurtured by her socialization and recognizes that the system itself is in conflict with her personal growth. In her enigmatic wisdom Hester has submitted to the eternal process of change. She does not cling to the patriarchy which would have redefined her as sinner or victim, but instead chooses to accept her "otherness" and so offers a model of heroic behavior which is superior to the pathetic moral victories bequeathed by Antigone and the daughters of patriarchy who choose death and leave only a ripple of puzzled disquietude as their boon to mankind.

Hawthorne does not speculate too profoundly on the nature of Hester's chthonic retreat, yet in presenting her rebirths, in stressing her arrogance and willingness to submit to further change, he presents a syncretistic figure who survives the dark passages of the soul and emerges with the strength to resist victimization. Bolen, in her speculations on feminine heroism, points out that "in every crisis, a woman is tempted to become the victim instead of the heroine."[14] The route taken by Antigone, and so many other feminine protagonists, romantically perpetuates the ancient Athenian call for the martyrdom of young women in the service of the polis. As a motif in fiction it has continued into the twentieth century as a facile twist which dispatches the rebellious daughters of patriarchy. But suicide is antithetical to the archetypal heroism of the goddess.

> Whether in myth or life, when a heroine is in a dilemma, all she can do is be herself, true to her principles and loyalties, until something unexpectedly comes to her aid. To stay with the situation, with the expectation that the answer will come, sets the inner stage for what Jung called "the transcendent function." By this he means something which arises from the unconscious to solve the problem of show the way to an ego [or heroine] who needs help from something beyond itself [or in herself].[15]

We can only speculate on the transcendent element in Hester's first ellipsis in prison. Hawthorne himself implies that Pearl's birth had given his heroine a raison d'être, and it is reasonable to assume that in the isolation of her imprisonment during which she endured pregnancy and gave birth, she entered into a knowledge and acceptance of the illogical, into the border region that makes synthetic considerations irrelevant. Perera writes of the border region of the mother-child bond, with its unique participation mystique, a fluidity so synergistic that "there is often no clear sense of objectivity and difference between the psychic boundaries of two persons."[16] The rewards of motherhood seemed to have served this transcendent function for this heroine and aided her in her transformation away from a psychotic break, away from victimization and toward her choice to embrace "otherness" and so emerge unbroken and reborn.

In more recent novels written by women the chthonic descents of the heroine are intelligibly described. Ellen Glasgow's *Barren Ground,* a realistic novel of the life of a Virginia farmgirl in the early part of the twentieth century offers another view of the archetypal heroine whose "spirit of fortitude has triumphed over the sense of futility."[17] Dorinda Oakley's story begins with the Kore's confrontation with patriarchy. Dorinda is a good girl, not beautiful, but sweet, a not atypical adolescent romantic who is dutifully filial, dutifully nurturing, competent, wholesome, and ostensibly deserving of reward. As the novel opens she enters into her first love, a passion unfortunately unconnected to merit. "She was facing the moment, which comes to all women in love, when life, overflowing the artificial boundaries of reason, yields itself to the primitive direction of instinct" (p. 24), Glasgow writes. Unfortunately, the vagaries of instinct and the ephemeral lure of romance draw Dorinda to the vapid Jason Greylock, even as her clearheaded introspection leads her to question the merits of marriage which she observes in various manifestations around her. Even as she gives herself to Jason, she asks if marriage can be but a futile exercise "to escape the endless captivity of things as they are" (p. 81).

Jason turns out to be without substance or character and he jilts the pregnant Dorinda a week before the ceremony. Glasgow does not equivocate in her description of Dorinda's subsequent descent into depression and rage. The awful process of disillusionment is graphically described. Dorinda stumbles through the broomsedge, the branches tearing her hair. Falling, she finds herself in a sentient abyss alone with raw pain, wood mould, and the smell of wet earth. "While life fought its way into her, something else went out of her forever—youth, hope, love—and the going was agony" (p. 123).

The sequence has psychological authenticity. Dorinda descends into the surreal region of trauma; she denies, flounders, attempts to flee, all the while becoming more intimate with the cruel psychic pain from which there is no escape. "The pain was more than she could bear. It was more than anyone could be expected to bear. In a flash of time it became so violent that she jumped up from her chair, and began walking up and down as if she were in mortal agony" (p. 125). In her rage and her youthful fear that the pain will never be relieved without some action, she is driven, but instead of turning on herself, she goes to murder Jason. Only unfamiliarity with the gun and her disabling agitation keep her from committing the murder. But the act of dropping the gun is a turning point in her crisis.

> Her will, with all its throbbing violence, urged her to shoot him and end the pain in her mind. But something stronger than her conscious will, stronger than her agony, stronger than her hate, held her motionless. Every nerve in her body, every drop of her blood, hated him; yet because of this nameless force within the chaos of her being, she could not compel her muscles to stoop and pick up the gun at her feet.
>
> [Page 129]

What Dorinda discovers is her own strength of character, that which Hester too discovered in her crisis. The realization that she had put her own superior self into the hands of a weak if charming man causes revulsion, but it is not translated into self-loathing. "Thoughts wheeled like a flight of bats in her mind, swift, vague, dark, revolving in circles" (p. 130). But from out of the chaos she will become stronger.

The psychological authenticity of Dorinda's descent continues. She passes in and out of denial; she obsesses; in her consuming grief she at first can conceive of no possibility of the lessening of pain; she views herself in absolutes, as finished, wasted, having lost both her youth and her beauty;

she craves escape. But through it all "her essential self was still superior to her folly and ignorance, was superior even to the conspiracy of circumstance that hemmed her in. And she felt that in a little while this essential self would reassert its power and triumph over disaster . . . she was not broken. She could never be broken while the vein of iron held in her soul" (p. 141). Faith in this "essential self" propels her to action. She flees, leaving the farm country of her youth, goes to the city, where she is further buffeted by erratic circumstance before happening into the care of the Faradays, who assist in her transcendence. But the descent has metamorphosed Dorinda. In the hospital after her accident and miscarriage, when Mrs. Faraday asks her if she likes children, she cannot answer. "In her other existence she had liked them; but that was so long ago and far away that it had no connection to her now" (p. 172). Yet she will subsequently be surrogate mother, *Kourotrophos* to the Faraday children and later to Nathan's son, John Abner. Her capacity for emotion disappears during this separation; she faces the world with a survivor's arrogance and ironic laughter. Recognizing that her psychological task is "to face . . . the wreck of her happiness . . . the loss of a vital interest in life" (p. 176), she nurtures her own autonomy and rejects marriage. In this she is like Demeter, cutting off the ritual homage so important to patriarchal vanity. Dorinda embraces the unconventional role of "otherness" in the community, while developing her pragmatism and her drive to know. In her dreams, aspirations, and actions during this period she continues to resemble Demeter in her period of grief. Dorinda's healing comes from empathetic investment in the Faraday family and in plans for helping her own back at Old Farm, although she deliberately rejects the option of an opportune marriage and does not long for a child of her own. Eventually she returns alone to Old Farm, supported by her indomitable pride and a ruthless realism: "Mother love was a wonderful thing, she reflected, a wonderful and ruinous thing! It was mother love that had helped to make Rufus the mortal failure he was, and it was mother love that was now accepting, as a sacrifice, the results of this failure" (p. 250). Her rejection of the pieta motif is a practical, intellectual judgment. She offers another kind of nurturance.

That same indomitable pride helps her to build a profitable business out of her daily venture at Old Farm. But her pragmatism and purpose do not lead her to deny the illogical in life. Although she regrets at points not having murdered Jason Greylock, and has repudiated all religious conceptions of sin and punishment, over and over again throughout her ongoing transformations she is "choked with the effluvium of the old despair." She is hardened but not broken or embittered by the experience and its recurring impact on her life. In fact, she recognizes an irrational connection between herself and Jason Greylock and in his final days she takes him to Old Farm to be nursed. Such an act of compassion was more a gesture of acceptance of the illogical in life than a moral display. Dorinda Oakley's strength is in her acceptance of the cycles of life, including the irrational passions. She has the goddess's wisdom, has faced her insignificance before the ongoing of broomsedge and barren land; she is supported not by religion, as her mother had been, not by her own philosophic ruminations, not by romantic or heroic ideals of individuation, but by the arrogant inner strength she has learned from crisis, adversity and change:

> it was nothing outside her own being that had delivered her from evil. The vein of iron which had supported her through adversity was merely the instinct older than herself, stronger than circumstances, deeper than the shifting surface of emotion; the instinct that had said, "I will not be broken." Though the words of the covenant had altered, the ancient mettle still infused its spirit.
>
> [P. 367]

Agnes Smedley's novel, *Daughter of Earth,* presents another manifestation of the goddess archetype. The first person protagonist, Marie Rogers, is thirty years old as the novel opens. She stands "at the end of one life and on the threshold of another. Contemplating. Weighing. About me lie the ruins of a life. . . . I gaze over the waters and consider. There have been days when it seemed that my path would better lead into the sea. But now I choose otherwise."[18] Marie rejects the romantic capitulation of suicide because "I belong to those who do die from other causes—exhausted by poverty, victims of wealth and power, fighters in a great cause" (p. 8). Marie is not an Andromache or a Brisies; hers is a fortune akin to those of the women in epic who were awarded as prizes in wrestling matches, their worth measured in oxen. The childhood she describes is a naturalist nightmare of poverty and abuse. Her mother, who is beaten by her father, beats Marie, arousing a "primitive hatred" in the child; Marie learns rage and cunning at an early age, she quickly comes to hate women and attempts to align herself with those who by virtue of their sex are allocated a higher place in the social hierarchy—status. It is of such a family that de Beauvoir wrote "marriage incites man to a capricious imperialism, the temptation to dominate is the most truly universal, the most irresistible one there is; to surrender the child to its mother, the wife to her husband is to promote tyranny in the world."[19]

The little girl curries favor with her father by intuitively crafting a place for herself in the masculine world. She becomes her little brother's protector against their mother. The goddess as mentor, she willingly facilitates the heroism of the male. But the father she attempts to please is unreliable, sometimes brutal, always dissatisfied and angry. In the awful tyranny allowed by marriage he exorcises his own hopelessness by asserting his mythic claim to dominion over his wife, which gives him license to be physically abusive of her and drives her to visit the same tyranny on her daughter. It is the familial dynamic Twain characterized so brilliantly with the reprobate Pap Finn, who would let no one take away from him his single unalienable right—to be "boss" over his own son.

The wretchedness of Marie's childhood is vividly described, along with her retreats into self-protective delusion. These are chthonic retreats into elaborate lies which help her battered ego to transcend and survive her childhood by creating a mythology of the self which is self-protective and allows for heroic possibility. Only poverty and uncertainty are to be counted so, so Marie retreats into daydreams not unlike her father's penchant for hyperbolic storytelling. In every retelling of his stories, John Rogers engages in more exaggerated self-aggrandizement. The accoutrements and props to his heroism eventually fade away. In revised myth the hero is more and more a superman single-handedly overcoming the limitations of the universe.

Marie, however, cannot lose herself in a similar mythology. She is too keenly perceptive, a characteristic which Alice Walker describes as "one of the cruelest products of poverty, for it is in fact an indication of unrelieved pain, a sign of an extremely loving and sensitive soul . . . being tortured to death."[20] But Marie Rogers from the beginning is equipped to survive because she does not deny herself rage, instead she is energized by it. Her earliest intuitive striving toward survival is expressed in a hatred of all women for their powerlessness, and a hatred of herself for being a woman, one who by an accident of sex is targeted for abuse and denigration. The significance of the individual in the hierarchy of power is a preoccupation from her earliest days: "I must have been no more than four . . . I killed a kitten . . . clodded it to death in the road because it was strange and I pretended it was dangerous" (p. 84). The birth of her brother brings home to her society's perception of the inherent superiority of the male. There is no logic and no justice to this peculiar social dynamic, and the intuitive attempts of her childhood to align herself with the men in her family are abandoned as she matures, but her empowering anger is not.

Her perspective changes as she accepts that the gender system is not just in conflict with her personal growth, it actually threatens her. She sees and experiences herself in her mother, whose hands are swollen and blackened from relentless labor. Her father comes and goes; it is her mother who remains working endlessly, however futilely, to feed the children who are her own existential entrapment. There is no discernible evidence of the ontogenetic or phylogenetic pleasures in this motherhood, no sweet bonding experience, no *participation mystique*. There is nothing in what Marie observes to tempt her to want a child. What she sees is motherhood as a desperate struggle, the yearning and hunger in children's eyes continuous evidence that the task is beyond her. The bond which develops between

Marie and her mother, is a "bond of misery." The solidarity she comes to feel with her mother, whom she eventually sees as weaker than herself, is at first a solidarity in labor, for Marie must help her at the laundry and the loom, but becomes a primitive protectiveness as Marie stands between her mother's weak body and her father's endless abuse. Even as she saves her mother's life she cannot touch her in affection, however, for "in our world no one was supposed to show affection or pain" (p. 90). Marie's perceptions and despair underscore the lessons of the early beatings. The self, especially when a woman, is awesomely small and insignificant in the machinations of the cosmos. Victimization is almost inevitable.

But women's vulnerability is exacerbated by the gender system. Rage is the only ethical and acceptable response possible once Marie understands the artificial and unnecessary nature of this injustice. Thus enraged, she rebels: most vituperatively she rebels against the victimization inherent in marriage. The memory of a "heart-corroding" scene in which the once autonomous Gladys is reduced by pregnancy to a supplicant before her husband's cruel, complacent taunts—"Give me back them clothes I bought you!"—repeats in a relentless motif throughout Marie's life. The autonomous woman, even as prostitute, has a better lot than a married woman. Marie's ferocity toward the institution extends to " disgust for women who are wives" (p. 93). She herself will survive by remaining unmarried, childless, self-supporting, for "only married women had to take orders" (p. 78). Motivated by her formative anger, Marie initially refuses the metaphoric significance of marriage. "My intellect, rough and unshod as it was, was wiser than my emotions. All girls married, and I did not know how I would escape, but escape I determined to. I remember that almost without words, my mother supported me in this" (p. 125).

Marie does not have the romantic inclinations of the young Dorinda. When she does come close to loving in her marriage to Knut, she cannot help but play the termagant even though she recognizes his supportive feminism. She cannot allow herself romance. There are interludes in her early years when she tries on romantic conventions, once briefly captivated by the special attention afforded the victim when she was ill, but she was abruptly robbed of the luxury when better. Another time she fantasized that her young boss, who worked closely beside her to teach her a skill, would metamorphose into a prince and take her away from the drudgery of work. Instead he fired her.

Marie's sustaining anger allowed no quarter to romance or self-delusion. She has the goddess's drive "to know," which is first manifest in school before the burdens of both work and school makes her sluggish and tired, and later in her relentless efforts to educate herself—from the tutelage of Robert Hampton, which she soon outgrows to her years of struggle at the university. It is a desire "to know everything in the world even if it hurt"

(p. 56). Like Dorinda, Marie has a keen, insightful mind which does not mitigate the realities around her. This drive is part of her inner core of strength, her essential self, in part a "native cunning" and it too feeds her rage, fueling her fearless refusal to capitulate to the conventions which would defeat her. Instead, she is transmuted through suffering, as well as through her cooperating will, into a position outside the conventions of patriarchal society, into "otherness."

She rejects the tyranny of the double standard in sex, of sexual practices as a method of social control. "Women had nothing but virginity to trade for a bed and food for the rest of their days. Fathers protected the virginity of their daughters as men guard their bank account" (p. 107). But she does not wish to keep her own because, "it had always shamed me that men judge women by such a standard" (p. 188). When she meets Knut and marries for the first time, she has not yet discovered her own passions. By the time she is in her late twenties, however, and divorced, she takes intermittent lovers without shame in what was "not so much a physical experience as a human adventure. They taught me very much of their work and intellectual interests, and I learned more from such experiences than I have from books" (p. 364). Like Hester Prynne or Dorinda Oakley, she judges herself in terms other than those of orthodox convention.

The chthonic retreats into rage from which Marie gains her prevailing strength are often complicated by difficult moral choices. The victimization of women is often linked to their inability to abandon children. But Marie will not be trapped by women's own affiliative ethics, victimized as her mother was. Her mother and sister Annie die within two weeks of one another. Left behind are Marie's two younger brothers and a younger sister. Although profoundly moved by their plight—they are alone with her shiftless, now alcoholic father—she cannot allow herself to be beguiled by conscience or guilt to remain with her brothers and Beatrice. She pulls away by an act of will, "I drew a dark curtain before my conscious memory and began to forget that I had a family at all" (p. 143). It is a ritual of withdrawal which she must repeat again and again. Yet she never ceases to be connected to them, and does manage somewhat to help George and Dan and to save Beatrice by pulling her out of poverty and supporting her through school.

Marie, like Dorinda, has overtly rejected the conventions of religion. Dorinda had seen it as an opiate used by her mother to assuage the misery of her life, but one without satisfaction. Marie, too, sees that piety mitigates rage and serves the tyranny which oppresses women in her class; she rejects it with a righteous fury. Both Marie and her prostitute Aunt Helen walk out of her mother's funeral when the preacher begins sermonizing that the deceased had been taken to punish the wickedness of the survivors.

> He looked accusingly at us all, one by one, and spoke to us without calling
> our individual names. We were not Christians, he said—and dared touch
> the coffin of my mother! He warned us that we were going the way of sin
> ... and some of us the way of scarlet sin ... his eyes swooped upon Helen
> as a vulture swoops upon its prey: God had punished us by taking my
> mother from us, but He would punish us still more!
>
> [Page 138]

Yet both women are propelled by their own intuitive ethics to take responsibility for the less able of their families. Like Dorinda, Marie contemplates
murdering with her own hands the man who abused her brother Dan. It
is a plan unrelated to sin or law; it is rooted in some less rational sense of
rightness. Dorinda's ethics are clearly rooted in her orderly upbringing,
despite her rejection of religion. The poverty, brutality, ignorance, and exploitation of Marie Rogers's childhood change her into an adult woman
who deliberately nurtures anger, who is unwilling to have children, hesitant
about love, one who vacillates between asceticism and love affairs, between
aloneness and political involvement, who quests restlessly and unceasingly
for unconditional acceptance yet who is invariably ethical, in character consistently informed by her sense of responsibility toward her younger
brothers and sister, even when she is least able. Both heroines disdain piety
and reject organized religion, yet both remain connected to the origin of
religion as an outgrowth of the tribe, and its function to conserve the life
of the tribe. The ethics to which they adhere are rooted in empathy and
responsibility to the group, to the voice of the divinity within.

Marie is only thirty when the novel closes, but she has learned the
strength that comes from acceptance of the chthonic aspect of the goddess
cycle. As she faces the collapse of her marriage to Anand, whom she deeply
loved, she ruminates on the inherent paradoxes of life:

> I think of the great loves that seem to have been great because they were
> hopeless; of the pain that is constant companion to joy; of the night that
> follows the day, of love and hate that are separated by less than a hair's
> breadth. And I think of annihilation that irrevocably follows creation. But
> above all I see that I have had to pay with my life's love for the one ex-
> perience for which I was least responsible.
>
> [Page 384]

It is this wisdom that allows her, at the end of the novel, to reject suicide,
and face aloneness again, this time unwelcome, if necessary, as yet another
season of her life. Bolen suggests that the heroic journey, a dark night of
the soul, is analogous to depression.[21] The chthonic heroine gains inner
strength from the experience and is further fortified to invest in others, to
metamorphose yet again, to continue in her acceptance of "otherness."

Dorinda Oakley and Marie Rogers provide clear and discernible figures of the archetypal goddess. With both these fictional characters the ebb and flow of change in their stories from the Kore aspect of the cycle onward are interspersed with defined periods of chthonic retreat. Unlike the ellipses of Hester Prynne, which are often left undescribed and remain somewhat enigmatic, Glasgow and Smedley have presented in realistic detail the deep emotional upheavals which the heroines cycled in and out of, and from which they gained their arrogance, their unusual strength. The pattern is suggested in other twentieth-century heroines as well.

Katherine Anne Porter's Miranda stories in *Pale Horse, Pale Rider,* present a heroine in the Kore cycle; this is the most commonly told story of women in American literature, often truncated by the redefinition of the feminine. The Kore becomes wife, and therefore backdrop in a story which has come to accept the centrality of the male. Miranda herself defies the expected marriage pattern in an almost perfunctory way. One experiences with Miranda her gradual disenchantment with the traditions of the romantic, chivalric South in "Old Mortality." As a process her disillusionment it is effectively completed through the almost distracted observations of the preanalytical Miranda rather than through any direct experience of her own. She is seemingly absorbed in prepubescent self-dramatization, "despair over her arithmetic" which causes her to fall "flat on her face on the classroom floor, refusing to rise until she was carried out,"[22] as well as the task of building a mythology of the self. It is not until "Part III: 1912" that she begins to evaluate experience, and by then she has already placed herself outside the conventional and expected, having eloped with someone whom her father does not approve of. This illicit marriage is but a detail in Miranda's larger rite of passage. Marriage is not the pivotal experience of Miranda's Kore cycle. It is merely a detail in her larger rejection of patriarchal culture which is focused in her father and his family. Miranda does not break with her heritage without regret; she grapples with the pain of isolation, of being without a tribe. "There was no welcome for her, and there had not been since she had run away. She could not persuade herself to remember how it would be; between one home-coming and the next her mind refused to accept its own knowledge" (p. 218). She becomes quite forlorn in her rebellion, initially unable to accept the loneliness inherent in becoming an outsider. The absurdly romantic legends of Amy had been fed to Miranda and her sister throughout their childhood, fairytales of their own unique subculture, and interspersed with the myth was the heavy-handed edict that this was what Miranda and Maria were to become in order to impress their father in the same sweeping, deathless way which Amy had. From the beginning, even as she absolutely accepts the romantic mythology spouted by her father, Miranda recognizes that it is in part illusion. When confronted with inconsistencies and contradictions, the sisters remain good girls, appropriately motivated by a stubborn desire to please:

"When they heard their father say things like that, Maria and Miranda simply wondered, without criticism, what he meant" (p. 174). It is difficult to abandon the goal of pleasing for the more nebulous process of becoming. The complications of a secure, romantically stimulating childhood linger to obfuscate Miranda's task of accepting herself as "other."

Again and again in novels written by women the heroine confronts her choices by reflecting on the lives of other women; some reincarnations of the compromised Olympians, some clearly representative of the goddesses who were relegated outside the confines of civilization, the Circes and Lilliths, some the shattered, shell-shocked descendants of Cassandra, the impuissant goddess. The heroine as Kore sees herself and her own experience in her mother; in archetype they are versions of the same figure. She sees herself also in alternative figures, as Dorinda sees herself in the madness of Jason's wife Geneva, or in the pointless martyrdom of Minnie May and her mother. Marie sees herself in the supplicant wife Gladys, in the self-destructing autonomy of her prostitute Aunt Helen, in the premature death of her sister Annie. The ancient process of fragmentation of the goddess continues as a motif in modern literature but one which provides the attentive heroine with models to reject in her own becoming. Miranda is without a mother to judge and reject. Her first model is the self-destructive Amy, who rebels briefly against the chivalric tradition, in pursuit of a more expansive life: — "And if I am to be the heroine of this novel, why shouldn't I make the most of it?" (p. 189) — is certainly not a sustaining model. Amy did not find sustenance for her rebellion. Her own mother counsels the necessity of adjustment. So Amy courts martyrdom. She capitulates, marries Gabriel, who she does not love and who she claims is petulant and vapid. Miranda sees herself that this was so, sees also the misery of the woman who became Gabriel's second wife.

But Miranda cannot completely abandon the romantic mythology by which her family would have her define herself. Even after her own rebellious marriage, she cannot quite accept the testimony of her cousin Eva that "Amy did away with herself to escape some disgrace, some exposure that she faced" (p. 214). Miranda is suspect of her feminist cousin Eva, who has gone to jail three times in the struggle to get the vote, a commitment which "almost made a pariah of me" (p. 210). The mythology of her childhood has neatly explained Eva's peculiarity. Eva was ugly, chinless, "a blot, no doubt about it, but the little girls felt she belonged to their everyday world of dull lessons to be learned, stiff shoes to be limbered up, scratchy flannels to be endured in cold weather, measles and disappointed expectations" (p. 178). Amy, self-destructive or not, belonged to the world of romance, poetry, and unworldly books. When Amy toys with the idea of remaining single, "a nice old maid like Eva Parrington," her brother proselytizes on patriarchal realities: "Oh, Eva—Eva has no chin, that's her trouble. If you had no chin, Amy, you'd be in the same fix as Eva, no doubt. . . . When women haven't anything else, they take a vote for consolation. A pretty thin bedfellow" (p. 183). No self-respecting daughter of patriarchy would opt to function in society in the role of Eva Parrington's "otherness." Eva herself testifies with "humorous bitterness" that this role was something she stumbled onto, because of her chinlessness, because her early categorization by her family sent her in search of something else. But Miranda hears in Eva's bitterness "a constant state of mind," and resists, as much as she is able, the wisdom that this outsider offers: "I'm glad you're going to use your mind a little, child. Don't let yourself rust away. Your mind outwears all sorts of things you may set your heart upon; you can enjoy it when all other things are taken away" (p. 210). It is the wisdom of the goddess, and although not fully lost on Miranda, it functions at this stage of her life, as another isolating factor. "It was a dreary prospect: why was a strong character so deforming? Miranda felt she truly wanted to be strong, but how could she face it, seeing what it did to one?" (p. 215).

Patriarchy deliberately inculcates rivalry between women; Eva speaks of this in her description of the mean-spirited rivalries between girls in the cotillion competition which her chinlessness had locked her out of. Yet it continues, as Miranda is as alienated from Eva as she is from Amy. But she is also propelled by Eva in that she echoes her realism, her dissatisfaction, her desire to know. As the first story ends, Miranda unwillingly accepts her own otherness, in "a vague distaste for seeing cousins." "She knew now why she had run away to marriage, and she knew that she was going to run away from marriage, and she was not going to stay in any place, with anyone, that threatened to forbid her making her own discoveries, that said 'No' to her" (p. 220).

When Miranda reappears in the third story, she has changed, become wiser, more emotionally autonomous, although still struggling in "a continual effort to bring together and unite firmly the disturbing oppositions of her day-to-day existence, where survival, she could see clearly, had become a series of feats of sleight of hand" (p. 270). Her survival had included a demotion at the newspaper after she and a fellow newspaperwoman had suppressed the facts of a juicy social scandal out of an ethical compassion for the girl and her family. The women reporters were considered "nice girls, but fools" by their colleagues. Miranda has clearly broken away from the confinement of desiring to please; she answers to her own ethical code, has begun her own course of "otherness."

But Porter presents a character whose vacillations are more pronounced than those of either Glasgow's Dorinda or Smedley's Marie. The illness which is a predominant aspect of this second story is a chthonic descent of the goddess cycle. Miranda's illness is death-threatening, totally absorbing, a primal passage into the border regions of the elemental

perceptions, a microcosmic confrontation of the individual with the unbending agenda of nature presented against the backdrop of war. The confrontation with death, her own death, is a confrontation with the implacable and profound, that which makes civilization with its pretense,
ideals, its artificial superego, and emphasis on heroic individuality irrelevant, even absurd.

> Silenced she sank easily through deeps under deeps of darkness until
> she lay like a stone at the farthest bottom of life, knowing herself to be
> blind, deaf, speechless, no longer aware of the members of her own body,
> entirely withdrawn from all human concerns, yet alive with a peculiar
> lucidity and coherence; all notions of the mind, the reasonable inquiries
> of doubt, all ties of blood and the desires of the heart, dissolved and fell
> away from her, and there remained of her only a minute fiercely burning
> particle of being that knew itself alone, that relied upon nothing beyond
> itself for its strength; not susceptible to any appeal or inducement, being
> itself composed entirely of one single motive, the stubborn will to live.
> This fiery motionless particle set itself unaided to resist destruction, to
> survive and to be in its own madness of being, motiveless and planless
> beyond that one essential end. Trust me, the hard unwinking angry point
> of light said. Trust me. I stay.
>
> [Pages 310–311]

When Miranda recovers, she finds that it is her friend Adam who has
died. The chivalric tradition has been inverted. The tender nurturing nurse
who has given life in the service of love is the hero, not the heroine. But
none of it matters. The lesson of her chthonic interlude has been a lesson
of negation. The romantic mythology of her childhood is at last rendered
irrelevant, but the knowledge gained is through the hard lesson of loss, accompanied by the wearisome regret that she had not had the wisdom to
recognize irrelevancy and so been honest while Adam lived. There is
nothing romantic about his death; he is "there beside her, invisible but
urgently present, a ghost more alive than she was," but, despite the bleakness of this juxtapositioning, she pulls herself forward with her own
strength, undoubtedly to be metamorphosed again.

Chapter XI

Chthonic Renewal: Irrational Modes in *Dinner at the Homesick Restaurant, The Good Mother,* and *The Color Purple*

Susan Sontag in *Illness as Metaphor* refers to illness as "the night-side of life"; it is "that other place" to which we all must acknowledge citizenship.[1] That illness is a dimension just beyond the familiar reality of everyday life is indisputable. Its character is alien, irrational. In fiction, as Sontag has demonstrated, illness has been employed as a metaphor for judgment, a manifestation not of the inescapable irrational interludes of life but of individual guilt and original sin.

Madness, that permanent or transitory condition which is viewed as illness of the mind, has also been utilized as a fictional device to perpetuate the male-dominated hierarchal structure of Western civilization. Barbara Hill Rigney in *Madness and Sexual Politics in the Feminist Novel* has suggested an alternative view of the experience of madness. Citing the work of R. D. Laing, Rigney points out that psychosis in either women or men can be a sane, self-protective response to life in an oppressive social situation. Furthermore, she correlates the hero's ritual of introspection with what has been labeled madness in others.[2] Rigney uses Margaret Atwood's protagonist in *Surfacing* to demonstrate this less popular view that madness is a necessary transitional step toward the wisdom that is beyond logic, here called the wisdom of the goddess.[3] Madness itself may be merely a pejorative term for categorization of irrational modes, including flights into the sensual or mystical, including passions whether eros or maternal love, grief or rage. All are aberrational conditions, not easily explainable within the narrow rational parameters of Western thought. They are too raw and nebulous, too volatile and unpredictable, yet intense and transformational enough that they might free one from internalized social norms. They threaten the existing social balance. So like Circe and Lillith, they are placed outside what is acknowledged as civilized. Except when used specifically in the service of civilization's accepted goals, such emotions or emotional interludes have been traditionally considered with suspicion, deemed irrational, sometimes uncivilized.

This tradition, reflected in linguistics as well as philosophy and litera-ture, is impacted by ideas of polarity and hierarchy,[4] in the habitual struc-turing of oppositional ideas which preclude the possibility that the illogical might coexist with the clearly logical and might in fact provide transfor-mative energy or illumination—the benefits garnered by the goddess dur-ing her cycle into the chthonic. The heroine of Atwood's novel demon-strates this. Her withdrawal is a chthonic retreat into autonomy, into the self-actualizing isolation which can be read in the original, premythic con-ception of virginity. It might be termed "madness" or "psychosis" by the dominant majority, but to the "discerning eye," as Dickinson wrote, "Much madness is divinest sense." When Atwood's protagonist surfaces, it is after she has located the divinity within herself, and has secured the vi-sion that follows "the failure of logic."

Obsessed with classification and hierarchization, Western logic has itself failed to conceptualize a wholeness which transcends the agonistic confrontation of opposites, or a vision of the goddess's seasonal cycle. The cycle, which appears more and more in contemporary fiction, especially that written by women, allows a fluidity and juxtapositioning of ideas pre-viously presented as polar, particularly the rational and irrational. It leads to wisdom which emphasizes the relativity of events and away from the judgment of them. It suggests that irrational interludes nourish the heroine, providing revelation or illumination which facilitates her arrogance, and so allows her to surface, as does Atwood's protagonist, with the strength to prevail.

Much of the experience of women is at odds with the phallocentric goals of culture. The social balance is often inimical to a woman's own need and to those of her children or her community. Attachment behavior itself, that merging of selves which is most intense in the participation mystique of the mother-child bond, is theoretically dangerous to the social balance in that it contradicts the priority of individuation; it challenges prevailing polarities; it threatens both the social hierarchy and the metaphoric cen-trality of the male. Yet it is vital to phylogenetic goals, and often immensely rewarding to the individual. This experience of mystical identification with another, of participation intimately in the life of another is a form of *eros* and is not limited to the mother-child pair. This eros is the love which is celebrated in fusion and intensifies with the blurring of the ego borders be-tween individuals. According to St. Augustine, it is the power that drives men toward God;[5] it is the manifestation of the drive toward life and inseparable from the first tribal conception of divinity, that of participation in what is larger than the self, in the nurturing tribal mother who gives birth to herself as well as to her children, who mothers herself as well as her children, who indiscriminately facilitates all life, takes all to her comfort in death.

Before Aristotle, Socrates struggled with the issue of the inner voice. He listened to his "daimon," that inner oracle which was the voice of divinity within him. As a concept this "daimon" has been construed to mean conscience, but the superego is designed by the learned mores of specific culture. Socrates' inner oracle was a precultural, preverbal voice rooted in nature and "the natural forces which go beyond the self and are felt as the grasp of fate upon us."[6] It's connection is to the prerational sentience which generated ideas of a maternal divinity. While the dominant tribe in the amalgamation that is Western culture has continued to insist on a civilization organized around the primacy and centrality of the male, and has produced aesthetics expressing his "universal" experience, the daemons of women have continued to be rebellious to these goals, suggesting an ethical code which is specific to women, and leading to a heroism which is also different. Contemporary writers have discovered an audience for this neglected story of women's experience. With growing insistence their novels reveal other "universals," including more discernible characterizations of the great goddess archetype who is comfortably familiar with irrational modes.

Anne Tyler's story, *Dinner at the Homesick Restaurant*, opens under the aegis of illness. Pearl Tull is dying, and her ruminations, made both lucid and borderless by her illness, allow the unraveling of the story of a family in which the irrational and illogical forces of life play a pivotal role. Ezra sits beside her; he is her second son, the one she'd convinced her husband to have as an "extra" when the illness of her oldest brought home to her the awful vulnerability inherent in motherhood. It was not until after the birth of Jenny, her third, that she sees the contradiction in her logic. "What she had now was not one loss to fear but three."[7]

Pearl Tull is a difficult protagonist to admire; fiercely independent, she is a woman who stubbornly denies anything which could weaken her. Propelled by "pride or spite or something," she prevails in her goals and at her death leaves behind a large and diversified clan which has evolved through the same stubborn force of will that motivated Hester Prynne, Dorinda Oakley, and Marie Rogers. It is a refusal to be victimized.

Pearl has little charm. She is not even particularly likable: at her funeral the minister eulogizes someone else. Her son Cody is shocked to hear her life called *full,* for he recognizes that it was more *stunted* than full; "espaliered" is Cody's assessment of it. He describes her to his father as "a raving, shrieking, unpredictable witch." Yet her story is so profoundly believable that she commands sympathy even as she oscillates between the ersatz archetypes of good and bad mother. Pearl Tull is quintessentially realistic, combining both good and bad traits and surfacing amid the contradictions as a good enough mother. As such, Pearl is a variation of the goddess archetype. Her arrogance is her power, her chthonic descents into rage somehow feed her essential self and allow her to prevail despite the odds. "It was unthinkable to cry in front of the children. Or in front of anyone. Oh, she had her pride! She was not a tranquil woman; she often lost her temper, snapped, slapped the nearest cheek, said things she later regretted—but thank the Lord, she didn't expose her tears" (p. 14). For Pearl, the odds against her include the inflexibility of her own difficult nature. She is a strong-willed woman, sometimes strong-willed to the point of absurdity. "'The doctor says I'm going blind,' she told the children, but privately, she'd intended to do no such thing" (p. 5). But she has created a mythology of the self which precluded victimization and allowed her to find great strength in her own ego. "'She's blind,' her doctor said, and she reported, 'He thinks I'm blind,' not arguing, but managing to imply, somehow, that this was a matter of opinion—or of will, of what you're willing to allow and what you're not" (p. 259).

Tyler's heroine is reflective and wise in her choice of self-delusions, and rituals. In her youth, in her Kore cycle, she had come up against repeated setbacks. Early on it looked as though she would not be asked to marry, that she would become a stereotype, the spinster living in her uncle's spare bedroom. But Pearl was stubborn; she refused his offer of an education, holding out for a late marriage. Eventually she was courted by the flamboyant Beck Tull, six years her junior, and "Her one mistake: a simple error in judgment" (p. 23). Together they had three children before he abruptly announced that he was leaving her and them. To avert this, she was prepared to change.

> "And the children," she said, clutching new hope. "You'll want to visit the children." . . .
> (He would come with presents for them and she'd be the one to open the door—perfumed, in her Sunday dress, maybe wearing a bit of rouge. She's always thought false color looked cheap, but she could have been wrong.)
> Beck said, "No."
>
> [Page 9]

A difficult change follows his departure. Pearl had been cut off from her own family by the nature of marriage itself; after Beck's departure, she cannot ask them for help, because in doing so she would have to admit her weakness. For months she tries to conceal Beck's abandonment from her children, fearing that confrontation will weaken her. Later when the difficult years of their childhood are over, she can admit that she was vulnerable: "All those years when she was the only one, the sole support, the lone tall tree in the pasture just waiting for lightning to strike" (p. 32). From the perspective of her last illness she comes to see the relativity and irrelevance of much of life. She recognizes that "she'd been an angry sort of mother. She'd been continually on edge; she felt too burdened, too much alone" (p. 19). But she resents the fact that her children, especially Cody, focus almost solely on those episodes of short temper, on their poverty and loneliness, forgetting the sweeter side of their childhood. "Honestly, she thought, wasn't there some statute of limitations here?" (p. 23). At her funeral it is Ezra who reminds his brother of the sweet times between those irrational explosions, reminds him of the Monopoly games, soft-shoe routines, cozy evenings listening to Fred Allen on the radio.

These "episodes of short temper" which Pearl in the wisdom of her age and illness can see, are relatively insignificant, as is much in life where the one certainty is change. Her children, however, reveal these episodes as "rampages" during which their peculiar mother engages in compulsive rituals of disruption: emptying Jenny's bureau drawers and closet, throwing Cody down a flight of stairs, pummelling Ezra with her fists. None of the three was safe from her hair pulling, her shrieking invective: "Parasites. . . . I wish you'd all die and let me go free. I wish I'd find you dead in your beds" (p. 53). With the selective hyperbole of childhood's perspective, her children see her as a crone, personification of the irrationally chthonic.

> Jenny knew that, in reality, her mother was a dangerous person—hot breathed and full of rage and unpredictable. The dry, straw texture of her lashes could seem the result of some conflagration, and her pale hair could crackle electrically from its bun and her eyes could get small as hatpins. Which of her children had not felt her stinging slap, with the claw encased pearl of her engagement ring that could bloody a lip at one flick? Jenny had seen her hurl Cody down a flight of stairs. She'd seen Ezra ducking, elbows raised, warding off an attack. She herself, more than once, had been slammed against a wall, been called "serpent," "cockroach," "hideous little sniveling guttersnipe." But here Pearl sat, decorously inquiring about Julia Caroll's weight problem. . . . But she never felt entirely secure, and at night, when Pearl placed a kiss on the center of Jenny's forehead, Jenny went off to bed and dreamed what she had always dreamed: her mother laughed a witch's shrieking laugh; dragged Jenny out of hiding as the Nazis tramped up the stairs; accused her of sins and crimes that had never crossed Jenny's mind. Her mother told her, in an informative and considerate tone of voice, that she was raising Jenny to eat her.
>
> [Page 70]

Pearl herself minimizes these rages, perhaps as part of her denial of everything that might weaken her, but also because of their relative insignificance when juxtaposed with her love for her children, the courage shown in her care of them. Without romanticizing such erratic behavior, one can also see that for Pearl these rages were necessary rituals for expiating the overwhelming vulnerability she denied, for managing the enormous stress of her effort to maintain her family.

Tyler does not focus solely on the mother's irrational eruptions. Pearl is the focal point, the matrix of this family, but emanating from her and around her are still other irrational entities which envelop, obfuscate, and propel familial relationships. Cody, the difficult older son, is crippled by his own unrelieved jealousy of the sweet Ezra. He plots to steal his brother's fiancee, and then spends years haunted by the unfounded fear that his wife and son are more attached to the gentle, unassuming Ezra than to Cody himself. Ezra himself is an endearing if somewhat fatalistic character, whose lack of will contrasts with his mother's forceful personality. *"Let it be* was the theme that ran through his life." But Ezra, unlike the unforgiving Cody, comes to recognize his mother's strength, without equivocating about her irrational outbursts.

Jenny, too, is a profoundly believable character, flawed in her judgments perhaps, as she moves from one marriage to another, avoiding intimacy, perhaps, yet overall a well-conditioned, self-motivated woman, who is "not capable of being destroyed by love" (p. 11). It is through Jenny's breakdowns while in school that Tyler underlines the less remembered, less sensational episodes of familial support which were as much generated by Pearl Tull's personality as was her craziness. It is to Pearl, the clan matrix, that Jenny runs for renewal.

"I don't understand you. Your mother has frightened and mistreated you all your life, and now you want to visit her for no apparent reason" (p. 103), Jenny's first husband grouses. But in Pearl's "wiry energy, the strength she had shown in raising her children singlehanded, and her unfailing interest in their progress" (p. 83), Jenny has located a vehicle of endless renewal. With her mother and the family she held together, Jenny "loosened; she was safe at last, in the only place where people knew exactly who she was and loved her anyhow" (p. 102). Reacting to her mother's intensity, Jenny evolves an almost perfunctory way of interacting in relationships; she emphasizes the ironic, the humorous, and develops perspective and a sense of the relativity of things. As an adult she tells her brother that the primary disease that plagues her young patients is "mother-itis."

Pearl Tull does know her children in a remarkably intuitive sense, can order the world for them, and does love them regardless of their flaws. When she confronts Cody with the inappropriateness of his obsession with his brother's fiancee, Ruth, she is not so much judgmental as practical:

"You don't fool me for an instant. . . . Why are you so contrary? You've got no earthly use for that girl. She's not your type in the slightest; she belongs to your brother, Ezra, and she's the only thing in this world he's ever wanted. If you were to win her away, tell me what you'd do with her! You'd drop her flat. You'd say, 'Oh, my goodness, what am I doing with *this* little person?'"

[Page 153]

When Cody complains that she does not understand his motives, Pearl disabuses him quickly: "'I understand you perfectly . . . with my three children, why not the least little thing escapes me. I know everything you're after. I see everything in your heart, Cody Tull.'

'Just like God,' Cody answers. 'Just like God,' she agreed" (p. 154). Omniscience, which eventually became the attribute of the god, is a function of eros, of the participation mystique which was the goddess's dominion. Its depreciated remnant is women's intuition.

Cody successfully absconds with Ezra's love and immediately feels heartbreaking regret. He does not leave Ruth, but commits himself to a life of senseless, complaining bitterness, continually torturing himself and Ruth and Ezra (and eventually his son) with irrational episodes, his own rituals of expiation. Pearl, however, focuses on the relative nature of the tragedy: "they might eventually smooth things over. Yes, after all, this choosing of mates was such a small, brief stage in a family's history" (p. 171). She valiantly perseveres in her obligation to facilitate ties, to preserve familial connections. Pearl does not believe that one can choose to sever such relationships, as Beck has done, as Cody would if she allowed it. This is Pearl's single ethical code, one which is unconnected to any larger cultural model. When she feels the family has failed as an entity because of the Cody-Ezra conflict she briefly attempts to blame herself, but then recognizes that there is no blame to be placed, that much is merely accidental. Ultimately, she has the satisfaction of not having given up, of having emphasized attachment over loss, and bequeathing that stubborn attachment to a then enlarged clan which remains after her death.

The motif of "homesickness" becomes a motif of the existential angst inherent in familial life, the contemporary tribe. Reality and longing are ever at odds in Pearl Tull's family, yet she manages to present the relativity of both. In contrast to her son Cody, who is irrationally attached to pain and hurt, and to Beck who simply leaves, Pearl remains rooted in the feminine ethics of empathy and attachment. She is syncretistic, fluid, and forgiving. She is at home with the irrational, which offers transformative energy both to herself and to the family. Within her peculiar, stunted, essential self Pearl Tull finds the arrogant courage that fortifies the chthonic heroine. Although outside the mainstream of orthodox patriarchally approved behavior, Pearl endures. Like Mrs. Scarlatti, Pearl recognizes that

"Life is a continual shoring up ... against one thing and another just eroding and crumbling away" (p. 99). The boon she leaves is a largely healthy family, "a clan" as Beck Tull, again on the verge of departing, defines them. "Like something on TV. Lots of cousins and uncles, jokes, reunions" (p. 294). Beck's is the observation of the outsider, more appearance than reality, but even to the insider, they are definable more by their empathy than their dissonance. Pearl's is the achievement of Danae, who though entombed with Perseus, was never allowed to articulate the story of her own heroism.

Like Pearl Tull, Anna Dunlap, the narrator and heroine of Sue Miller's novel *The Good Mother,* is an unlikely model of the archetypal goddess. This narrator tells her story in retrospect; she is still a young woman at the point when she recounts the story of the loss of her daughter, yet what she describes is the familiar story of the Kore who comes up against the expectations of patriarchal culture, fails to develop in the way which has been prescribed, and so begins evolving in a different pattern, one which employs modes of the irrational as sources of the transformative energy; the result is yet another manifestation of the syncretistic heroine who prevails.

Anna Dunlap's initial failure is in her own perception of herself. Before patriarchal society, represented by her mother's demanding family, makes any judgment about Anna, she gives up on herself. From the pre-adolescent whose "dream of making music ... infused my life with a sense of limitless possibility,"[8] she became a benumbed adolescent whose yearning for intimacy and unconditional acceptance propelled her into a series of masochistic sexual encounters. The young Anna was clearly no fighter. Her estimation of herself was predicated completely by her own sense that she had failed to measure up to the standards of musical achievement set by her grandfather. What self-respect she had was intricately interwoven with music and it was when she turned her back on music, that she began her tentative and self-abusive quest for intimacy. Both her elliptical immersions in her music and her eventual self-realization through the achievement of rare and passionate intimacy with Leo serves as modes of the irrational which provide Anna with the strength (she herself is too self-deprecating to call it arrogance) to change in ways which allow her to sustain her relationship with Molly, who is Anna's unquestioned raison d'être.

Throughout her narrative, but particularly in the beginning, Anna assesses herself as a particularly conservative woman, a willing daughter of patriarchy who had adhered to the values inculcated by culture. Her discontent materializes in an almost decorous revolt when she initiates the divorce from Brian. But it is an ill-considered rebellion, an almost perfunctory action. Anna had married Brian because he offered a "moral safety net," an escape from her self-destructive search for acceptance and intimacy. Although she describes them as friends, there is no element of passionate commitment between Anna and her husband. Yet she is a passionate, keenly sensitive mother who is profoundly moved by every aspect of the bond between herself and Molly. Yet she accepts that passion in herself without rumination. She is unable to define the lack that characterized her union with Brian, yet she recognizes the mutual nourishment inherent in the intimacy of her relationship with Molly. The daughters of patriarchy, however, are suppose to be devoted mothers; both she and Brian see that passion as appropriate. After her divorce, Anna strives in a mild-mannered way to be independent and self-supporting, but she remains motivated to conservative ladylike goals; she is essentially compliant rather than restive, and certainly neither arrogant nor strong. The strength Anna gains from her independence is tenuous at best. Then she encounters Leo and the wellspring of strength in *eros*.

In *Love and Will*, Rollo May, taking his lead from the ancient Greeks, delineates the genres of love and decries the cultural dangers in confusing them. He defines eros as "the drive to procreate or create—the urge as the Greeks put it, toward higher forms of being and relationship."[9] It is eros which Anna has yearned toward all her life. After judging herself in terms of her failure as a musician, she is no longer nurtured by an immersion in music. It is only in her relationship with Leo that she enters into the cycle of chthonic retreat and renewal. Later, when eros is lost, music becomes a substitute.

The relationship between Anna and Leo is infused with high passion; it is irrational, ecstatic, wonderful, rare. "It felt like some shift in dimension" (p. 190) to Anna. For the receptive, conservative Anna, who had previously viewed her participation in love as in work as a matter of "utility," this new dimension, this charmed union facilitates a growth and transformation which sustains her even after the relationship itself is stunted by the machinations of the patriarchy. May writes: "It is *eros*, the power in us yearning for wholeness, the drive to give meaning and pattern to our variegation, for to our otherwise impoverishing formlessness, integration to counter our disintegrative trends. Here we must have a dimension of experience which is psychological and emotional as well as biological."[10] Eros allows Anna to rethink her definition of herself; she abandons her suburban dress, her self-destructive episodes, her entrapping fastidiousness, even her self-doubts with such celebratory ease that her desire to merge not just with Leo, but to fuse herself with both Molly and Leo is profoundly believable. It is a transcendent syncretism toward which Anna strives.

> Our lives seemed magically interpenetrated, commingled, even as we each separated into all the day's complicated activities. I had never expected it

to seem so graceful and easy, but Molly's seemingly complete comfort with Leo was like a benediction on all aspects of the relationship, even the sexual.

[Page 193]

I can remember feeling a sense of completion as though I had everything I wanted held close, held inside me; as though I had finally found a way to have everything. We seemed fused, the three of us, all the boundaries between us dissolved.

[Page 195]

May points out that eros is the yearning for mystic union, the power which drives man toward God.[11] Although recognized as an irrational force since Plato first wrote of eros as a daimon,[12] it is none too surprising that as an entity eros has lost its place as a legitimate topic of metaphysical discourse, has been attenuated when not denied; as an irrational force it is suspected, misunderstood, denigrated by an orthodox culture which prides itself on having passed firmly and irrevocably through a rite of passage into an age of reason. This rational blindness characterizes the patriarchy in *The Good Mother*. When Anna comes up against the tragic consequences of her own metamorphosis and finds herself in a desperate battle with the inflexible rules of the established order, her first temptation is a traditional defense. Dazed with shock, she attempts to recapture her earlier self; she returns to the costume of her preerotic self, paints her face, curls her hair, but finds someone else, "nearly unrecognizable, someone pretty and brittle and utterly cold" (p. 239). Despite her desperate situation, she recognizes the growth and enhancement of her evolved self.

Yet the subsequent scenes present Anna in conflict with an inflexible antagonist. The staid and rational orthodoxy is represented by her morally outraged ex-husband, a lawyer, as well as by her disapproving grandfather, who controls through money, and by her sympathetic but realistic defense attorney, Muth. It is Muth who cuts Leo loose, allowing Anna's sensitive lover to appear the villain who has victimized not just Molly but her naive mother as well. Leo is placed outside the confines of the definably civilized so that Anna can remain within. For Leo is a deliberate bohemian, a discardible component; he must be repudiated, at least ostensibly, in order for Anna to regain legal custody of Molly. In this phase, Anna's grief generates alienation from Leo and eros, both catalysts to this awful vulnerability; she is motivated also by a paradoxical desire to placate Leo whose complicity with her own compromise is necessary. Anna's deepest ethics are inflexible, and intuitively, stubbornly rooted in the mother-child bond, the elemental root of all sociality. Hers is a preverbal compulsion expressed by a centrality of focus which is unshaken by distractions of either orthodox culture or overt rebellion. It is so absolutely and unquestionably inherent to Anna that Miller does not allow her to either ruminate or debate.

Instead, Anna Dunlap enters into a new role, without Molly, without passion, without the playful wonder of eros. In this phase she is not rebellious, as Ursula and Leo would have her be; she is instead compliant, receptive, manipulative, a consummate actress playing to the rules of the marketplace, appearing with false dependent femininity. She functions as a mystic, an aesthete, stripping herself of all emotional accoutrements in the service of her primal connection to her daughter. Her concentration is almost palpable.

But Anna loses Molly. There is nothing allegorical in the nature of this twist of plot. Issues of guilt and punishment are secondary. Anna's response to Payne, the psychiatrist who attempts to address her feelings on this topic, is opaque. "He waited for a response. 'You know, this legal stuff, it says if this one's right, this one's wrong. If this one wins, this one loses.' He shook his head and smiled ruefully at me. 'Don't buy into that. That's not life. O.K.?'" Ursula voices for her the alternative way of looking at the experience, reminding her of the relativity of events. Anna's central focus is on connection rather than culpability.

Anna's response to the loss of legal custody is grief over the crimping of her access to Molly. The chthonic retreat that follows the end of the trial is fraught with rage and self-abuse, but resolved with the rite of shooting Leo's gun into the sands on the beach. When Anna returns to Cambridge she cuts her fingernails, returning to music as an alternative to the self-destructive ritual of her trip to Plum Island. Immediately and without hesitation, she prepares to reinvest her life in Molly's.

In the years that follow, Anna adapts to the fact that Molly is to live with her father. Although pained by Molly's initial difficulty with their separation, Anna does not seriously contemplate challenging the arrangement in court. Her energies are invested in perpetuating and strengthening her participation in Molly's life, despite the handicap of having lost legal custody of her. Molly herself "began to seem better, more used to the different rhythm of what we could have together" (p. 447).

Anna is not the overt rebel who Ursula and Leo would have her be; she does not wish to challenge the patriarchy for the sake of challenge. The memory of the dissembling and playacting of the court ritual with its "forced intimacy," further dissuades her. But Anna exhibits a prevailing strength of purpose which allows her to compromise in ways which facilitate her primary goal. The novel is a retelling of the myth of Demeter. Like the goddess, Anna never escapes her own grief over losing Molly, but compromises toward the goal of retaining as much of the connection as she can. The lost child is reunited with her mother because of her mother's ingenuity and power; the mother accepts the cycles inherent in life, cycles of grief and joyousness. The ethics which motivate Anna or Demeter are the ethics of connection and empathy leading to a central emphasis on the relationship between mother and child. Experiencing eros, first in her relationship with her daughter and later in her relationship with Leo, has been transforming and illuminating for Anna. The result is that she prevails despite oppression, accepting an unconventional "otherness" outside the roles prescribed by orthodox culture but one which is not confrontational. Anna resists victimization and looks to the possibility that Molly will come to live with her mother by choice when she is allowed that option as an adolescent. She redefines herself to this end, refusing to be weakened. "I've made do with a different set of circumstances—with our distance, our brief times together, with all that's truncated, too little, too small in what we have. And I take a certain pride in how well I've done this, in thinking that perhaps I'm suited to it in some way as other, more passionate people might not be" (p. 460). Without Anna's voice to tell this story, the experience might well have become the raw material of revisionist allegory. Having failed to be consistently cooperative to the goals of the dominant culture, Anna is punished by the righteous powers. The revisionist version would include despairing judgment, perhaps even Anna's suicide. Anna, like Pearl Tull, is only one step removed from the mainstream, only marginally out of line with the revised views of appropriate feminine behavior. Anna's obligations to internalized social systems are presumably made more intense by the proximity. Like Demeter, Anna Dunlap could have claimed a place on Olympus if she had been more cooperative. Like Danae, Pearl Tull might have become a mute supporting actress in her son's story. Other versions of the goddess/heroine have been completely excluded from the primary narrative of Western aesthetics. Daphne's desire to escape the will of Apollo makes her completely incomprehensible to patriarchy; so her metamorphosis is revised into nightmare. Lillith's scorn for the requirements of the revision of the feminine necessitated her ostracism from the narrative itself. But even in her most oppressed and exotic, the goddess has found a voice in contemporary fiction.

Alice Walker ends her novel, *The Color Purple*, thus: "I thank everybody in this book for coming. A. W., author and medium." It is a novel which allows full play to the irrational aspects of life. Intuition and eros as well as bizarre coincidence all work with the protagonist. This author "and medium" presents characters who attend to such forces and completely reevaluate the concept of God. The process of redefinition replays the archetypal process described by Harrison. The conception of divinity which emerges is an outgrowth of eros. It is grounded in the sensual, the aesthetic, and the mystical, and is expressed in a morality of responsibility to human connection and sensual pleasure rather than any abstract code of restrictions propelled by guilt.

The god of Celie and Shug in *The Color Purple* arises in response to the needs of the tribe, a tribe which is a circle within a circle of oppression.

This community is a small group of Afro-American women who are the innermost ring of a relentlessly repressive reality. Amid violence and chaos they live on the verge of extinction as individuals, but as a collective they strive toward life in the ancient manner, conceptualizing something which is larger than themselves but to which each belongs. In this each can find comfort from abuse and existential angst. For this particular group, black women in the South in the first half of the twentieth century, such striving necessitated a seachange in conception. To find the divinity within which would sustain them, they had first to abandon their traditional notion of God.

Celie is the central voice of the narrative, and through her one can trace the gradual process of changing God. It comes with the abandonment of piety and the birth of rage. In her first few letters Celie is a preanalytical reporter who has been brutalized into passivity. Before the novel opens the fourteen-year-old Celie had endured such atrocity that she has been numbed. As an afterthought to his cruelty, her stepfather, who has raped her and abducted their infant, tells her that she can tell no one about the violation and loss except God. It is the pieta motif he offers and she accepts. For Celie the idea of God is associated with comfort and motherhood: her own cruelly aborted motherhood, and the loss of her own mother's comfort. "You better not never tell nobody but God. It'd kill your mammy."

For Celie these letters to God are rituals of self-protection: God is an idea which she associates with empathy and the care of others. When her mother asks her the father of her babies, she tells her they are God's. "I don't know no other man or what else to say." When her mother asks where the baby is, she tells her, "God took it," although she believes that her stepfather killed her daughter and will try to kill her son. When she realizes that her sister is the new object of her stepfather's lust, she promises to protect her, "With God help."

At the bottommost circle of Celie's hell, women are raped by men in their own families, killed by their boyfriends and husbands; babies are sold or killed by their fathers; women are worked to death by their menfolk or they die from their misplaced faith in patriarchy, as Celie's mother did. "I don't even looks at mens. That's the truth. I look at women, tho, cause I'm not scared of them. Maybe cause my mama cuss me you think I kept mad at her. But I ain't. I felt sorry for mama. Trying to believe his story kilt her" (p. 6). Celie operates by pitiful instinct, without anger, dressing up in horsehair, feathers, and high heels so that her stepfather will use her and not rape Nettie when his new wife is too sick for copulation. Celie's stepfather negotiates her disposal to Mr. _____ even as she lies in bed recovering from his last attack. She escapes into the eyes of Shug Avery, that say "Yeah, it *bees* that way sometime" (p. 9).

Except for her piety, Celie is mired in defeat. She is without anger; is utterly passive and accepting of the abuse visited on her. Even children are stronger than Celie, and so they brutalize her too. Other women, Nettie and later Mr. _____'s sisters Kate and Carrie, counsel her that in this society of brutal gender polarity, Celie has to learn to resist. But she does not know how, does not have the will. When beaten she escapes into a mythology of the self: "It all I can do not to cry. I make myself wood. I say to myself, Celie, you are a tree." Celie's tree metaphor is an expression of her passive intransigence, but it also connects her to the ancient myth of Daphne as her unconscious erects a similar defense, envisioning an escape from victimization into prevailing earth, the intransigent tree. It is a metaphor for Celie's obstinance which will flourish into self-will and fortify rebellion as she herself metamorphoses. But her life is worse than death when the story begins. She clings to her tree myth, to the company of God, and to the fantasy that surrounds a picture of Shug Avery. Eventually, however, her dogged resolution to survive will be fueled by retreats into rage and she will be transformed into the chthonic heroine.

Despite the monotony of her brutal life, Celie begins to become analytical. The experiences of Harpo, her stepson, help her in this. In Sophia, Harpo's girlfriend, who defiantly claims she is not "in trouble" when she becomes pregnant with Harpo's baby, and who is backed up by a bevy of strong-willed belligerent sisters, Celie sees a new way of dealing with the experience of being a woman. Primitively resentful at Sophia's pity for her and at the monotonous brutality of her own experience, Celie at first advises Harpo to beat Sophia, just as his father had advised, just as his father beats Celie. But when it is done, Celie is haunted by her sin against Sophia's spirit, her violation of inherent ethics of empathy. When confronted, she is ruthlessly honest, self-deprecating: "I say it cause I'm a fool, I say. I say it cause I'm jealous of you. I say it cause you do what I can't. What that? she say. Fight. I say" (p. 42).

And from Sophia and her sisters, Celie sees the strength in unity, the need to substitute anger for piety.

You ought to bash Mr. _____ head open, she say. Think about heaven later.

Not much funny to me. That funny. I laugh. She laugh. Then us both laugh so hard us flop down on the step" (p. 44).

Humor becomes a conduit of Celie's redemption, humor and Shug Avery, who all through this novel is intricately interwoven into Celie's evolving conception of divinity. Shug is "the color purple," a combination of red and blue, colors associated with royalty and passion; but she is also an available aesthetic, one in which even the impoverished Celie can immerse herself for comfort.

Shug herself begins as a chthonic heroine, and it is through her intervention that Celie is led to discover the divinity within herself. When

Shug first appears in Celie's life, she is an icon in a photograph, a model too lofty for Celie to emulate. Shug is a sacred, inaccessible figure, a Christ-figure to Celie who wishes only to be allowed to minister to her. The letters which tell of Shug's first appearance in Celie's life describe a young zealot's pleasure in submerging herself in service of a guru. "I wash her body, it feel like I'm praying. My hands tremble and my breath short" (p. 51). Celie collects Shug's hair from the hairbrush like a believer gathering relics. But this is the multiple goddess and service to her is service to all her cycles: "I work on her like she a doll or like she Olivia—like she mama" (p. 55). Shug herself is no long-suffering patient, no pious Christ imitator; instead she is syncretistic, protean, and volatile. "Shug halfway between sick and well. Halfway between good and evil, too. Most days now she show me and Mr. _____ her good side. But evil all over her today. She smile, like a razor opening" (p. 59). But when Shug deigns to step into Celie's sphere, to quilt with her, Celie is transfixed. In her relationship with Shug, Celie discovers eros.

Eros is the yearning toward another, toward participation in another's life. May writes that "eros seeks union with the other person in delight and passion, and the procreating of new dimensions of experience which broaden and deepen the being of both persons."[13] It is the force behind Pearl Tull's devotion to her children, behind Anna Dunlap's devotion to first her daughter and then her lover, and it is here the force which pulls Celie toward Shug. Eros is "the longing to establish union, full relationship," as May says;[14] it is not restricted by any orthodox sense of appropriate pair bonding.

Celie's sufferings have depleted her energy. She is at best apathetic before her relationship with Shug, although she longs for Nettie and her children. But in concentrating on survival, Celie has held her analytical abilities in abeyance, has conserved her emotional energy, without anger, adrift in self-deprecation. She allowed others to name and define emotional needs for her. When Mr. _____'s sisters first suggest that Celie deserves more than she has, tentatively but immediately she agrees. She initially allows other women to suggest what should be, but when she has contributed to Sophia's beatings, she feels guilt, and learns from that. Others, first Nettie, then Kate and Carrie, later Shug and Sophia, all define for her her own needs, even the need to fight.

Shug has done much of her own fighting before the novel begins, and we learn from Mr. _____ that Shug has done much of her fighting alone. Shug herself has suffered. She has been rejected by Albert, whom she had once loved passionately, been rejected by her parents, been demeaned and condemned by the community, and been pressured to give over the raising of her own three children. Shug presumably descended into chthonic retreat, hit rock bottom, and gave up any desire to please the patriarchy before Celie's story begins in *The Color Purple*. Where Shug found her own transcendence is not made absolutely clear, but the connection is made between wisdom and suffering in this syncretistic figure. Shug can accept her "otherness" because her singing allows her autonomy and acceptance on another level of community life. But she has clearly made her peace with the illogical, has been nurtured by both eros and the sensate, is motivated by intuitive ethics rather than orthodox conceptions of morality. It is in this that she blesses Celie. Despite oppression, Celie has not felt rage, but instead has bowed to the agonistic authority of her oppressors. Celie accepts the hierarchy because "sometimes it bees that way." It is Shug who articulates a credo of the sensate and irrational. When Celie is abruptly disabused of her outworn piety, and is about to abandon God altogether, it is Shug who refocuses Celie. Shug suggests that God is misunderstood when associated with power; instead, the two women realign the concept of God, creating something from which to feed their own souls and to find self-affirmation. This new deity is associated with the celebration of life's natural and sensual pleasures and all aspects of eros: maternal nurturance, sexual intimacy, and friendships between people. Their god is beyond gender and unconnected to social order; it is akin to roofleaf and the use of marijuana as a religious ritual, a deity much closer to the ancient goddess of the earth than to any of the gods who came to prominence after the merging of tribes and the fusing of divinity and inflexible authority.

Shug functions as facilitator of an essential transcendence for Celie. Shug is a maternal figure as well as Celie's lover: in a metaphoric sense she gives Celie life. Initially Shug also gives unconditional love and support but later she encourages Celie toward autonomy. Her love for Celie is generous; she sees in Celie another version of herself. The goddess mother gives birth to herself as Kore. Their love is primarily psychological and emotional rather than sexual, but it employs sex as the "sacrament of intimacy." It is clearly a more complex and loftier relationship than the male-female couplings which are juxtaposed to it.

But Shug is not absolutely generous. She is touchingly human, sometimes needy herself. Shug is a powerful heroine, having purpose, passion, perception, and power, all unrelated to goals of self-aggrandizement. Shug's only goal is personal fulfillment, becoming, and her wisdom is in her knowledge that this can be done only by accepting one's otherness and by investing in others. That is the boon she offers womankind.

Shug is the central figure in a larger community of support. Celie first felt the comfort of connection in her relationship with Nettie, and memory of that continued in her longing for Nettie. Eventually this empathy is revitalized in her gradual affiliation with the other women, and brings Celie out of her apathy and bleak acceptance. When Sophia leaves Harpo because he beats her, she goes to live with her sister Odessa, a scenario which touches Celie profoundly. She thinks of escaping to or with Nettie, "Thought so sharp it go through me like a pain. Somebody to run to. It seem too sweet to bear." But with it, Celie began to think analytically and in terms of options rather than of simply enduring. Emotion begins to return to Celie as she begins to feel sisterhood for women other than Nettie.

Sophia herself, the marvelous Amazon of the first section of the novel, had learned in her babyhood that there was some chance of prevailing if women fought, and so she continues to fight. Sophia is broken not by the oppressors within her own circle of hell, but because of the larger oppression, the larger tribal conflict, where white men and women oppress black men and women and always win. In that ring Sophia must learn to bend beneath oppression or die. To this end she transforms herself into Celie: "Every time they ast me to do something, Miss Celie, I act like I'm you. I jump right up and do just what they say" (p. 93). But Sophia is more analytical than the early Celie; she knows already that no obsequiousness will ever fully satisfy, and so she must kindle her own energy: "Good behavior ain't good enough for them, say Sophia. Nothing less than sliding on your belly with your tongue on they boots can even git they attention. I dream of murder, she say, I dream of murder sleep or wake" (p. 94). Moved but unaware of the irony, Celie escapes Sophia's testimony into a fantasy of God, "all white too, looking like some stout white man work at the bank" coming in his chariot to ferry Sophia to safety.

Later, when Celie learns of Mr. _____'s ultimate act of cruelty, the concealment of Nettie's letters, she transforms herself into Sophia. "All day long I act just like Sophia. I stutter. I mutter to myself. I stumble bout the house crazy for Mr. _____'s blood. In my mind he falling dead every which a way" (p. 125). In these letters the heroine reveals her own ominously chthonic withdrawals as she summons transformation, nurtures her rage by remaining calm, unthinking, a blank of gestative energy. Celie gives birth to her own anger, and only Shug keeps her from murdering Mr. _____ by reminding her of the larger rings of oppression, of the consequence of Sophia's crime and the promise of Nettie's return. But as part of this transformation, Celie gives up writing to God, that white man who looks like a banker, and "act just like all the other mens I know. Trifling, forgitful and lowdown" (p. 199).

This is a novel which assaults the reader in an intimate, personal way in the first few pages and then seduces with its awful, enchanting drive. It begins not with a hero striving for self-aggrandizement, but with the goddess's suppressed knowledge that the individual is immutably insignificant before the workings of the cosmos; however, the individual woman is not inconsequential before the factitious codings of the oppressor civilization unless she accepts herself as such. It is the novel as oxymoronic, being simultaneously beautiful and ugly, simultaneously raw and sensitive. From the very core of the suffering, it refocuses the reader on the horror of that single, relentlessly ongoing pattern of human behavior, agonistic ethno-centrism, and the gender polarity that is its psychological mutation. But there at the center of the violence and chaos is the hedonic goddess herself, syncretistic and protean, indiscriminately nurturing, prevailing, powerful, irrational. She blesses only empathy and acknowledges only change. The bearded white banker God disappears into her, as does the Harpo who would have beaten his wife to conform to the coding, as does the petulant and vapid Eleanor Jane who learns to abandon the oppressor's coding, as does Mr. _____ who suffers, gains wisdom, and so is given a name by the reempowered goddess.

Chapter XII

The Chthonic as Metaphor: Manifestations in *Beloved*, *Seachange;* Revision in *The Witches of Eastwick*

In the novels already discussed, the irrational forces which nurture the heroine have been discernible although essentially ephemeral. Emotions have been the catalysts of the power inherent in the goddess archetype, not only emotions which have been generated by culturally acceptable ethical underpinnings—care, commitment, and attachment—but also those which have been traditionally suspected by rational culture: rage, grief, and eros. The incorporation of these forces as elements of fiction which is otherwise realistic, in fact potentially naturalistic, is a notable characteristic of contemporary fiction, particularly fiction by women, a forum in which increasing alienation from traditional restrictions facilitates revelation of the goddess's story. The novels are grounded in social reality with heroines functioning in assertive and authoritarian ways previously associated with heroes. Their goals, however, differ from those of the hero and are much more tribal in nature. In pursuit of those goals, the heroines come up against external antagonists which are connected to social institutions, but the conflict is rooted in the clash of ethical systems with the voice of the feminine divine remaining distinct and tenacious. Deference to the cultural paradigm that insists on only a masculine divinity and the social hierarchy which evolved along with that emphasis, has been abandoned. As the goddess's voice becomes more articulate her internal conflicts are more clearly related to feminine ethics than to social oppressions.

A related yet more radical variation is a genre which uses techniques associated with expressionism. This genre expedites the goddess's story on the one hand, but it also offers evidence that the contrary process of manipulating aesthetics toward validation of the revised feminine is ongoing. Novels such as Toni Morrison's *Beloved*, Lois Gould's *Seachange*, and

185

John Updike's insidious *The Witches of Eastwick*, present chthonic heroines who are renewed through less ephemeral modes. These are stories of believable women in realistic situational conflicts, but they offer metaphoric characterizations of the supernatural: grief materializes as a ghost in *Beloved*, rage is a catalyst to metamorphosis in *Seachange*, eros leads to preternatural powers in *The Witches of Eastwick*. The effect is surreal, the impact disconcerting.

Toni Morrison's *Beloved* is another story of the chthonic mother. Her central character, the archetypal goddess figure, is Sethe, an American slave who, in the tradition of Medea and Hecuba, is motivated by profound love and absolute outrage to seize the last and only power left to her, the power to horrify. When Schoolteacher and his nephews, the brutal white slave owners who violated her, appear to return Sethe and her children to the bleakness of Sweet Home, Sethe chooses the last possible escape. She attempts to kill her sons, does kill her infant daughter, planning all the while also to kill herself, and so escape to the safety of death: "She just flew. Collected every bit of life she had made, all the parts of her that were precious and fine and beautiful, and carried, pushed, dragged them through the veil, out, away, over there where no one could hurt them. Over there. Outside this place, where they would be safe."[1]

The novel, which is set in Kentucky and Ohio during the period just before and just after the Civil War, pivots on this event. Like the characters in the fictional world of *The Color Purple,* the characters in *Beloved* live on the verge of extinction, oppressed by ever enlarging, ever more powerful oppressors. Many, like Sethe's mother-in-law Baby Suggs and Paul D., have chosen the carapace of apathy, withholding love and will, suspending commitment in order to ensure their individual survival. For them the answer, before emancipation, was to love nothing, or to "protect yourself and love small," immerse oneself in the comfort of the simplest aesthetics available, in color and the smallest stars. Alone against the rings of oppression, the individual as shown in these novels is passionless or crushed. But apathy leads to fragmentation, which Sethe is compelled to resist.

Oppression also functions to free the individual from internalized social codes as in *The Color Purple* and *Daughter of Earth.* Oppression can realign individuals into alternative communities, groupings akin to the ancient tribes whose conception of divinity sprang from participation in that group and whose religious rituals consisted of exercises to avert that which threatened and to lure that which benefited the group. In *Beloved* Sethe's tribe is her children and her affiliation with them so absolute as to obviate her other considerations, including those of a learned morality. In her efforts for her children Sethe is returned to the ethics generated from precultural sentience.

Sethe does not cut herself off from emotional commitment, but clings to it. On the verge of extinction, she strives toward life in the ancient manner, conceptualizing something to which she belongs which is larger than herself. Harrison points out that it was not the mystery of the universe which generated the first conception of divinity, but something more concrete, "The thing greater than man, the power not himself that makes for righteousness."[2] Sethe finds her own righteousness, her own divinity in her love for her children. Her participation in them generates courage and power, power which she herself claims is equal to the powerful anger of the murdered baby who haunts 124 Bluestone Road. Propelled by the intensity of her commitment to her children and by the intensity of her outrage when the whitemen "take her milk," she is compelled to action over apathy.

She tells Lillian Gardner of the milking, and is whipped for it. A chokecherry tree is engraved on her back. But again, brutality moves her to action. She escapes Sweet Home alone and on foot, badly injured, about to give birth, leaving behind Halle, the husband who is broken by brutality, and going toward her children in Ohio. Sethe creates by her actions a narrative of courage which generates still greater courage, generates a prodigious arrogance and willful independence which at its most awesome results in the death of Beloved, but which also sustains her during the eighteen years of social ostracism which follow her act, an act which was preverbal, and which cost much, but which she did not repudiate: "If they didn't get it right off—she could never explain" (p. 163).

Sethe's survival, Denver's miraculous birth, the fact that her children *are* kept from Schoolteacher and the nephews, Beloved's death, her sons' disappearance, her mother-in-law's misery—all came about because of Sethe's unquestioning commitment to something larger than herself, to her children. The commitment to the safety of the group also allows Sethe to view her own actions with a sense of their relativity rather than in terms of sin. She did not conceive of boundaries between her babies' lives and her own. She chose to ensure their safety "with a handsaw," seemingly unaware of "where the world stopped and she began" (p. 164).

At Sweet Home Sethe had learned the strength of community, a community defined by racial hierarchy more than gender polarity, but a community which had been allowed a modicum of pride. In the days before Gardner's death blacks at Sweet Home called themselves men, were a tribe unto themselves, giving each in belonging a special strength, a self-affirmation which would fail them as individuals when change occurs. After his death brutality descends and severs the community of slaves at Sweet Home. Sethe, Sweet Home's only woman, is the one who surfaces unbreakable. Having learned her own lessons; having heard stories of herself, including her mysterious birth (her mother had kept only her, while "throwing away" the children the white crew of the slave ship conceived in her); having listened to Baby Suggs "A man ain't nothing but a man, . . .

But a son? Well now, that's *somebody*"; having known the power of her own love for her children who were not sold away from her, Sethe has developed a sustaining ethic. Convinced of the centrality of the mother-children connection, Sethe has grounded herself in this commitment and there found the transcendent energy to escape and survive.

Sethe's is not a learned but an inherent ethic. There is nothing about her experience, about the social institution in which she was raised that rewards the kind of intensive mothering which characterizes Sethe. There is no stable social structure from which she can take models of behavior or which allocate social rewards. Within the larger ring of oppression she is supposed not to be capable of the same level of attachment to her children which white women have to theirs. Beyond that the situational conflict places her outside the influence of any dominant culture and allows her to manifest innate compulsions.

Like other chthonic heroines, she becomes an aberrational figure among her own people, the Negro community. To them, Sethe's actions are too assertive, too stubborn, too arrogant for a people who have cultivated apathy, have protected themselves by not loving too much. The passion of Sethe's motherlove embarrasses her own people; they are more comfortable with known patterns, with tragedy and loss. Sethe's emotion seems incontinent, it disquiets them, but it is Sethe's prevailing arrogance, her unwillingness to become contrite, to seek their merciful forgiveness after her release from jail that makes her a permanent outsider. "Sethe's crime was staggering and her pride outstripped even that," Ella asserts (p. 256). But Sethe answers only to her own daemon.

Sethe first discovers the power of her rage when she is facing death by the Ohio River, "trying to get to her three children, one of whom was starving for the food she carried; that after her husband had disappeared; that after her milk had been stolen, her back pulped, her children orphaned" (p. 31). At that point, as she later tells Denver, "*something* came up out of the earth into her—like a freezing, but moving too, like jaws inside" (p. 31). Sethe is metamorphosed, she becomes a snake, and in her rage, she is eager to kill the whiteboy she expects will appear before her. Instead it is Amy, the white girl who is Sethe's almost supernatural deliverer. Amy is mother to the weak and wounded Sethe, midwife to her newborn daughter. Together the three form a peculiar tableau: "two throw-away people, two lawless outlaws—a slave and a barefoot whitewoman with unpinned hair—wrapping a ten-minute-old baby in the rags they wore" (p. 84).

Sethe herself acknowledges that brutality first changed her. She had been "once soft, trusting," before Schoolteacher. But her courageous escape also changed her. In a world where to love anything too much was dangerous, Sethe's "too thick love" strengthened her, allowing her to manage the miraculous escape from Sweet Home to Ohio and her children which their father, Halle, could not. Once having done it, the act itself expanded her and seemingly validated her intuitive ethics. In those twenty-eight days between her arrival and Schoolteacher's, Sethe's love for her children seemed to become even more intense. It was a force so enlarging, so inherently ennobling, that Sethe never repudiates it, not when her neighbors shun her, not when the ghost of the child herself comes back to haunt her. For Sethe there is in that love a spiritual comfort which is more traditionally associated with religious faith. Even her mother-in-law, Baby Suggs, once called "holy" by the Negro community, cannot "approve or condemn Sethe's rough choice" (p. 180), although Baby Suggs does repudiate God. Even when Paul D. is horrified by the story of Beloved's death, Sethe is unmoved: "Too thick, he said. My love was too thick. What he know about it? Who in the world is he willing to die for?" (p. 203). Willing to die to take them to "the other side," to be with her own mother who was kept from her, Sethe's focus blurs the edges of separateness between herself and her children; and even when her dead daughter returns and the antics of the ghost drive away her sons, she sustains herself with the recollection of the power she had held in her hands which forced Schoolteacher to back away: "she had something in her arms that stopped him in his tracks. He took a backward step with each jump of the baby heart until finally there were none" (p. 164). It is the same hedonic aggression shown by Hecuba and Medea, an aggression which the oppressors fail to understand and so categorize. Schoolteacher abandons Sethe and her three living children, comforting himself that freedom has returned this Negro family to "the cannibal life they preferred." Despite the cost and the consequences, Sethe continues to believe in the absolute rightness of her action: "I took and put my babies where they'd be safe" (p. 164), she tells Paul D., who is frightened of such arrogance. Later Stamp Paid will come to understand this hedonic aggression and try to explain it to Paul D. Sethe had tried to "outhurt the hurter," a strategy which the oppressed can fathom if not approve.

For Paul D., Stamp Paid, and Ella, all representatives of the social community to which Sethe belongs, "more important than what Sethe had done was what she claimed" (p. 164). But for Sethe, who answers only to herself, the results justify the action. The compulsion was something in her blood and the end, horrible though it was, justified the means. Despite Beloved's death: "They ain't at Sweet Home. Schoolteacher ain't got them," she tells Paul D., emphasizing the relativity of the events rather than accepting guilt for the death. Sethe's ethic is unconnected to any larger cultural model; it sets her outside her own community, yet it emphasizes attachment over loss, relationship over individuation.

Sethe bequeaths her strength to Denver, contributing to Denver's self-image by infusing in her a mythology of herself that did not allow for victimization, surrender, or defeat. It is Sethe's idea that Denver saved herself, "pulled the white girl out of the hill" (p. 42), when it became clear that her mother would not survive to give birth to her. Denver takes strength also from her mother's oddness, from their position outside the dominant culture. "Denver had taught herself to take pride in the condemnation Negroes heaped on them; the assumption that haunting was done by an evil thing looking for more. None of them knew the downright pleasure of the enchantment, of not suspecting but *knowing* the things behind things" (p. 37). Denver is nourished by her mother's story and the irrational thing it produced. Eventually Denver finds the strength to save them both.

The narration allows the reader an intimacy with Sethe which precludes any judgment that she is either a crazy or an unloving mother. When Paul D. proposes that they have a baby together, a clearheaded, logical assessment of that responsibility frightens Sethe. She ruminates without irony: "Needing to be good enough, alert enough, strong enough, *that* caring-again. Having to stay alive just that much longer. O Lord, she thought, deliver me. Unless carefree, motherlove was a killer" (p. 133). For Sethe, motherhood compelled responsibility, motherhood was a commitment to life, but also to sanity. Sethe is envious of others, particularly Halle, who seem to have been able to allow themselves the option of a psychotic break. As part of something larger than herself, Sethe cannot consider a destructive separation from her community, cannot consider embracing either apathy or madness: "Other peoples' brains stopped, turned around and went on to something new, which is what must have happened to Halle. And how sweet that would have been . . . what a relief to stop it right there. But her three children were chewing sugar teat under a blanket on their way to Ohio and no butter play would change that" (p. 71). There is an unexamined exasperation in Sethe's reflection upon her husband, whose break came because he was helplessly concealed in the barn when Schoolteacher's nephews took Sethe's milk. Such sensibility offends Sethe. In fiction some characters are broken, driven to madness, or escape into apathy. Only the heroine acts constructively, if with awful consequences.

The remaining conflict is an internal one. The ghost who eventually materializes is a manifestation of Sethe's own grief. It is the individual child, sacrificed as part of a larger plan to get her children safely out of a brutal life. That Beloved alone died was accidental, and only related to the larger good. Sethe claims: "I'll explain to her, even though I don't have to" (p. 201). But the child herself, Denver, and Sethe's sons as well, are invested in the task of becoming individuals. They are unable to comprehend Sethe's desperate actions, unable to fathom the horror escaped at Sweet Home, and perceive only that she is a threat to each of them as individuals. Despite the evidence of her everyday love, Denver dreams of her mother killing her, fantasizes romantically that her father will come and save her, engages in dissembling to protect herself: I spent all of my outside self loving Ma'am so she wouldn't kill me" (p. 207). Eventually it is Denver, strengthened by both her mother's bequest of rebellious arrogance and her grandmother's bequest of anxious wisdom—

> But you said there was no defense.
> "There ain't."
> Then what do I do?
> "Know it, and go on out the yard. Go on."

—who becomes the link back to the community for herself and her mother.

Sethe's conflict with Beloved is something which Denver believes she can understand: "Sethe was trying to make up for the handsaw; Beloved was making her pay for it." It has all the characterizations of grief work, with the bereaved mother reluctant to work through the grief because it is all that is left of the child: "Sethe's greatest fear was the same one Denver had had in the beginning—that Beloved might leave." Curiously, Sethe confronts her grief twenty years after the death, just when she has been freed of her responsibility to her other children, just when Denver is old enough. The conflict has been waiting in the center of Sethe's life; the baby has been haunting the house, but did not demand full attention until Sethe is on the verge of yet another change, this one heralded by the arrival of Paul D., a "singing man."

Sethe's refusal to be victimized or to allow whites to "dirty" her "best thing, her beautiful magical best thing" has been deemed "misdirected" by her own larger community. Despite Sethe's integrity, she is haunted by the demands of the individual child whom she herself had to make a victim. When the baby arrives, a full grown woman demanding an explanation, Sethe asks forgiveness, but does not really want it. It would be the last letting go; her daughter would be lost to the "disremembered and unaccounted for." Denver and eventually Paul D. have to help Sethe make the final transition out of the constrictions of maternal eros which for Sethe has included twenty years of anger from a daughter whose throat she cut, a daughter who was a part of herself.

The novel ends with an emphasis on healing, empathy, and change. Sethe has metamorphosed yet again, as has Denver and Beloved. Sethe's long chthonic cycle is over; she has resolved both her isolation and grief itself, has disappeared. Denver has grown up and now mothers her mother. The new season is one of harmony and order. It appears to be logical, rational, and temporary.

Lois Gould's novel *Seachange,* like *Beloved* and *The Color Purple,* presents a heroine whose metamorphosis is in reaction to brutality. It is a contemporary version not of Daphne's metamorphosis, but of Caenis's, whose transformation came after violation. "Caeneus the Lapith, who had once been a woman," is listed among those who went on the Calydonian boar hunt with Atalanta.[3] She was probably once the local goddess of Lapith; her metamorphosis is told of in Apollodorus but Ovid claims that Caenis had "turned blank all thoughts of marriage" and was walking alone on a beach when Neptune appeared and raped her. He "mounted her before she caught her breath. He was well pleased and thought that she was too."[4] Caenis herself was not pleased, and would have wished to resist the victimization, the defeat of the will, but was not as fortunate as Daphne. Caenis's metamorphosis comes after the rape, as the victim envies the power of the rapist and is driven to merge herself with the ascendant tribe. By the time that Ovid tells the story, metamorphosis is the power of the god and Caenis asks Neptune to make her a man so she will never be "taken" by one again. She becomes Caeneus, subscriber to the heroic ideal, celebrant of the violent rites of bonded males, hunters, and warriors.

Lois Gould presents a contemporary version of Caenis's story. Her novel opens as her heroine, Jessie Waterman, is held captive by a black gunman who has broken into her apartment and raped her with the gun. The reader enters the consciousness of the bound woman after the rape as she lies on the floor in her bedroom awaiting the arrival of her husband, who is due momentarily. The rapist, "tranquillized by her clever use of nonstruggle, which he took as abject surrender," has gone to amass booty from other rooms. In her nether world of detachment and terror, Jessie contemplates the metaphoric centrality of the male in culture, recalling images of historic women who died with or for their husbands. She tries to "conjure some brave and selfless act that she might yet commit, without hope of escape," that would save Roy from coming unexpectedly upon the black gunman. As she rummages around in her mind past the comfortably familiar image of herself as the victim, now trying to pull out a rationale for *not* dying to save Roy, she discovers her resentment.

> Jessie would have made a conscious choice—save me, not him. Let it happen, whatever it is. Let it happen to *him*. Or, if he's lucky, let him kill the other one. Or both of them, scuffling for the gun. Not my fault, not my responsibility; look, my hands were tied. I couldn't help it. Anyway, I hate Roy. (*Hate* Roy? She had never thought that before. She took it calmly.) If B. G. killed him I'd be free. Then B. G. would kill me too. I'd still be free. She repeated the sequence several times. It sounded right. Almost musical.[5]

Jessie squirms under the options; she has never developed skill at decision-making, nor at establishing priorities other than the deferring to men.

"Crazy cunt" her husband calls her with gruff affection. Her friend Kate, however, describes her differently: "Quite apart from her physical perfection, she was a strange and wonderful creature, full of sudden discomforting insights and improbable passions." Kate values her, but to Roy and the patriarchy he represents, Jessie is the disempowered goddess, Cassandra, her intuition considered irrational, her power reduced by patronizing. A dutiful daughter of patriarchy, she has never expressed resentment at the epithet. Instead she endures it wryly: "She was not, after all, a new woman, but an 'old' woman in a new time. . . . Yet there was something, had been something, askew all along. A sense of displacement, or of never having been placed" (p. 22).

The fictional world of Jessie Waterman, which is urban, monied, and sophisticated, is revealed as another reign of the phallus. Sexual violence is a common crime. Although considered traumatic, rape is something which Jessie is expected to recover quickly from. Instead, the experience transforms and energizes Jessie. She comes to see that the threat of sexual violence is the main tool of social control and that it perpetuates and infuses the established hierarchy. The overt sexual violence of the gunman is only different in degree from the covert behavior of her husband. The gun used to rape Jessie becomes synonymous with her husband's phallus. Roy himself has a "negative pull on women" and is "a relic from the golden age of misogyny." His sensitivity has atrophied from lack of use: it is an unnecessary accoutrement in the aggressive male world, even a liability. Roy's participation in the agonistic ethic of that world makes him as much a part of Jessie's victimization as the armed intruder.

Following the rape, which apparently included her husband's successful participation at gunpoint, Jessie withdraws into a chthonic depression, moves to a cottage on Andrea Island outside New York City, and responds to her husband's intrusive questions with a lengthening silence. The silence of women in chthonic interludes is disquieting. It is ominous, as was Persephone's. Like Persephone, Jessie's silence is a response to victimization, to displacement, to the loss of choice. Jessie talks only to her daughters and to her friend Kate: "I feel like Persephone, except I can't even get pomegranates. They're out of season," she tells Kate.

Jessie Waterman had been a beautiful Madison Avenue model, successful wife and mother, apparently well adjusted enough, sophisticated enough to integrate the experience of rape, and expected to return promptly to her otherwise perfect life. She had well developed hedonic qualities, and was appropriately uncomfortable with anything agonistic, denying aggression in herself. But rage surfaces during the depression following rape, and Jessie develops a passionate interest in the dynamics of power. Like Atwood's heroine in *Surfacing*, she understands suddenly that her own complicity is necessary if she is to be a victim. She reflects on the issues of femininity and power, concluding that female power is circular, oozing, gestative, but lacking the power to self-start. She envisions herself as split, receptive, feminine, a victimized self as occupant of an internal space in an otherwise malleable whole, and capable of being destroyed from within as well as without. Concentrating on the development of her will, dormant from lack of cultural demand, Jessie begins the process of metamorphosis. Bent on purging herself of the weakness that allowed victimization, she determines to "kill" the feminine, vulnerable Jessie and deliberately develop her masculine, agonistic side. It is the violence of feminine power within herself that facilitates this transformation. The goddess is ever regenerative. Rape substitutes for the missing self-start mechanism.

The physical violation of the gunman is juxtaposed with Roy Waterman's possessive and compulsive touching of his wife and daughters. The male touch is deprecating, whether father's or husband's or rapist's. There are no sensitive men in this novel, even the meteorologists who strive to subdue the hurricane Minerva are presented as rapists, violators of the irrational, deprecators of the feminine. They are bent on subduing through assault, on controlling and defining: "They would capture her and make her civilized" (p. 65). Jessie feels an intense sympathy for the hurricane whose destruction is analogous to her own:

> They would bottle their ejaculate in bomb casing and send it flying into her warm center. The bombs would go off in there, setting fire to her. It had been done successfully a number of times. Gang rape as a tool of basic research. Twelve of them, thirteen — all heroes — attacking her repeatedly at regular intervals.... They would tame the bitch; that was how they thought of it. They knew if they could hurt her enough — if they could change her internal form — she would weaken. She would destroy herself.
> [Page 66]

To avoid victimization or self-destruction Jessie takes on the accoutrements of dominating masculine behavior. Her tone becomes icy and patronizing; her manner develops an ominous undertone. Jessie has perceived that it is not enough for men to dominate by tradition, they must also perpetuate the threat of violence. Her analysis of the social institutions she lives in is not unlike Keuls's view of ancient Athens. Social order, which is necessarily hierarchical to preserve the status of the dominant tribe, is perpetuated through dynamics of control and obedience. The subliminal threat of rape maintains the social hierarchy at every step. Issues of ownership and need are enforced through the threat of physical punishment. "Do *exactly* as I say, and you won't get hurt." Women come to believe that they are protected by the balance of social power; in exchange they are needed by men. It is much the same dynamic as between parents and children. Polarized pairs remain the organizing factor. The lesser of the pair accepts subjugation and potential victimization as the natural and righteous disposition of the hierarchy.

Gould suggests that the intensity of Minerva's destruction might well have been a response to the attempts of civilized man to disempower her. Under cover of the hurricane—with which Jessie feels an intimate connection—Jessie repudiates her own femininity along with her social disposition as victim. She merges herself with Kate Saville, having become grudgingly aware of the need for the female in life. But like Hesiod and Semonides, she banalizes and resents the feminine, devalues emotion, deprecates intuition, goading Kate but at the same time compelling her attention. By embracing the masculine constellation of violence-power-sex, Jessie becomes a part of the dominant tribe, her rite of passage a violent copulation with the Coastguardsman and the rape of Kate.

Jessie understands that part of the banalization of feminine power has been in the act of rendering women defenseless. All the acceptable weapons are male. Coded into appropriate femininity is repulsion at violence, queasiness at guns, repression of rage. Women perceive themselves as potential victims, prepare and expect to be protected, accept that their own powers, intuition, and gestative energy, are silly, irrational, childlike. She offers the same revelation to Kate. "As for the weapon, she understood that too. His power had less to do with the gun he was using than with her reaction to it. Her repulsion, her rage, her hostility. He had made her see that they were all his weapons, not hers. He had used them all against her" (p. 137).

Responding to the violation, to her new insights into the order of things, Jessie metaphorically transforms herself through force of will. She organizes a new tribe because she believes she has the right to do it. She escapes the dominant culture as she symbolically abandons her earlier self. When she surfaces on Reef Island with her daughter, stepdaughter, and eventually Kate, not even Roy recognizes her. She has given birth to herself as a man, a ruling figure of the dominant tribe, misogynist, patronizing, violent. Jessie's new tribe is a miniature of the larger social model, except that there is the promise that Diane and Robin will grow up to be women of a different order, women unlike Kate or the old Jessie. Instead of passive daughters of patriarchy who are powerless and primed for victimization, Diane and Robin will have seized their own weapons, developed the will and allowed the violence within themselves. Autonomous outsiders by choice, like the ancient Amazons, like Circe and Calypso, they live just beyond the parameters of civilization, but in their isolation they have escaped the violence and power of the prevalent order. Jessie Waterman is another fictional embodiment of the motif of the banished goddess, but her story is told without the revisionist's deprecation. Her seachange is a change in perception of the righteous order of civilization; it leads to a developed defense and to the choice, like Lillith's, to live outside.

Theoretically, archetypes reappear in literature, regardless of the author's sex and even when they are distorted for allegorical purposes. The male tribe who composed mythology into its firm form were not disposed to present the goddess sympathetically. Her concerns were opposed to their cultural ascendancy. When she was given voice as with Medea and Hecuba and Antigone, she reveals herself as disquieting and enigmatic. Since her ethics and motives are unclear and her behavior rebellious to the interests of a civilization convinced of its own righteousness, she is dismissed as either dangerous or fatuous. Her discrete ethical motivation put her in conflict with patriarchal goals and made her baffling in a way that Sethe or Jessie is not. Revision was inclined to evaluate her in terms of the evolving polarities of Western discourse. Medea did not serve civilization; she was therefore a barbarian as Sethe is not. Hecuba's behavior was unfathomable to Agamemnon, so he defined her as inhuman and turned away in horror as Schoolteacher did. Deprecation is still a comfortable, serviceable response when confronted with what is feminine and alien. Even Antigone, whose ethics were indisputably lofty and who did not engage in any distasteful display of hedonic aggression, was perfunctorily dispatched in what might well be the single socially accepted act of hedonic aggression, suicide.

When the goddess appears in the work of a male author, as with Homer's Circe, or Hawthorne's Hester, she is an entity outside the confines of the acceptably civilized. But recent scholarship has allowed for more understanding of the heroine's ethics and presumably released even male writers from the proscriptions and expectations of traditional gender polarity. So the archetypal heroine may appear more discernibly in novels by men as well as women. John Updike's *The Witches of Eastwick* is a case in point.

The three women of Updike's novel represents figures for whom the ethical systems are to conflict. The novel opens with "The Coven" in chthonic retreat from the preoccupations of the dominant culture. Jane Smart, Sukie Rougemont, and Alexandra Spofford, three divorcees in their middle and late thirties, have discovered in their community and their position outside the mainstream of patriarchal concerns that they have certain supernatural powers. Ostensibly free from the imposed requirements of patriarchal concerns, these women have powers which seem to be the rewards of having located the divinity within, a discovery made possible after divorce, after "being left . . . or doing the leaving" (p. 178). As the novel opens, Alexandra is annoyed by a crowd on the beach so she conjures up a thunderstorm by summoning transformative energy within herself. She does this with much the same perfunctory arrogance that Circe used to clear her island of intruders. Alexandra's power flowed from this mere reappropriation of her assigned self, achieved not until midlife. Not until midlife did she truly believe she had a right to exist, that the forces of nature had not created her as an afterthought and companion—bent rib as the infamous *Malleus Maleficarum* had it—but as the mainstay of the continuing Creation, as the daughter of a daughter and a woman whose daughters in turn would bear daughters.[6]

Alexandra makes her living by sculpting Venus figures which bear a remarkable resemblance to the Paleolithic goddess figurines uncovered by archaeologists. She is the most maternal of the three witches as well as the most sympathetic, in part because of her sensitivity to traditionally accepted ethics as well as to her own rogue daemon. In the first third of the novel the three women are united into an insulated alternative community characterized by the tribal eros which fortifies such groups; but this one also has a preternatural dimension as well as an aura of opprobrium.

Nina Auberbach has pointed out that fraternities are traditional bastions of privilege while "a community of women may suggest less the honor of fellowship than an antisociety, an austere banishment from both social power and biological rewards"; yet membership in certain of these groups, including Updike's coven, allows the participants an unexpected power.[7] Auberbach points to the shared vision of the mythological Graie; that trinity was another of those which had its roots in the matriarchal constellation and appeared in pictorial art which predated mythology. In revision, the Graie became a gothic anomaly. Auberbach notes that mythology placed groups of women outside the parameters of civilization and used them as backdrops in the drama of the hero, "as raw material, from which a solitary adventurer will chisel his heroism."[8]

A community of women is knit together by social instincts as is any tribe; and by its nature such a community evolves a sense of the group, its nascent divinity, which is not masculine and does not subscribe to the conventional expectation that women attain adulthood through masculine approval. Auberbach suggests that the ethics of women's communities are associated with irrational modes, with sources of transformation and birth.[9] That which strengthens and empowers the group is a manifestation of eros, intimate participation in the lives of others and therefore of the group.

As with more familiar forms of eros—between lovers or mother and child—the women of the coven are acutely sensitive to aura and nuance among themselves, but in Updike's fictional world their omniscience extends into the outside community as well: "In the right mood and into their third drinks they could erect a cone of power above them like a tent to the zenith, and know at the base of their bellies who was sick, who was sinking into debt, who was loved, who was frantic, who was burning, who was asleep in a remission of life's bad luck" (p. 33). Their sensitivity is individual, but they are empowered by participation in "the infrangible triangle, the cone of power." Through Sukie it is revealed that in the three of them, this "triune body" has a maternal quality, a coziness "being the closest approach to a mother she had ever had" (p. 133). Alexandra calls it "Mother-power." Significantly, however, no one of the three is personally involved with her own biological children. This void is persistently disturbing. One cannot help but note the absence of maternal affections; but the design of this fictional community is specific. The exclusion of their children testifies to the anomalous, vaguely reprehensible nature of the group. As a device of plot this characterization is akin to abstract expressionism; a deliberate and effective stroke, it delineates the author's evaluation of such a community. The fact that children are perfunctorily excluded marks the group as scurrilous as well as aberrational.

Updike's genuine affection for his witches, particularly Alexandra, sometimes obfuscates an artful deprecation. Ultimately this sisterhood is derisively presented. The women are pitiable if sympathetic souls. Updike characterizes their sexual adventures by foisting on the reader the notion of the divorcee as vamp. Their behavior is relentlessly irresponsible; Updike makes it analogous to the trivial distraction of a board game. They do not have consuming passions, or flights into eros, instead they "land on all the properties." These affairs with married men are banal at best, dangerous at worst. The lovers they choose are bumblers; Alexandra's wears a hat during intercourse; Sukie's bludgeons his wife to death. While the friendship between the women is to be accepted as the source of their unusual powers, the community itself is viable only until a male interloper arrives to interrupt the rhythm of their weekly gatherings, to weaken the potency of the coven by imposing his own brand of evil. Darryl Van Horne captivates not one, but each of the witches. While sharing them he tempts them away from each other, diffuses their unity, attenuates their newly gained insight into their essential selves, and seduces them back into offering homage to the metaphoric centrality of the male. That the coven becomes a cult of personality around this reincarnated Lucifer testifies to its inherent lack of integrity. In mythological revision the dance of the Maenads could not remain the inexplicable joyousness of the feminine divine, of participation in the feminine group and the flux of phenomena. Instead, it demanded explanation in terms of a masculine catalyst; so aesthetics created the latercomer Dionysus, himself a somewhat enigmatic divinity, yet one conjured by the accepted formula; androgynous or not, Dionysus is the son of the god.

There is much in Updike's characterization of the witches which touches on the authentic archetype. During her marriage Alexandra's chthonic retreats had been depressions. She had grown to loathe her body and to yearn toward that which was outside her window, the earth, the larger world that expanded beyond the claustrophobia of her marriage.

Outside, she could take flight, her astral self leaving behind its heavy shell. It was this yearning as if toward her "other self" that propelled her to divorce. Eventually, freed from patriarchal constraint and living outside the orthodox community of married America, Alexandra became more transformative. She began to see the rhythms of nature repeated in herself. Ceasing to be goal oriented, she engaged herself in the seasonal process. She perceived the onset of fall not as the death of summer but as a rebirth of the self which "answered to something diffuse and gentle within Alexandra, her sense of merge, her passive ability to contemplate a tree and feel herself a rigid trunk with many arms running to their tips with sap, to become the oblong cloud oddly alone in the sky or the toad hopping from the mower's path" (p. 97). Yet her transformation is tentative, and her sense of her essential self precarious. While empathetic in his portrait of her dissatisfactions, Updike still manages to imply that her current transformation is a lark, a detour into irresponsibility rather than manifestation of some permanent or enlightened rebellion, of the acceptance of otherness. Alexandra's powers and the strength of the coven disintegrates before the specters of competition and guilt.

A second coven materializes in Eastwick; like adolescent cliques, the popularity and power of one increases as the other fades. The competition between women interferes with Alexandra's sculpting as well as with the efforts of the original witches to remain bonded. Questions of individual guilt help splinter the original group. With their relationship with Darryl Van Horne, a relationship which shifts their focus from the group to the individual male, they begin their cycle back into patriarchy where women are powerless, unsure of themselves, and defined by society in terms of their relationships to men. The relationship with Darryl leads first to petty jealousy among women and then to betrayal among women. The trinity of the Charities of ancient vase painting became the competitive goddesses in Paris's story. The Graiae became not the goddess as trinity but this gothic trio who facilitate Perseus's achievement.

Alexandra is most pained by their betrayal of Jenny, a Kore version of themselves. She was "a version of each mature, divorced, disillusioned, empowered woman's younger self." Updike describes the young woman as an ingenue, one of their own daughters perhaps who had "trusted them, had confided herself to them as a woman usually first confides herself to a man, risking destruction in the determination to *know*" (p. 209). Once a welcomed novice who was privy to the illicit antics of the witches and Van Horne, Jenny abruptly ended their idyll by marrying Van Horne. Angry and vengeful, the trio of witches direct the "teeniest-weeniest psychokinetic push" toward Jenny's fear of cancer and the disease materializes. Jane and Sukie appear to grow "strong on Jenny's death," though Alexandra wilts. She is overcome by guilt, as Celie had been when she betrayed Sophia. Both women have betrayed their own ethics, sinned against the goddess's morality which fosters young life indiscriminately and is rooted in the tribe. Alexandra throws away the poppet which had represented Jenny, hoping to banish the Ker and to repudiate her own power, but Jenny's illness continues without abatement. As Alexandra struggles with the issue of individual responsibility, the less emotional, more perfunctory Jane dismisses their part in Jenny's demise, stressing the relativity of power, the impossibility of severing the continuum of life and death, and the possibility that their efforts to fertilize her illness had been an act of merge with the immutable plan of nature.

In contrast to other heroines, Updike's witches seemed to have gained little from their chthonic retreat. They are not strengthened, have not gained more validated egos or a sense of comfort with the ubiquitous irrational. Instead, the witches reject "otherness," which in Updike's fictional world is fraught with irresponsibility. They repudiate their community and their powers and flee back into the "socially sanctioned existential cowardice" of marriage. Updike does not leave them split off and enigmatically sagacious as Hawthorne did Hester; instead, he has them scurry back into the shelter and moral dependency of orthodox feminine behavior. These women fall into older patterns of characterization in American fiction. They forsake knowledge of the world and return to a prelapsarian mould. In mythological revision the powerful goddess, giver of all gifts, became the dangerously irresponsible Pandora; in contemporary revision she is banal and silly, with just enough good sense to repudiate her own power.

The novel ends as does *Beloved*, with a sense of the transitional nature of all experience, the relativity of all perception. The witches of Eastwick have cycled back into the separateness of women in patriarchy. Their powers are merely a memory, exaggerated perhaps, legendary, ephemeral, ripe for allegorical revision: "The witches are gone, vanished; we were just an interval in their lives, and they in ours" (p. 307). Their witchery was a manifestation of the unruly, irrepressible feminine divine. Its appearance and disappearance, therefore, is characterized by an ethos of transition and transformation. In Updike's rendition their story is in the ancient tradition of mythological revision. The syncretistic goddesses surface from the objective universe, puzzle the spectators with their "otherness," their dissatisfactions, and their power, but eventually they disappear, or merge docilely with the agenda of civilization. In this case they surrender their "wise craft" much as a child might precociously determine that she is not ready for a dangerous toy; they comply with their own vitiation. The return of the patriarchal order at the close of the novel comes about through their own complicity. The hallowed, tangible constructions of civilization are again in tact. A reliably rational order has returned and the voice of the goddess is again rendered mute. Revision insists that she prefers the silence.

Afterthought

Human beings are the only species which has cerebral encounters with abstract issues, the only species which asks metaphysical questions. Such confrontations are potentially overwhelming. Propelled by this anxiety and the drive for life, the species adapted by evolving the process of religious ritual and mythmaking. Thus imaginative defenses were created to meet a specific and universal need, and human tribes envisioned spirits which they might placate, banish, or lure, and subsequently evolved a conception of divinity which was an aspect of the participation mystique, of eros, that powerful emotional sanction that comes of belonging to something larger than the self. The tribal divinity and the stories that came from that were at first closely connected to the primary anxieties: what can be done to guarantee food and fertility, what can be done to protect the children, what happens after death. Presumably the tribal ancestors of slaves evolved storytelling in the same self-affirming pattern as did the tribal progenitors of kings, both propelled by the same phylogenetic and ontogenetic urgency. Presumably the mothers of children in all tribes did as well.

Eventually other concerns, social and ecological, entered into the continuum of mythmaking with disparate peoples justifying their claims to land and prominence in their own stories about their own gods but continuing always to conceptualize themselves as heroic, as chosen. Eventually tribes conquered and amalgamated and affiliations realigned themselves; the process of conceptualizing divinity as an outgrowth of the favored collective mutated and the imaginative ability to envision oneself as heroic and intimately connected to that divinity was limited by culture although not by inherent need or tendency. The descendants of heroes continued to identify themselves with that potential. He who is the repository, the embodiment of community values takes his imaginative influence from that status. But while women certainly remain heroic in the stories of their own becoming, when they turn to test their mental constructs against those allocated significance by the recorded tradition of their culture, they find that the heroic event itself has been drastically curtailed and no longer includes the familiar elements of feminine experience. The fictional events

201

in which Daphne escapes victimization, in which Danae gives birth alone and takes her child to safety, in which Atalanta proves herself the autonomous equal of the male hunters, have all been eliminated from contention.

The indisputable significance to the species of the mother's heroism in saving her child makes it difficult not to acknowledge the artifical nature of these restrictions. Traditional exegesis, however, does not. But such a conceptual limitation was pivotal to the changing of the gods, and to the acceptance by women themselves of the insignificance if not the stigma of their group experience. Presumably when the slave is freed from slavery, he willingly abandons his stigmatization and returns himself to his legacy of heroism, declares himself once again righteously empowered, a son of god. But for women the internalization of vulnerability, culpability, and secondary status prescribed by these archaic constructs of gender has no such facile exit, no conceivable end. The new laws of the tribe, tradition, include the nonheroism of women. "The savage who is breaking the laws of his tribe has all the world—totem, tabus, earth, sky and all—against him. He cannot be at peace with God," Murray writes,[1] yet that is where women have been left, alienated from both divinity and heroism. When the ever-optimistic, archetypal strivings of the individual imagination clash with this ungiving tradition, the individual retreats, wanting to be at peace with theological and cultural order, accepting guilt, wanting to avoid the social punishment of ostracism and further alienated from her own imaginative possibilities by the fact that extant literature offers no transcendent models of autonomous affirmation, no daughters of the goddess.

But the elimination of the feminine divine and the revision of her myth are really quite discernible innovations in the course of cultural history, a course which does not necessarily reflect conceptual or moral progress. These innovations were implemented as mankind grappled with abstract concerns over authority and civilized order and resolved them in ways which were often primitive and unjust, which were always self-serving to the empowered. At the height of his conceptual tyranny he enshrined his own transcendent, infrangible signifier, an angry, ominous god who rewarded his constituency by sanctioning their archaic social hierarchy which included man's control over women's sexual practices, and his right to deprecate her heroism. Simultaneously, this took from women the essential function of myth itself, self-affirmation.

Cultural concepts of heroism continue to affect people's inner realities. Let us return to a contemporary scenario. An airplane encounters engine trouble as it descends. Two passengers sit side by side, seatbelts buckled, alone with their own defenses. One immediately constructs scenarios of action and heroism, envisions escaping through the nearest window, of rescuing two or three others on the way out. The other thinks only in blasts of hopeless panic, envisioning vulnerability, hoping to be saved, having no legacy of imaginative power, having been schooled only in the "clever use of non-struggle." Behind them sits a mother with her small children, empowered not by culture but by her own preverbal, irrational motherlove its own unyielding, transcendent force.

Although initially it appears that there is little left in Western verbal tradition from which to build an image which is both feminine and powerful, there is evidence of a continuum in mythmaking that suggests itself as the solution. The pursuit of the image must be done by reversing the process of revision by which she was buried under patriarchal interpretation. Mankind clings to his theological order, this male monotheism, in part because it remains a comfortable, self-serving paradigm which allows the tacit endorsement of his sexual tyranny and makes all subsequent diminishment of that tyranny an act of largesse. But beyond that, subscribing to this order places man outside the flux of phenomena, insulates him from the irrational, seemingly overwhelming aspects of human life. In imagination, at least, man has control and all he need do is continue his tenacious condemnation of the pagan deities, including the goddess, and the chthonic religions. From the lofty height of his ordered, rational monotheism they are labeled base and primitive, connected as they are to the accidental and passionate, to pregnancy, childbirth, copulation, conception, illness, death, eros, motherlove, and blind rage, all those things to which the individual must periodically submit despite his will. To another view of experience, these chthonic interludes are not chaotic regression, but merely another aspect of ongoing human experience—one which may strengthen the will, validate the ego, enhance the future. Such experience may offer a conduit to wisdom.

Literary analysis must reevaluate the significance of revision in the bastardization of both myth and divinity. The thousand years which separate the story of the Judgment of Paris from the legendary war celebrated in the epic, the hundreds of years which separate it from the original Homeric composition suggest something other than a progressive clarification of what is archetypal. What is clarified by specific focus is that the myth of the goddess, and therefore the feminine immanence as a component of abiding significance, has been deprecated and that act has stunted the imagination of Western culture. The goddess's heroism in escaping rape into her own schema has become the story of the hero god, and revised again tracks a regression, with the goddess rendered first human and then progressively less powerful, less autonomous, less mature. Finally she is a girl-child with no claim to "significant affirmative action" who flees from conjugal violence back to paternal tyranny. While tradition has indiscriminately amassed the details of overlay and declared the final product archetypal, the original spirit of feminine heroism—its ethics and motivation—

have been further and further displaced. But this is true only if the continuum is entered at its extant beginnings and only so much as we continue to insist that allegorical revision has been definitively interpreted and all modern attempts to reinterpret or explicate it in relation to more clearly articulated feminine experience are ersatz if not heretical.

Notes

Introduction: In Search of the Heroine

1. Joseph Campbell, *Hero with a Thousand Faces*, Bollingen Series (Princeton, N.J.: Princeton University Press, 1972), 17:61.

2. Ibid., p. 40.

3. Annis Pratt, *Archetypal Patterns in Women's Fiction* (Bloomington: Indiana University Press, 1981), has pointed to the "rape-trauma archetype" as one of the most frequent plot structures in women's fiction. Pratt, p. 81.

4. Mary Ellman, *Thinking About Women* (New York: Harcourt Brace Jovanovich, 1968), p. 44.

5. Carl Gustav Jung, *Man and His Symbols* (New York: Doubleday, 1964), p. 67.

6. Gerda Lerner discusses the historic discrepancy between women's actual contributions to culture and their "marginality in the meaning-giving process of interpretation and explanation." The resulting tension she calls "the dialectic of women's history." Gerda Lerner, *The Creation of Patriarchy* (New York: Oxford University Press, 1986), p. 5.

7. Gloria Steinem, Introduction to *Goddesses in Everywoman: A New Psychology of Women*, Jean Shinoda Bolen (New York: Harper and Row, Colophon edn., 1985), p. x.

8. Leo C. Curran, "Rape and Rape Victims in the Metamorphosis," *Women in the Ancient World: The Arethusa Papers*, John Peradotto and J.P. Sullivan, eds., Series in Classical Studies (Albany, N.Y.: State University of New York Press, 1984), p. 266.

9. Lerner points out that in history and its interpretation, that which succeeded and survived was by the very fact of its survival considered superior to that which vanished and thus "failed," p. 15.

10. Lerner suggests that in the protohistoric period military elites developed alongside temple elites and eventually rivaled them. Lerner, p. 57.

11. Northrop Frye, *The Great Code* (New York: Harcourt Brace Jovanovich, 1981), p. xvii.

12. Elaine Pagels, *Adam, Eve, and the Serpent* (New York: Random House, 1988), p. 146.

13. Hesiod, *Hesiod, the Homeric Hymns, and Homerica*, "To Demeter," trans. Hugh G. Evelyn-White, Loeb Classical Library (New York: Macmillan, 1914), p. 323.

Chapter I: Motherhood in Prehistory:
Attachment Patterns and the Origin of Religion

1. Herbert J. Muller, *Freedom in the Ancient World* (New York: Harper, 1961), p. 14.

2. Elaine Morgan, *The Descent of Woman* (New York: Stein and Day, 1972), p. 171.

3. Nancy Tanner, *On Becoming Human* (Cambridge: Cambridge University Press, 1981), p. 222.

4. Muller, *Freedom in the Ancient World*, p. 8.

5. Joseph Campbell, *The Masks of God: Primitive Mythology*, rev. edn. (New York: Viking, 1969; reprint, New York: Penguin, 1976), p. 313.

6. Ibid., pp. 319–20.

7. Ibid., p. 388.

8. Ibid., p. 401.

9. James Mellaart, *Earliest Civilizations of the Near East*, Library of Early Civilizations, ed., Stuart Piggott. Reprint edn. (New York: McGraw-Hill, 1978), p. 77.

10. Bodies buried in Catal Huyuk were primarily those of women and children, who had been excarnated before burial under the floors. Mellaart concludes that the excarnation was a deliberate religious ritual and that vultures were employed. Skeletons were then arranged in fetal positions and buried in containers. Mellaart *Earliest Civilizations*, pp. 87–89.

11. Anne Barslow, "The Prehistoric Goddess," *The Book of the Goddess, Past and Present* (New York: Crossroad, 1983), p. 11.

12. Campbell, *Primitive Mythology*, p. 202.

13. Ibid., p. 401.

14. Joseph Campbell, *The Masks of God: Occidental Mythology* (New York: Viking, 1964), p. 7.

15. Henry Morgan Lewis, *Ancient Society* (Cambridge, Mass.: Harvard University Press, 1965), p. 397.

16. Campbell, *Occidental Mythology*, p. 6.

17. Elizabeth Fisher has suggested that agriculture was the beginning of women's repression as it brought with it property ownership and the need for a familial labor force, thus reducing women to baby makers and children to the labor force of the property-owning man. Elizabeth Fisher, *Woman's Creation: Sexual Evolution and the Shaping of Society* (Garden City, N.Y.: Anchor/Doubleday, 1979).

18. Muller, *Freedom in the Ancient World*, p. 21.

19. Ibid., p. 23.

20. Ibid., p. 24.

21. Fisher, p. 110.

22. Johann Jakob Bachofen, *Myth, Religion, and Mother Right: Selected Writings of J. J. Bachofen*, trans. Ralph Manheim, Bollingen Series (Princeton, N.J.: Princeton University Press, 1967), 84:79.

23. A detailed review of this debate is presented by Gordon Rattray Taylor, Introduction to *The Mothers* by Robert Briffault, abridged edn. (London: Allen and Unwin, 1959), pp. 110–11.

24. Joseph Campbell, Introduction to *Myth, Religion, and Mother Right*, p. xlv.

25. A comprehensive review of the mother-child tie in psychoanalytical literature is given by John Bowlby in *Attachment and Loss*, Appendix (New York: Basic, 1969), pp. 361–78.

26. A fascinating study of the origins of love and characteristics of mother-

infant attachments in other species is Konrad Lorenz, *On Aggression* (New York: Harcourt Brace and World, 1967).

27. Bowlby, p. 57.
28. Ibid., pp. 198–209.
29. Ibid., p. 202.
30. Ibid., p. 62.
31. Gilbert Murray, *Five Stages of Greek Religion*, (Garden City, N.Y.: Doubleday, 1955; 3rd edn., Beacon, 1951), pp. 3–5.
32. Jane Ellen Harrison, *Prolegomena to the Study of Greek Religion*, Meridian edn. (Cleveland: World Publishing, 1903), p. 7.
33. Bowlby, p. 330.
34. Ibid., pp. 16–19.
35. Ibid., p. 166.
36. Jane Ellen Harrison, "Themis" in her *Epilegomena and Themis* (New Hyde Park, N.Y.: University Press, 1962; reprint ed., *Epilegomena*, Cambridge: 1921, reprint edn. of 2nd revised edn., *Themis*, Cambridge: 1927), p. 484.
37. Harrison, *Prolegomena*, p. 172.
38. Ibid., p. 169.
39. Harrison, *Epilegomena and Themis*, p. xxii.
40. Harrison, *Prolegomena*, p. 156.
41. Ibid., p. 490.
42. Harrison, *Epilegomena and Themis*, p. 138.
43. Ibid., p. 142.
44. Murray, *Five Stages of Greek Religion*, p. 5.
45. Harrison, *Epilegomena and Themis*, p. 141.
46. Ibid., p. 129.

Chapter II: The Nature of the Goddess: Ominous, Transformative, Nurturing; Three Persons in One Goddess

1. Sir James Frazer, *The Golden Bough* (New York: Macmillan, 1922), p. 423.
2. Aeschylus, *Choephori*, 1.127.
3. Jane Ellen Harrison, *Mythology* (New York: Cooper, 1963), p. x.
4. Sylvia Brinton Perera, *Descent to the Goddess: A Way of Initiation for Women* (Toronto, Canada: Inner City, 1981), p. 21.
5. Edwin Oliver James, *The Ancient Gods: The History and Diffusion of Religion in the Ancient Near East and Eastern Mediterranean* (New York: G. P. Putnam's Sons, 1960), p. 99.
6. Apuleius, *The Golden Ass*, trans. by W. Adington, book XI; cited in Campbell, *Primitive Mythology*, p. 56.
7. Marija Gimbutas, in *The Goddesses and Gods of Old Europe, 7000–3500 B.C. Myths, Legends and Cult Images*, revised edn. (Berkeley: University of California Press, 1982), presents a detailed argument for an Old European culture, of pre–Indo-European tribes who were agricultural, matrifocal, and worshiped tribal goddesses, but who had orginated around Vinca rather than Anatolia. Her evidence that this culture also influenced Minoan Crete is impressive.
8. James, *The Ancient Gods*, p. 105.
9. Gimbutas, p. 18.
10. Will Durant, *The Story of Civilization*, vol. 2, *The Life of Greece* (New York: Simon and Schuster, 1939), p. 20.

11. Gimbutas, pp. 55, 66.

12. From the Old European pantheon comes the prototype Mistress of the Waters, a Bird and Snake Goddess associated with the generative power of primordial water. The periodic drought so catastrophic to the Balkan Peninsula, Greece, Anatolia, and the Levant led to the crystallization of a divinity who governed upper and lower waters and who was affiliated with bird and snake, bear and chevron, rain and mother's milk, and the meander or labyrinth, an ancient symbol of water which was later the home or palace of the goddess. In this manifestation, the divinity nurtured the world and was consequently mother or nurse. Artifacts from Old Europe, Cyprus, Mycenaean Greece, as well as Minoan Crete, present the Snake or Bird Goddess cuddling a human baby. See Gimbutas, pp. 112–46.

13. Harrison points to the etymology of *herm*, the rude pillar or grave marker which, like the tree, is rooted in the womb of the earth, where the tribe's dead were buried. Tribes appealed to the dead to work magic for the good of the living. Hermes was initially a *herm*, who developed into one of the later young gods who first attended the goddess and later usurped her. He retained his chthonic connection by the fact that he remained the escort of the dead, even after his metamorphosis into an Olympian sky god. See Harrison, *Mythology*, pp. 3–13.

14. Martin Pearson Nilsson, *A History of Greek Religion*, 2nd rev. edn. (New York: W. W. Norton, 1964), p. 13.

15. Lewis Richard Farnell, *The Cults of the Greek States* (Chicago: Aegaean, 1985), 1:13.

16. Harrison, *Prolegomena*, p. 267.

17. Harrison, *Mythology*, p. 67.

18. Farnell, 1:123.

19. Ibid., 1:120.

20. Harrison points out that later in mainland Arcadia Demeter had two surnames and two statues, and when she was benign, she was Louisa. See Harrison, *Prolegomena*, p. 214.

21. Edwin Oliver James, *Tree of Life: An Archaeological Study*, Studies in the History of Religions (Leiden, Netherlands: Brill, 1966), 11:199.

22. Harrison, *Prolegomena*, p. 274.

23. Sinclair Hood, *The Minoans: The Story of Bronze Age Crete*, Ancient People and Places Series (New York: Praeger, 1971), 75:139; Nilsson, *History of Greek Religion*, p. 130; and Farnell, 1:23.

24. Plato, *Apology*, 41d.

25. Farnell, 1:30.

26. Harrison, *Prolegomena*, pp. 269–72.

27. Peter Warren, *The Aegean Civilizations* (New York: Dutton, 1975), p. 42.

28. Campbell, *Occidental Mythology*, p. 62.

29. Warren, p. 38.

30. Merlin Stone, *When God Was a Woman* (New York: Dial, 1976), p. 31.

31. Hood, 75:117.

32. Nilsson, *History of Greek Religion*, p. 27.

33. Murray, *Five Stages of Greek Religion*, p. 27.

34. Campbell, *Primitive Mythology*, p. 469.

35. Harrison suggests that cult objects of the goddess religion, specifically the Gorgon's head, were misunderstood by the conquering patriarchal culture and were so awesome that they lent themselves easily to patriarchal reshaping of the goddess into a villainness or bogey who was necessarily tamed by a hero. See Harrison, *Prolegomena*, p. 187.

36. Gimbutus, p. 66.

37. Harrison, *Prolegomena*, pp. 153, 161.

38. Murray, *Five Stages of Greek Religion*, p. 29.

39. Farnell, 1:17; and James, *Ancient Gods*, p. 29.

40. Homer, *Iliad*, 18.590–92.

41. Harrison, *Epilegomena*, p. 493.

42. Earl A. Grollman, ed., *Explaining Death to Children*, with Introduction by Louise Bates Ames (Boston: Beacon, 1967), p. 5.

43. Durant, p. 189.

44. Hesiod, *Hesiod, Homeric Hymns, and Homerica*, "To Demeter," 480–84, p. 323.

45. James, *Ancient Gods*, p. 79.

46. Perera identifies Inanna as the first dying divinity whose "sacrifice redeems the wasteland earth. Not for mankind's sins did Inanna sacrifice herself, but for Earth's need for life and renewal. She is concerned more with life than with good and evil." Perera, p. 21.

47. James, *Ancient Gods*, p. 79.

48. Edwin Oliver James, *Comparative Religion*, rev. edn. (New York: Barnes and Noble, 1961), p. 125.

49. Charles Seltman, *The Twelve Olympians*, Apollo edn. (New York: Crowell, 1962), p. 148.

50. Harrison, *Mythology*, p. 58.

51. Homeric, *Hymn to Demeter*, 8–11.

52. Gimbutas, p. 196.

53. Christine Dowling, "The Mother Goddess Among the Greeks," *The Book of the Goddess, Past and Present*, ed. Carl Olson (New York: Crossroad, 1983), p. 50.

54. Homeric, *Hymn to Demeter*, 493–91.

55. Hesiod, *Hesiod, Homeric Hymns and Homerica*, "To Earth the Mother of All," p. 457.

56. Farnell, 1:116.

57. Robert Graves explains the Cretan practice of saining as a dance of aversion in which sacred torches were paraded around newborns to ward off evil spirits. Robert Graves, *The Greek Myths*, revised edn. (New York: Viking, Penguin, 1955; reprint edn., 1986), 1:95.

58. Carol Gilligan, citing Nancy Chodorow, *In a Different Voice: Psychological Theory and Women's Development* (Cambridge, Mass.: Harvard University Press, 1982), p. 8.

59. Ibid., p. 17.

60. Campbell, *Hero with a Thousand Faces*, p. 58.

61. Gilligan, p. 17.

62. David McClelland, *Power: The Inner Experience* (New York: Dell, 1969), cited by Gilligan, p. 22.

63. Philip Slater, *The Glory of Hera: Greek Mythology and the Greek Family* (Boston: Beacon, 1968), p. 36.

64. Harrison points to the successful usurpation of this ancient prerogative of the mother as a sign of fully established patriarchy. Harrison, *Epilegomena*, p. 495.

65. Gilligan, p. 23.

66. Page DuBois, *Centaurs and Amazons: Women and the Pre-History of the Great Chain of Being* (Ann Arbor: University of Michigan Press, 1982), p. 90.

67. Campbell, *Occidental Mythology*, p. 70.

Chapter III: Fiction as Process and the Deprecation of the Goddess: Atalanta, Cassandra, and Ariadne

1. Elaine Morgan, in *The Descent of Woman*, expands on Michael Chance's theory that primate politics revolve around two types of aggression, *agonic* which strives for dominance and *hedonic* which is more concerned with what primatologists call "display." Morgan sees human primates as tending to have more nuance in their patterns, but also as having been originally hedonic in their most ancient social groupings. Adoption of agonic modes came later as the need arose. See Morgan, pp. 186–90.

2. Campbell, *Occidental Mythology*, p. 65.

3. Durant, p. 28.

4. Lionel Tiger, *Men in Groups* (New York: Random House, 1969), p. 41.

5. Tiger, quoted in Morgan, p. 200.

6. Tiger, p. 44.

7. Frye, *The Great Code*, p. 7.

8. Northrop Frye, *The Educated Imagination* (Bloomington: Indiana University Press, 1964), p. 73.

9. Frye, *The Great Code*, p. 47.

10. Nilsson, *History of Greek Religion*, p. 27.

11. Hesiod, *Hesiod, Homeric Hymns, and Homerica*, "To Artemis," p. 453.

12. Harrison has pointed out that virginity in its original sense meant autonomy; patriarchal concerns altered its meaning and included it as an aspect of moral order. Harrison, *Epilegomena and Themis*, p. 505.

13. Apollodorus, *The Library*, trans. Sir James Frazer (Cambridge, Mass.: Harvard University Press, 1921), 1.8.2. for his unconsionable misogyny.

14. Graves, *The Greek Myths*, 1:265.

15. Apollodorus, 1.8.2–3.

16. Ibid., 1.8.2.

17. Tiger, quoted by Morgan, p. 200.

18. Morgan, p. 200.

19. Durant, p. 30.

20. Harrison, *Mythology*, p. xii.

21. Harrison, *Prolegomena*, p. 325.

22. Frye, *The Great Code*, p. 6.

23. Ibid., p. 8.

24. See Marlo Thomas et. al, *Free to Be You and Me* (New York: McGraw-Hill, 1974).

25. Muller, *Freedom in the Ancient World*, p. 3.

26. Durant, p. 30.

27. Lerner, p. 56.

28. Ibid., p. 9.

29. Muller, *Freedom in the Ancient World*, p. 90.

30. Ibid., pp. 90–91.

31. Nilsson, *History of Greek Religion*, quoted by Campbell, *Occidental Mythology*, p. 53.

32. Campbell, *Occidental Mythology*, p. 54.

33. James, *Comparative Religion*, p. 123.

34. Perera contrasts the patriarchal idea of death, "a rape of life, a violence to be feared and controlled as much as possible with distance and moral order," with the matriarchal idea of death as not a destruction of life but "a transformation

to which, like the grain to the reaper, the goddess willingly surrenders and over which process she rules." Perera, pp. 21–22.

35. Lerner, p. 16.

36. Lerner points out that as women and children became significant economic assets under developed agricultural systems, the male elders of the tribe came to control food, women, and the once sacred "mysteries" of the harvest, Lerner, p. 49.

37. Harrison, *Prolegomena*, p. 325.

38. Ibid., p. 312.

39. Ibid., p. 281.

40. Harrison, p. 386.

41. Ibid., pp. 384–86.

42. DuBois, pp. 28–29. The birth of the centaurs is associated rather loosely with Hera, but not until after she had lost her status as an autochthonic great goddess and become, through trickery, rape, and shame, the unwilling and unhappy wife of Zeus. By the time the myth was composed, the Indo-European Zeus was in full control, and up to his usual tricks. He deceived Ixion, himself a scurrilous fellow, into believing that a cloud form is really Hera, whom he then impregnated. The association with the great goddess is a remnant; in the overlay it is the cloud form, called Nephele, not Hera, who gives birth to "the outcast child Centaurus," who then sires the rest of the breed, according to Graves, *The Greek Myths,* 1:208.

43. Appollodorus, 1.9.17.

44. Harrison, *Prolegomena*, pp. 187–232.

45. It is curious that this antediluvian bias is still passed along by scholars. Sinclair Hood writes of the Paleolithic mothers as representing "with an intensity which verges on the horrible, the deification of motherhood." Sinclair Hood, *The Minoans: The Story of Bronze Age Crete*, vol. 75, Ancient People and Places Series (New York: Praeger, 1971), p. 242. Muller claims the Indo-European gods had "loftier ethical possibilities than the amoral Mother, who encouraged a degrading obsession with phallus or fertility rites, and characteristically was served by temple prostitutes and eunuch priests." Muller, *Freedom in the Ancient World,* p. 91.

46. Harrison, *Prolegomena*, p. 194.

47. Muller, *Freedom in the Ancient World*, p. 88.

48. James, *Comparative Religion*, p. 21.

49. Robinson, Cyril, *History of Greece* (New York: Crowell, 1965), p. 11.

50. Ibid., p. 12.

51. James, *Comparative Religion*, p. 121.

52. Harrison, *Epilogomena*, p. 387.

53. Harrison, *Prolegomena*, p. 594.

54. Campbell, *Occidental Mythology*, pp. 145–46.

55. Harrison, notes that he is the son of Poseidon, a Cretan god, and therefore a son of Minoan mainlanders who settled in the vicinity of Athens, and championed its ascendancy in the coastal federation. Harrison, *Mythology*, p. 54.

56. Campbell, *Occidental Mythology*, p. 48.

57. Campbell, *Hero with a Thousand Faces*, p. 61.

58. Campbell, *Occidental Mythology*, p. 86.

59. Ibid., p. 150.

60. Curran, "Rape and Rape Victims," *Women in the Ancient World: The Arethusa Papers*, p. 266.

61. Campbell, *Occidental Mythology*, p. 80.

62. Edith Hamilton, *Mythology*, (Boston: Little, Brown, 1940, 1942; reprint ed., New York: New American Library, Mentor, 1953), p. 173.

63. Ibid., p. 115.

64. Graves, *The Greek Myths 1*, p. 78.

65. Campbell, *Occidental Mythology*, p. 80.

Chapter IV: Self-deprecation and Ostracism in Homer

1. Slater suggests that the autochthonic concern with fertility was altered through Indo-European overlay into the preoccupation with personal immortality that is reflected in the epics. Slater, p. 216.

2. DuBois, p. 60.

3. Harrison notes that "Homer himself is ignorant of, or at least avoids all mention of the dark superstitions of a primitive race; he knows nothing at least obstensibly." But she goes on to point out that the substratum based on worship of fertility and the dead came to him already crystallized in language and legend and so remnants appear in the epics. Harrison, *Prolegomena*, p. 335.

4. Samuel Butler theorized at the end of the nineteenth century that Homer, at least the author of the *Odyssey*, was actually a woman. Samuel Butler, *The Authoress of the Odyssey* (London: A. C. Fifield, 1897; reprint ed., London: J. Cape, 1922). Robert Graves considered this possibility in the fictional *Homer's Daughter* (Garden City, N.Y.: Doubleday, 1955).

5. Eva C. Keuls, *The Reign of the Phallus: Sexual Politics in Ancient Athens* (New York: Harper and Row, 1985), cites Solon as "codifier of the double standard of sexual morality," since his reforms included such repressive measures as state-controlled and price-controlled brothels, harsh and intrusive laws for "safeguarding the chastity of citizen women, including the notorious statute that a father could sell his daughter into slavery if she lost her virginity before marriage," and was probably the initiator of the Women's Police. Keuls, p. 5.

6. Richmond Lattimore, Introduction to *The Iliad of Homer*, trans. Richmond Lattimore (Chicago: University of Chicago Press, 1961), p. 21.

7. Eva Cantarella, *Pandora's Daughters: The Role and Status of Women in Greek and Roman Antiquity*, trans. Maureen B. Fant, Foreword by Mary R. Lefkowitz (Baltimore: Johns Hopkins University Press, 1987), p. 24.

8. Lattimore, *Iliad*, p. 29.

9. Ibid., pp. 33–35.

10. Ibid., p. 29.

11. It is essential to note that Homer, while condemning Clytemnestra through both Zeus and Agamemnon, nowhere attributes her death of matricide. Throughout the *Odyssey* Orestes is set before Telemachus as a model of one who had correctly avenged the wrongs done to his father, but his achievement was in killing Aegistus, not his mother. Nestor reported to Telemachus on the murder of Agamemnon, but describes his death at the hands of Aegistus, not Clytemnestra. In fact, Nestor suggests Aegistus had beguiled Clytemnestra into complicity, despite her initial unwillingness. "Now in time before, beautiful Klytaimestra would not consent to the act of shame, for her own nature was honest . . . but when the doom of the gods had entangled her and she must submit . . . Aegistus took her back to his house, and she was willing as he was." (*Odyssey*, 3.265–73.)

12. Harrison suggests that Helen was a local goddess of the Minoan tree cult tradition, with sanctuaries at both Sparta and Rhodes. The rape or abduction of

Helen was probably the theft of a sacred cult object from its sanctuary, indicative of the triumph of an invading Indo-European tribe over the autochthonic cult of the goddess. Harrison, *Prolegomena*, pp. 322–23.

13. Michael Grant, *Myths of the Greeks and Romans* (New York: New American Library, Mentor, 1962), pp. 43–44.

14. Lattimore, *Iliad*, p. 24.

15. Cantarella, p. 31. She points to Odysseus's brutal execution of his unfaithful maidservants as evidence that the Homeric man had power not only over the life and death of his servants, but may also have expected sexual fidelity from them or at least the right to determine who their partners would be. The story of Eurycleia, nursemaid to Odysseus, supports this idea. The epic tells of Laertes' decision not to take her as a concubine out of respect for the wishes of his wife. The fact that it is mentioned at all suggests that it was an unusual choice.

16. Sarah Pomeroy, *Goddesses, Whores, Wives, and Slaves: Women in Classical Antiquity* (New York: Schocken, 1975), pp. 22–23. Also, S. B. Pomeroy, "Andromaque, un exemple méconnu du matriarcat," *REG* 88 (1975): 16–19.

17. Cantarella, p. 28.

18. Ibid., p. 31.

19. Lattimore points out that this is another aspect of the legend to which Homer nowhere alludes, which suggests that it was a later embellishment. Lattimore, *Iliad*, p. 27.

20. There are mentions made by others—Athena, Nestor, and Odysseus himself—of the possibility that Telemachus is not Odysseus's son, but they reflect lingering confrontations between patrilineal and matrilineal traditions, as well as the continuing process of asserting patriarchal mores by infusing as a cultural motif the distrust of women. Monogamous women are the only ones who can testify with assurance to the paternity of their children and allowing women the sexual freedom they had once had, or that men continued to have, was inconsistent with the desire to establish a hierarchial, polarized society which perpetuated male hegemony. *Marta certa, patra semper incertus.*

21. The peculiar fact reported in the *Iliad*, that ransom was paid for Andromache's mother rather than her father, has suggested to some that she was the actual ruler of her kingdom, and there is still argument over whether Arete or Alcinous was the actual ruler of Phaeacia. The attention paid to the future marriage of their daughter and the urgency of securing for her a royal consort has led some scholars to believe that if Nausicaa was not to become queen, it was at least through marriage to her, that rule of Phaeacia was determined.

22. Helene P. Foley, "'Reverse Similes' and Sex Roles in the *Odyssey*," Peradotto and Sullivan, *Women in the Ancient World: The Arethusa Papers*, p. 73.

23. Ibid., p. 63.

24. Cantarella, p. 29.

25. Richmond Lattimore, Introduction to *The Odyssey of Homer*, trans. Richmond Lattimore (New York: Harper and Row, Colophon edn., 1975), pp. 5–7.

26. Campbell emphasizes Circe's chthonic nature and points to her use of her sexuality as part of her power to destroy and her power to comfort and guide; she is an Underworld ogress but also, like Persephone, giver of immortal life. Campbell, *Occidental Mythology*, p. 171.

27. Campbell points to Tiresias *(sic)* as another figure who has been both male and female and so "assimilated what is substantial of life and are, so, eternal." Campbell, *Occidental Mythology*, p. 171.

28. Harrison, *Prolegomena*, p. 177.

Chapter V: The Reconstructed Divinity:
Danae, Athena, and Pandora

1. Graves offers a footnote about Ajax in *The Greek Myths* where he points out that Ajax was of Lelegian stock and what has traditionally been viewed as his rebellious atheism was more likely a tenacious attachment to the ancient goddess worship. Graves, *The Greek Myths*, 2:287.

2. Campbell, *Occidental Mythology*, p. 168.

3. Harrison, *Prolegomena*, p. 292.

4. Campbell, *Occidental Mythology*, p. 168.

5. Harrison, *Prolegomena*, p. 292.

6. Lattimore, Introduction to *The Iliad of Homer*, p. 24.

7. Harrison, *Prolegomena*, pp. 176–77.

8. Graves, *The Greek Myths*, 2:27.

9. Harrison, *Prolegomena*, pp. 214–16.

10. Ibid., p. 214.

11. Ibid., p. 232.

12. Slater, p. 318.

13. Harrison notes that the Medusa-Perseus myth is a Libyan myth, with the hero a human counterpart of the winged Pegasus: Harrison, *Mythology*, pp. 41–42; while Graves identifies her as a Pelasgian pre–Achaean goddess at Argos: Robert Graves, *The White Goddess* (New York: Farrar, Straus and Giroux, 1980), p. 64. According to Graves, one version of her story masculinized her to Danaus, son of Belus, who brought his daughters from Libya to Greece; they were originally three, a trinity of goddesses who later became fifty. Harrison points to Herodotus's idea that the Eleusian Mysteries came from the daughters of Danus who then taught them to Pelasgian women. Harrison, *Prolegomena*, p. 121. Piecing these fragments together puts Danae back in Crete.

14. Harrison, *Mythology*, pp. 41–42.

15. Slater, p. 314.

16. Campbell, *Occidental Mythology*, p. 154. Elsewhere, Campbell points out that chthonic forces were perceived as antigod by the Indo-European schema: "daemons that formerly had symbolized the force of the cosmic order itself, the dark mystery of time, which licks up heroes like dust: the force of the never-dying serpent, sloughing lives like skins, which pressing on, ever turning in its cycle of eternal return, is to continue in this manner forever, as it has already cycled from all eternity, getting absolutely nowhere." It is an idea which could not coexist with the warrior principle; an idea which offered itself for polarity with the rising values of the heroic culture. Campbell, *Occidental Mythology*, p. 24.

17. Merlin Stone points out that Leto appeared in many ancient lands, including Canaan, Arabia, Egypt, Malta, and Crete. Hellenic Greeks attempted to diminish Leto as a passing dalliance of Zeus, "still they spoke of Lato as the mother of the moon and the sun," and her daughter Artemis was honored at Ephesus and elsewhere as one "who roamed free and independent in forests—as Amazons were said to do." Merlin Stone, *Ancient Mirrors of Womanhood: Our Goddess and Heroine Heritage* (New York: New Sibylline Books, 1979), p. 202.

18. Graves points to the story of the death of Selene, also called Semele, as an explanation for the violent wresting of her power by her once subservient son, Dionysus. This is similar to Apollo's usurpation of power at Delphi; Appollodorus also tells of Dionysus's descent into Hades to secure the release of his mother, who then returns with him to Artemis's temple where she is afterward honored as his

mother. Graves, *The Greek Myths*, 1:106–7. The stories rob the goddess of her prodigiousness while shoring up the consciences of their sons through imposition of gallantry as recompense. The gallantry is lauded, the original larceny downplayed.

19. James, *Comparative Religion*, p. 124.
20. Graves, *The Greek Myths*, 1:44–45.
21. James, *Tree of Life*, 11:193–94.
22. Karoly Kerenyi and Carl Gustav Jung, *Essays on a Science of Mythology: The Myth of the Divine Child and the Mysteries of Eleusis*, trans. R. F. C. Hull (Princeton, N.J.: Princeton University Press, Bollinger Series, 1969), 22:106.
23. Harrison, cited by Graves, *The Greek Myths*, 1:46.
24. Graves, *The Greek Myths*, 1:46.
25. Oswyn Murray, *Early Greece* (Stanford, Calif.: Stanford University Press, 1983), p. 23.
26. F. A. Wright, *Feminism in Greek Literature: From Homer to Aristotle* (Port Washington, N.Y.: Kennikat, 1969), p. 25.
27. Linda Sussman, "Workers and Drones; Labor Idleness and Gender Definition in Hesiod's Beehive," Perodotto and Sullivan, *The Women in the Ancient World: The Arethusa Papers*, pp. 82–86.
28. Harrison, *Prolegomena*, pp. 283–84.
29. Ibid., pp. 284–85.
30. Hamilton, *Mythology*, p. 63.
31. Ibid., p. 70.
32. Graves, *The Greek Myths*, 1:99.
33. Ibid., 1:169–70.
34. Ibid., 1:60.
35. Ibid.
36. Pomeroy, p. 115.
37. Lerner, p. 121.

Chapter VI: The Feminine Principle in Classical Athens: Cultural Imprimatur of Second Stratum Archetypes

1. Frye, *The Great Code*, p. 50.
2. Wright, p. 1.
3. Pomeroy, p. 59. Pomeroy points out that in contrast to Wright's view, A. W. Gomme published a "radical" essay in 1925, "The Position of Women in Athens in the Fifth and Fourth Centuries B.C.," and that until very recently scholars chose positions on the issue according to their acceptance of the views of Wright or Gomme. Contemporary scholars have broken off from this narrowly defined debate by bringing in evidence from new sources.
4. Ibid., p. 60.
5. Semonides of Amorgos was a poet-philosopher of the 7th century B.C. The fragments of his work which remain indicate a remarkably virulent misogyny. His poetic comparisons juxtapose women with various animals and indubitably contributed to that continued association which would come to ugly fruition in the writing of Aristotle. Like Hesiod, Semonides described women as vile, duplicitous, and base. Only one type, the woman like the bee, was worthy and part of her worth came from her aloofness from other women, her immersing of herself in the patriarchal family. See Cantarella, pp. 35–37.

Wright reviews the fragments left by the Lyric Poets and concludes that

Archilochus (714–650), Semonides (556–468), and Hipponax (c. 550) exhibit the "same mixture of sensual desire and cynical distaste for women" although "The paucity of material, probably no great loss either in an artistic or moral sense, has obscured the facts, but there seems little doubt that in this period literature was definitely used for the first time to degrade the position of women." Wright, p. 23. Murray, *Early Greece,* p. 24, seems to agree; as does Sussman, p. 81.

6. Keuls, p. 5.

7. Slater, pp. 7–9.

8. Ibid., p. 29.

9. Lerner points out that the existence of laws which regulate sexual conduct and limit economic power by gender and class indicate that these issues were conceptually linked and continued to pose problems. Lerner, p. 103.

10. Durant, p. 117.

11. Generation of Animals II, 3 (737a, 28–31) Aristotle, *Repro. An.* 3.3.

12. Cyril E. Robinson, *A History of Greece* (New York: Crowell), p. 251. Robinson and others point out that Thucydides had a habit of putting words into the mouths of the characters in his history, while Pericles was famous for a simplistic style. The consensus of historians leads to the conclusion that the funeral oration was the product of what Thucydides thought Pericles might have said. Thucydides lived 471–399 B.C. His assessment of virtues of fifth-century Athenian women is certainly representative if not authentically Periclean.

13. Keuls, p. 88, quoting Thucydides 2, 45, 2.

14. Naomi R. Goldberg, *Changing of the Gods* (Boston: Beacon, 1979), p. 29.

15. Keuls suggests that in addition to the evidence of pictorial art, there were plays which depicted rape and sexual treachery by gods. The titles of lost stayr plays imply such themes. These may have been destroyed by monastic Christian scribes in a later era. Keuls, p. 3.

16. Pomeroy's citations of archaeological studies of skeletal remains support Keuls's assessment. Evidence suggests that average adult longevity was five to ten years longer for males than for females in Classical Athens. Pomeroy, p. 68.

17. Campbell, *Occidental Mythology,* p. 160.

18. Keuls, pp. 183–86.

19. Keuls, p. 367, is supported by Sheila McNally, "The Maenad in Early Greek Art," Peradotto and Sullivan, *The Women in the Ancient World: The Arethusa Papers,* p. 107. DuBois also wrote at length about the agon between Amazons and Athenian heroes in art and how the superwomen represented the antithesis of the ideal Athenian wife. DuBois, pp. 3–40.

20. K. J. Dover, "Classical Greek Attitudes to Sexual Behavior," *Women in the Ancient World: The Arethusa Papers* (Albany, 1984), p. 147.

21. Keuls, pp. 183–86.

22. Keuls cites Sir Kenneth J. Dover's study, *Greek Homosexuality* (Cambridge, Mass., 1978) which adheres to the traditional view that Athenians in Classical times "sanctioned and even glorified" homosexuality as a "useful institution." Keuls, p. 275.

23. Keuls, p. 275.

24. DuBois, pp. 57–58, reviews the works of other scholars concerning this overlay, including G. Karl Galinsky, *The Herakles Theme: Adaptations of the Hero in Literature from Homer to the Twentieth Century* (Oxford, 1972), M. Bowra, *Greek Lyric Poetry,* 92nd edn., Oxford, 1961) as well as Nilsson, *Cults, Myths, Oracles and Politics in Ancient Greece* (Lund, 1951).

25. DuBois, pp. 59–67.

26. DuBois, p. 79.

27. Ibid., p. 68.

28. Hamilton, p. 155.

29. Froma Zeitlin, "The Dynamics of Misogyny: Myth and Mythmaking in the *Orestia*," *Arethusa* 11.1,2 (Spring and Fall 1978): 149–84.

30. DuBois, p. 90.

31. Philip Vellacott, Introduction to Aeschylus's *The Oresteian Trilogy*, trans. Philip Vellacott (New York: Penguin, 1956), p. 25.

32. Harrison, *Mythology*, pp. 72–74.

33. For the suggestion that the story of Athena's goading Odysseus and his son to the gratuitous violence of the last scenes represents later justification rather than initial aspects of the story. See Lattimore, Introduction to *The Odyssey of Homer*, p. 17.

34. Frye, *The Great Code*, p. 9.

35. DuBois, p. 139.

36. Ibid., p. 135; and also Keuls.

37. Edith Hamilton, *The Greek Way* (New York: W. W. Norton, 1930), p. 157.

38. Ibid., pp. 159–60.

39. Keuls, p. 147.

40. Campbell, *Occidental Mythology*, p. 258.

41. Karl Reinhardt, trans. Hazel Harvey, David Harvey and Basil Blackwell, *Sophokles*, 3rd edn. (Frankfurt: Klostermann, 1979), p. 88.

42. Bertolt Brecht, *Vorwort zu "Antigonemodell"* 1948, p. 100, quoted in Kate Hamburger, *From Sophocles to Sartre: Figures from Greek Tragedy, Classical and Modern*, trans. Helen Sebba (New York: Frederick Ungar, 1969), p. 163.

43. Hamilton, *The Greek Way*, p. 161.

44. Ibid., p. 163.

45. Graves, *The Greek Myths*, 2:194.

46. Morgan has pointed out that all governance is based on principles of male bonding and the agonic drive. Morgan, p. 202.

Chapter VII: Euripides

1. Hamburger, pp. 8–10.

2. Vergil, *The Aeneid*, trans. Patrick Dickinson (New York: New American Library, Mentor, 1961), p. 46.

3. Ibid.

4. Plato, *Apology*, 39d.

5. Hamilton, *The Greek Way*, p. 165.

6. Cantarella, pp. 67, 69.

7. Hamburger, p. 14.

8. Graves, vol. 2, p. 237.

9. DuBois, pp. 110–15.

10. Ibid., p. 118.

11. Gilbert Murray, *Euripides and His Age* (New York: Henry Holt; London: Williams and Norgate; Cambridge: University Press Home University Library of Modern Knowledge, 1913), no. 73, p. 88.

12. Hamilton, *The Greek Way*, p. 168.

13. I have used Lattimore's translation of *The Trojan Women*, except where

noted by asterisk where I have used Michael Cacoyannis's 1972 film, A Joseph Shaftel Production, *Trojan Women.*

14. In Euripides' *Andromache*, he has taken this characterization one step further: "O dearest Hector, for your sake I even welcomed your loves, when Cyris sent you fumbling. I was wet nurse to your bastards many a time only to make your life a little easier. And for such conduct he approved and loved me" (222–25). In *Iphigenia at Aulis* it was he who added a little-remembered element to the legend of Clytemnestra. According to her own testimony, Agamemnon had forced her to marry him after he had murdered her first husband and her infant. Graves, *The Greek Myths*, 2:52.

15. Richmond Lattimore, Introduction of Helen, *The Complete Greek Tragedies: Vol. III, Euripides*, ed. David Grene and Richmond Lattimore (Chicago, University of Chicago Press, 1959), p. 485.

16. Keuls, p. 341.

17. Grene and Lattimore, Introduction to *Helen*, p. 483.

18. Ibid., p. 485.

19. Grene and Lattimore, Introduction to *Hecuba*, p. 488.

20. Ibid., p. 489.

21. Durant, p. 532.

Chapter VIII: Merging Traditions of Goddess Deprecation: The Heroism of Eve

1. Mary Ellmann, *Thinking About Women*, p. 28.

2. Ibid., pp. 32–33.

3. Campbell, *Hero with a Thousand Faces*, p. 59.

4. Ibid., p. 62.

5. Ibid., p. 64.

6. Ibid., p. 136.

7. Ibid., p. 40.

8. Ibid., p. 119.

9. Ibid., p. 71.

10. Ibid., p. 72.

11. Ibid., p. 116.

12. Stone notes that the disenthronement of the goddess which was initiated by the Indo-European invaders was eventually accomplished by the Hebrew, Christian, and Moslem religions that arose later. Stone, *When God Was a Woman*, p. 228.

13. Dorothy Dinnerstein, *The Mermaid and the Minotaur: Sexual Arrangements and Human Malaise* (New York: Harper and Row, 1976, Colophon edn., 1977), pp. 124–29.

14. John A. Philips, *Eve: The History of an Idea* (San Francisco: Harper and Row, 1984), p. 7.

15. Philips, p. 12. Mary Ellmann points out that in creating the Hebrew god actions are "profoundly intellectual and self-directed. Adam is formed out of dust, Eve out of Adam's rib: God plays the first sculptor and the first surgeon. He begins Art and Science." Ellmann, p. 64.

16. Lerner, p. 200.

17. Ibid., p. 179.

18. Dinnerstein interprets both the Pandora and Eve myths as reflective of women's membership in "an intelligent, playful, exploratory species, inhabiting an

expanding environment which it makes for itself and then adapts to. Dinnerstein, p. 200.

19. Philips, p. 102.

20. Ibid., p. 14.

21. Ibid., p. 180, where Philips points out that except for Isa. 34:14–15, "Lillith has been completely exorcised from Scripture." Pagels notes that Lillith remained a legendary figure connected to the hierarchic order. She was said to be responsible for infant death when the infant's mother had not been appropriately submissive to her husband. Pagels, p. 263.

22. Philips, p. 32.

23. Ibid., p. 30.

24. Stone, quoting Campbell, *When God Was a Woman*, p. 7.

25. Philips, p. 22.

26. Hamilton, *Mythology*, p. 70.

27. Ellmann, p. 96.

28. Philips, p. 14.

Chapter IX: Rediscovering the Goddess

1. Charlene Spretnak, *Lost Goddesses of Early Greece: A Collection of Pre-Hellenic Myths* (Boston: Beacon, 1978), pp. 28–37.

2. Harrison, *Epilegomena and Themis*, p. 505.

3. Perera, p. 16.

4. Judi M. Roller, *The Politics of the Feminist Novel*, Contributions in Women's Studies, no. 63 (New York: Greenwood, 1986), p. 118.

5. Dinnerstein uses this apt phrase to summarize what in Simone de Beauvoir's view was the "central bribe to which woman succombs" in the gender arrangement of traditional marriage. Dinnerstein, p. 211.

6. Carolyn G. Heilbrun, *Toward a Recognition of Androgyny* (New York: Alfred A. Knopf, 1973, Colophon ed., 1974), p. 91. She credits Francis Fergusson, *The Idea of a Theatre* (Garden City, N.Y.: Doubleday, 1953).

7. Heilbrun, p. 49.

8. Dinnerstein, quoting de Beauvoir, pp. 220–21.

9. Dinnerstein, quoting de Beauvoir, pp. 220–21.

10. Leslie A. Fiedler, *Love and Death in the American Novel* (New York: Criterion, 1960), pp. xviii, xix.

11. Linda Ray Pratt, "The Abuse of Eve by the New World Adam," *Images of Women in Literature: Feminist Perspectives* ed. Susan Koppelman Cornillon (Bowling Green, Ohio: Bowling Green University Popular Press, 1972), p. 165.

12. Campbell indicates that the hero's "first step, detachment or withdrawal, consists in a radical transfer of emphasis from the external to the internal world, macro- to microcosm, a retreat from the desperations of the waste land to the peace of the everlasting realm that is within," in fact, the divinity within. For the heroine this necessitated a kind of chthonic retreat, and then the discovery of what had been culturally denied, the feminine divinity within. It is not surprising that the male author handles this through ellipsis. Campbell, *Hero with a Thousand Faces*, p. 19.

13. Dinnerstein, p. 221.

14. Nathaniel Hawthorne, *The Scarlet Letter*, Centenary Text (New York: Harper and Row, 1968), p. 72.

15. Hawthorne, p. 225.

16. Campbell, *Hero with a Thousand Faces*, p. 20.

Chapter X: The Chthonic Aspect as a Source of Strength in Twentieth-Century American Heroines

    1. Jean Shinoda Bolen, *Goddesses in Everywoman: A New Psychology of Women* (New York: Harper and Row, 1984; Colophon edn., 1985), p. 285.
    2. Perera, p. 12.
    3. Ibid., p. 14.
    4. Ibid.
    5. Perera, p. 23.
    6. Ibid., p. 25.
    7. Freud cited in Gilligan, p. 7.
    8. Perera, p. 24.
    9. Dinnerstein, pp. 129–30.
    10. Perera, p. 34.
    11. Ibid., pp. 43–44.
    12. Ibid., p. 45.
    13. Ibid., p. 50.
    14. Bolen, p. 290.
    15. Ibid.
    16. Perera, p. 71.
    17. Ellen Glasgow, *Barren Ground* (New York: Harcourt Brace, 1925; New York: Hill and Wang, First American Century Series ed., 1957), p. vi.
    18. Agnes Smedley, *Daughter of Earth* (New York: Feminist Press at the City University of New York, 1987), p. 8.
    19. De Beauvoir, p. 519.
    20. Smedley, Foreword by Alice Walker, p. 3.
    21. Bolen, p. 289.
    22. Katherine Anne Porter, *The Collected Stories of Katherine Anne Porter* (New York: Harcourt Brace and World, 1965), p. 195.

Chapter XI: Chthonic Renewal: Irrational Modes in Dinner at the Homesick Restaurant, The Good Mother, *and* The Color Purple

    1. Susan Sontag, *Illness as Metaphor* (New York: Farrar, Straus and Giroux, 1977), p. 3.
    2. Barbara Hill Rigney, *Madness and Sexual Politics in the Feminist Novel* (Madison: University of Wisconsin Press, 1978), p. 8.
    3. Ibid., p. 11.
    4. Gayle Greene and Coppelia Kahn, eds., *Making a Difference: Feminist Literary Criticism* (New York: Methuen, 1985), citing the theories of Helene Cixous, p. 82.
    5. Rollo May, *Love and Will*, New York: Dell, 1969.
    6. Ibid., p. 124.
    7. Anne Tyler, *Dinner at the Homesick Restaurant* (New York: Alfred A. Knopf, 1982), p. 4.
    8. Sue Miller, *The Good Mother* (New York: Dell, 1986), p. 197.
    9. May, p. 37.
    10. Ibid., p. 78.

11. Ibid., p. 79.
12. Ibid., p. 122.
13. Ibid., p. 74.
14. Ibid.

Chapter XII: The Chthonic as Metaphor: Manifestations in Beloved, Seachange; *Revision in* The Witches of Eastwick

1. Toni Morrison, *Beloved* (New York: Alfred A. Knopf, 1987, p. 163.

2. Harrison, *Prolegomena*, p. 490.

3. Graves, *The Greek Myth*, 2:217.

4. Ovid, *The Metamorphoses*, translated with Introduction by Horance Gregory (New York: Viking, 1958; reprint edn., New American Library, Mentor, 1960), p. 330.

5. Lois Gould, *Seachange* (New York: Avon, 1977), p. 16.

6. John Updike, *The Witches of Eastwick* (New York: Alfred A. Knopf, 1984), p. 14.

7. Nina Auerbach, *Communities of Women: An Idea in Fiction* (Cambridge, Mass.: Harvard University Press, 1978), p. 3.

8. Ibid., p. 4.

9. Ibid., p. 10.

Afterthought

1. Murray, *Five Stages of Greek Religion*, p. 5.

Selected Bibliography

Aeschylus. *The Oresteian Trilogy*. Translated with Introduction by Philip Vellacott. New York: Penguin, 1956.

Agonito, Rosemary. *History of Ideas on Women: A Source Book*. New York: G. P. Putnam's Sons, 1977; Paragon, 1979.

Apollodorus. *The Library*. Translated by Sir James Frazer. 3 vols. Loeb Classical Library. Cambridge, Mass.: Harvard University Press, 1921.

Appolonius Rhodius. *The Argonautia*. With English translation by R. C. Seaton. 2 vols. Loeb Classical Library. Cambridge, Mass.: Harvard University Press, 1961.

Apuleius. *The Golden Ass*. Translated by W. Adington.

Aristophanes. *The Complete Plays of Aristophanes*. Edited and Introduction by Moses Hadas. New York: Bantam, 1962.

Atwood, Margaret. *Surfacing*. New York: Warner, 1983.

Auerbach, Nina. *Communities of Women: An Idea in Fiction*. Cambridge, Mass.: Harvard University Press, 1978.

Bachofen, Johann Jakob. *Myth, Religion, and Mother Right: Selected Writings of J. J. Bachofen*. Translated by Ralph Manheim. Preface by George Boas. Introduction by Joseph Campbell. Vol. 84. Bollingen Series. Princeton, N.J.: Princeton University Press, 1967.

Bolen, Jean Shinoda. *Goddesses in Everywoman: A New Psychology of Women*. New York: Harper and Row, 1984; Colophen edn., 1985.

Bowlby, John. *Attachment and Loss*. New York: Basic, 1969.

Briffault, Robert. Abridged with Introduction by Gordon Rattray Taylor. London: Allen and Unwin, 1959.

Butler, Samuel. *The Authoress of the Odyssey*. London: A. C. Fifield, 1897; reprint edn., London: J. Cape, 1922.

Cameron, Averail, and Amelie Kuhrt. *Images of Women in Antiquity*. Detroit: Wayne State University Press, 1983.

Campbell, Joseph. *Hero with a Thousand Faces*. Vol. 17. Bollingen Series. Princeton, N.J.: Princeton University Press, 1972.

————. *The Masks of God: Occidental Mythology*. New York: Viking, 1964.

————. *The Masks of God: Primitive Mythology*. Revised ed. New York: Viking, 1969; Reprint, New York: Penguin, 1976.

Cantarella, Eva. *Pandora's Daughters: The Role of Women in Greek and Roman Antiquity*. Translated by Maureen B. Fant. Foreword by Mary R. Lefkowitz. Baltimore: Johns Hopkins University Press, 1987.

Cornillon, Susan Koppelman, ed. *Images of Women in Literature: Feminist Perspectives*. Bowling Green, Ohio: Bowling Green University Popular Press, 1972.

Chodorow, Nancy C. *The Reproduction of Mothering: Psychoanalysis and the Sociology of Gender.* Berkeley: University of California Press, 1978.

Christ, Carol. *Diving Deep and Surfacing: Women Writers and Spiritual Quest.* Boston: Beacon, 1979.

Coser, Rose, Judith Lauber, Alice S. Rossi, and Nancy C. Chodorow. "On *The Reproduction of Mothering:* A Methodological Debate." *Signs* 6 (Spring 1981): pp. 482–514.

Cuddy, Lois. "Mother-Daughter Identification in *The Scarlet Letter.*" *Mosaic* XIX/2 (Spring 1986): 102–15.

Davidson, Cathy N., and E. M. Broner. *The Lost Tradition: Mothers and Daughters in Literature.* New York: Frederick Ungar, 1980.

De Beauvoir, Simone. *The Second Sex.* Translated and edited by H. M. Parshley, 1953; reprint edn., New York: Random House, 1974.

Dinnerstein, Dorothy. *The Mermaid and the Minotaur: Sexual Arrangements and Human Malaise.* New York: Harper and Row, 1976, Colophon edn., 1977.

Dowling, Christine. "The Mother Goddess Among the Greeks." *The Book of the Goddess, Past and Present.* Edited by Carl Olson. New York: Crossroad, 1983.

DuBois, Page. *Centaurs and Amazons: Women and the Pre-History of the Great Chain of Being.* Ann Arbor: University of Michigan Press, 1982.

Durant, Will. *The Story of Civilization.* Vol. 2, *The Life of Greece.* New York: Simon and Schuster, 1939.

Ellman, Mary. *Thinking About Women.* New York: Harcourt Brace Jovanovich, 1968.

Euripides. *Ten Plays by Euripides.* Translated by Moses Hadas and John McLean. Introduction by Moses Hadas. New York: Bantam, 1960.

Farnell, Lewis Richard. *The Cults of the Greek States.* Vol. 1. Chicago: Aegaean, 1895.

Fiedler, Leslie. *A Love and Death in the American Novel.* New York: Criterion, 1960.

Fisher, Elizabeth. *Women's Creation: Sexual Evolution and the Shaping of Society.* Garden City, N.Y.: Anchor/Doubleday, 1979.

Foley, Helene P., ed. *Reflections of Women in Antiquity.* New York: Gordon and Breach, 1981.

Fraiberg, Selma. *Every Child's Birthright: In Defense of Mothering.* New York: Basic, 1977.

Frazer, Sir James. *The Golden Bough.* Abridged edn. New York: Macmillan, 1923.

Frye, Northrop. *The Educated Imagination.* Bloomington: Indiana University Press, 1964.

————. *The Great Code.* New York: Harcourt Brace Jovanovich, 1981.

Gilligan, Carol. *In a Different Voice: Psychological Theory and Women's Development.* Cambridge, Mass.: Harvard University Press, 1982.

Gimbutas, Marija. *Goddesses and Gods of Old Europe, 7000–3500 B.C.: Myths, Legends and Cult Images.* Revised edn. Berkeley: University of California Press, 1982.

Goldberg, Naomi R. *Changing of the Gods.* Boston: Beacon, 1979.

Glasgow, Ellen. *Barren Ground.* New York: Harcourt Brace, 1925; New York: Hill and Wang, First American Century Series ed., 1957.

Gould, Lois. *Seachange.* New York: Avon, 1977.

Grant, Michael. *Myths of the Greeks and Romans.* New York: New American Library, Mentor, 1962.

Graves, Robert. *The Greek Myths.* 2 vols. New York: Viking, Penguin, 1955; reprint edn., 1986.

_____. *Homer's Daughter.* Garden City, N.Y.: Doubleday, 1955.

_____. *The White Goddess.* New York: Farrar, Straus and Giroux, 1980.

Greene, Gayle, and Coppelia Kahn, eds. *Making a Difference: Feminist Literary Criticism.* New York: Meuthen, 1985.

Grene, David, and Richmond Lattimore. *The Complete Greek Tragedies: Vol. III, Euripides.* Chicago: University of Chicago Press, 1959.

Grollman, Earl A., ed. *Explaining Death to Children.* Introduction by Louise Bates Ames. Boston: Beacon, 1967.

Hamburger, Kate. *From Sophocles to Sartre: Figures from Greek Tragedy, Classical and Modern.* Translated by Helen Sebba. New York: Frederick Ungar, 1969.

Hall, Nor. *The Moon and the Virgin: Reflections on the Archetypal Feminine.* New York: Harper and Row, 1980.

Hamilton, Edith. *The Greek Way.* New York: W. W. Norton, 1930.

_____. *Mythology.* Boston: Little, Brown, 1942; reprint edn., New York: New American Library, Mentor, 1953.

Harrison, Jane Ellen. *Epilegomena to the Study of Greek Religion and Themis: A Study of Social Origins of Greek Religion.* New Hyde Park, N.Y.: University Books, 1962.

_____. *Mythology.* New York: Cooper, 1963.

_____. *Prolegomena to the Study of Greek Religion.* Meridian edn. New York: World Publishing, 1903.

Hawthorne, Nathaniel. *The Scarlet Letter.* The Centenary Text. Introduction by Stephen Black. New York: Harper and Row, 1968.

Heilbrun, Carolyn G. *Toward a Recognition of Androgyny.* New York: Alfred A. Knopf, 1973, Colophon edn., 1974.

Herodotus. *History.* With English translation by A. D. Godley. 4 vols. Loeb Classical Library. Cambridge, Mass.: Harvard University Press, 1957–61.

Hesiod. *Hesiod, the Homeric Hymns, and Homerica.* With English translation by Hugh G. Evelyn-White. Loeb Classical Library. New York: Macmillan, 1914.

Hillman, James. *The Myth of Analysis: Three Essays in Archetypal Psychology.* New York: Harper and Row, 1972; Colophon, 1978.

_____, ed. *Facing the Gods.* Irving, Texas: Spring Publications, 1980.

Homer. *The Iliad of Homer.* Translated and Introduction by Richmond Lattimore. Chicago: University of Chicago Press, First Phoenix edn., 1961.

_____. *The Odyssey of Homer.* Translation and Introduction by Richmond Lattimore. New York: Harper and Row; Colophon edn., 1975.

Hood, Sinclair. *The Minoans: The Story of Bronze Age Crete.* Vol. 75. Ancient People and Places Series, New York: Praeger, 1971.

James, Edwin Oliver. *The Ancient Gods: The History and Diffusion of Religion in the Ancient Near East and Eastern Mediterranean.* New York: G. P. Putnam's Sons, 1960.

_____. *Comparative Religion.* Revised edn. New York: Barnes and Noble, 1961.

_____. *The Cult of the Mother-Goddess.* New York: Praeger, 1959.

_____. *Prehistoric Religion: A Study in Prehistoric Archaeology.* New York: Barnes and Noble, 1957.

_____. *Tree of Life: An Archaeological Study.* Studies in the History of Religions. Vol. 11. Leiden, Netherlands: Brill, 1966.

Jung, Carl Gustav. *Man and His Symbols.* New York: Doubleday, 1964.

Kerenyi, Karoly, and Carl Gustav Jung. *Essays on a Science of Mythology: The Myth of the Divine Child and the Mysteries of Eleusis.* Translated by R. F. C. Hull. Vol.

Bollingen Series. Revised edn. Princeton, N.J.: Princeton University Press, 1969.

Keuls, Eva C. *The Reign of the Phallus: Sexual Politics in Ancient Athens.* New York: Harper and Row, 1985.

Lerner, Gerda. *The Creation of Patriarchy.* New York: Oxford University Press, 1986.

Lewis, Henry Morgan. *Ancient Society.* Cambridge, Mass.: Harvard University Press, 1965.

Lorenz, Konrad. *On Aggression.* New York: Harcourt Brace and World, 1967.

McClelland, David. *Power: The Inner Experience.* New York: Irvington, 1975.

May, Rollo. *Love and Will.* New York: Dell, 1969.

Mellaart, James. *Archaeology of Ancient Turkey.* Totowa, N.J.: Rowman and Littlefield, 1978.

_____. *Earliest Civilizations of the Near East.* Stuart Piggott ed., Library of Early Civilizations. New York: McGraw-Hill; reprint edn., 1978.

Mechinger, Siegfried. *Euripides.* Translated by Sam Rosenbaumn. New York: Ungar, 1966.

Miller, Sue. *The Good Mother.* New York: Dell, 1986.

Moi, Toril. *Sexual/Textual Politics: Feminist Literary Theory.* New Accents. London: Methuen, 1985.

Morgan, Elaine. *The Descent of Woman.* New York: Stein and Day, 1972.

Morrison, Toni. *Beloved.* New York: Alfred A. Knopf, 1987.

Muller, Herbert J. *Freedom in the Ancient World.* New York: Harper, 1961.

_____. *A History of Ancient Greek Literature.* New York: Ungar, 1966.

Murray, Gilbert. *Euripides and His Age.* New York: Henry Holt; London: Williams and Norgate; Cambridge: Cambridge University Press Home University Library of Modern Knowledge, 1913.

_____. *Five Stages of Greek Religion.* 3rd edn. New York: Beacon, 1951.

_____. *A History of Ancient Greek Religion.* New York: Frederick Ungar, 1966 (1989).

Murray, Oswyn. *Early Greece.* Stanford, Calif.: Stanford University Press, 1983.

Neumann, Erich. *The Great Mother: An Analysis of the Archetype.* Translated by Ralph Manheim. Vol. 47. Bollingen Series. Princeton, N.J.: Princeton University Press, 1964.

Nietzsche, Friedrich. *The Birth of Tragedy.* Translated with commentary by Walter Kaufman. Vintage Books, 1967.

_____. *The Will to Power.* 1904. Translated by Walter Kaufman. New York: Random House, 1968.

Nilsson, Martin Persson. *A History of Greek Religion.* Revised edn. New York: W. W. Norton, 1964.

_____. *The Mycenaean Origin of Greek Mythology.* Vol. 8. Sather Classical Lecture, Berkeley: University of California Press, 1932.

Olson, Carl, ed. *The Book of the Goddess, Past and Present.* New York: Crossroad, 1983.

Ovid. *The Metamorphoses.* Translated and Introduction by Horace Gregory. New York: Viking, 1958; reprint ed., New York: New American Library, Mentor, 1960.

Pagels, Elaine. *Adam, Eve, and the Serpent.* New York: Random House, 1988.

Peradotto, John, and J. P. Sullivan, eds. *Women in the Ancient World: The Arethusa Papers.* Series in Classical Studies. Albany, N.Y.: State University of New York Press, 1984.

Perera, Sylvia Brinton. *Descent to the Goddess: A Way of Initiation for Women.* Studies in Jungian Psychology. Vol. 6. Toronto, Canada: Inner City, 1981.

Philips, John A. *Eve: The History of an Idea.* San Francisco: Harper and Row, 1984.

Pindar. *The Odes of Pindar.* Translated by Richmond Lattimore. Loeb Classical Library. Chicago: University of Chicago Press, 1959.

Plato. *Apology.*

Pomeroy, Sarah. *Goddesses, Whores, Wives, and Slaves: Women in Classical Antiquity.* New York: Schocken, 1975.

Porter, Katherine Anne. *The Collected Stories of Katherine Anne Porter.* New York: Harcourt Brace and World, 1965.

Pratt, Annis. *Archetypal Patterns in Women's Fiction.* Bloomington: Indiana University Press, 1981.

Pratt, Linda Ray. "The Abuse of Eve by the New World Adam." *Images of Women in Literature: Feminist Perspectives.* Susan Koppelman Cornillon, ed. Bowling Green, Ohio: Bowling Green University Popular Press, 1972.

Preston, James J., ed. *Mother Worship: Themes and Variations.* Chapel Hill: University of North Carolina Press, 1982.

Reinhardt, Karl. *Sophocles* trans. Hazel Harvey, David Harvey and Basil Blackwell, 1979.

Rigney, Barbara Hill. *Madness and Sexual Politics in the Feminist Novel.* Madison: University of Wisconsin Press, 1978.

Robinson, Charles Alexander, Jr., ed. *An Anthology of Greek Drama.* Second Series. New York: Holt, Rinehart and Winston, 1965.

Robinson, Cyril E. *History of Greece.* New York: Crowell, 1965.

Rogers, Katherine M. *The Troublesome Helpmate: A History of Misogyny in Literature.* Seattle: University of Washington Press, 1966.

Roller, Judi M. *The Politics of the Feminist Novel.* Number 63. Contributions in Women's Studies. New York: Greenwood, 1986.

Seltman, Charles. *The Twelve Olympians.* Apollo edn. New York: Crowell, 1962.

Simon, Bennett. *Mind and Madness in Ancient Greece: The Classical Roots of Modern Psychiatry.* Ithaca, N.Y.: Cornell University Press, 1978.

Slater, Philip. *The Glory of Hera: Greek Mythology and the Greek Family.* Boston: Beacon, 1968.

Smedley, Agnes. *Daughter of Earth.* Foreword by Alice Walker. Afterword by Nancy Hoffman. New York: Feminist Press at the City University of New York, 1987.

Sontag, Susan. *Illness as Metaphor.* New York: Farrar, Straus and Giroux, 1977.

Sophocles. *The Complete Plays of Sophocles.* Translated by Sir Richard Claverhouse Jebb. Introduction by Moses Hadas. New York: Bantam, 1967.

Spitz, Rene A. *The First Year of Life: A Psychoanalytic Study of Normal and Deviant Development of Object Relations.* New York: International University Press, 1965.

Spretnak, Charlene. *Lost Goddesses of Early Greece: A Collection of Pre-Hellenic Myths.* Boston: Beacon, 1978.

Steiner, George, and Robert Fagles, eds. *Homer: A Collection of Critical Essays.* Englewood Cliffs, N.J.: Prentice-Hall, 1962.

Stone, Merlin. *When God Was a Woman.* New York: Ungar, 1976.

_____. *Ancient Mirrors of Womanhood: Our Goddess and Heroine Heritage.* New York: New Sibylline Books, 1979.

Tanner, Nancy. *On Becoming Human.* Cambridge: Cambridge University Press, 1981.

Thomas, Marlo, et al. *Free to Be You and Me.* New York: McGraw-Hill, 1974.

Tiger, Lionel. *Men in Groups.* New York: Random House, 1969.

Tyler, Anne. *Dinner at the Homesick Restaurant.* New York: Alfred A. Knopf, 1982.

Updike, John. *The Witches of Eastwick.* New York: Alfred A. Knopf, 1984.

Vergil. *The Aeneid.* Translated by Patrick Dickinson. New York: New American Library, Mentor, 1961.

Walker, Alice. *The Color Purple.* New York: Harcourt Brace Jovanovich, 1982.

Warren, Peter. *The Aegean Civilizations.* New York: Dutton, 1975.

Wright, Frederick Adam. *Feminism in Greek Literature: From Homer to Aristotle.* Port Washington, N.Y.: Kennikat, 1969.

Zeitlin. "The Dynamics of Misogyny: Myth and Mythmaking in the *Orestia*," *Arethusa* 11.1, 2 (Spring and Fall 1978): 149–84.

Index